PLAYING AND REALITY
REVISITED

International Psychoanalytic Association's
Psychoanalytic Classics Revisited Series

Series Editor: Gennaro Saragnano

PLAYING AND REALITY REVISITED

edited by

Gennaro Saragnano and Christian Seulin

Routledge
Taylor & Francis Group
LONDON AND NEW YORK

First published 2015 by
Karnac Books Ltd.

Published 2019 by Routledge
2 Park Square, Milton Park, Abingdon, Oxon OX14 4RN
52 Vanderbilt Avenue, New York, NY 10017

Routledge is an imprint of the Taylor & Francis Group, an informa business

British Library Cataloguing in Publication Data

A C.I.P. for this book is available from the British Library

ISBN 978-1-78220-025-3 (pbk)

Edited, designed and produced by The Studio Publishing Services Ltd
www.publishingservicesuk.co.uk
e-mail: studio@publishingservicesuk.co.uk

CONTENTS

IPA PUBLICATIONS COMMITTEE

The aim of this new series of books, which comes after the four successful series previously published under the auspices of the International Psychoanalytic Association, is to make available to psychoanalysts, and other scholars in related fields, a reinterpretation of the classics of psychoanalysis by authoritative colleagues from various countries and with different theoretical approaches, in the light of the more recent developments in contemporary psychoanalysis.

In a historical period characterised by the increased internationalisation of psychoanalysis, and its fast spread in Eastern Europe and Asia, we believe that there is an increased demand for psychoanalytical culture and for further investigating the great classics of this discipline, whether books or single papers, which have marked the history of the theoretical and clinical development of psychoanalysis. We think that the word "Classics" includes all those contributions which, far from being comprehensible only if viewed against a specific historical and cultural backdrop, are capable of continuously revealing to us their capacity of stimulating psychoanalytical thought in a creative and anti-dogmatic manner, and therefore remain as inalienable theoretical and clinical landmarks, regardless of the personal opinions and approach of each psychoanalyst.

We decided to open this new series of books with *Playing and Reality* by Donald W. Winnicott, undoubtedly a great classic of psychoanalysis. Published in London in 1971, this key works has since represented an endless source of clinical insights and theoretical investigations, becoming one of the principal textbooks in the training of all psychoanalysts. Christian Seulin and I asked thirteen eminent colleagues to personally "reinterpret" Winnicott's thought, based on his most important book, revisiting his well-known concepts of transitional objects and phenomena, playing, creativity, cultural experience, the use of an object and mirroring, in the light of contemporary psychoanalysis. We are, therefore, confident that this first book in the series of Psychoanalytic Classics Revisited may help the scholars and students of psychoanalysis and of human behaviour in general.

Gennaro Saragnano, MD
Series Editor
Chair, IPA Publications Committee

ABOUT THE EDITORS AND CONTRIBUTORS

Editors

Gennaro Saragnano, MD, is a member and former Secretary of the Italian Psychoanalytical Association and psychiatrist and psychoanalyst in private practice in Rome. He served the International Psychoanalytical Association as a member of the Website Editorial Board from 2005 to 2009, and has been a member of the Publications Committee of the International Psychoanalytical Association since 2009. He was appointed Chair of the Publications Committee during the Mexico City IPA Congress in August 2011. He is co-editor of *On Freud's On Beginning the Treatment* (Karnac, 2012).

Christian Seulin, MD, is training and supervising psychoanalyst of the Paris Psychoanalytical Society (SPP), and a member of the International Psychoanalytical Association. He is former Secretary of the Executive Council of the Training Commission of the SPP and former President of the Lyon's group of the SPP. He is living and practising in Lyon. He has authored more than 50 articles and chapters, and one book. He has been a member of the Publications Committee of the IPA since 2009.

Contributors

Jan Abram is a psychoanalyst in private practice; Training and Supervising Analyst of the British Psychoanalytical Society; Board Member of the International Journal of Psychoanalysis; Chair of the Scientific Committee, British Society; author of *The Language of Winnicott* (1996 and 2007) and Editor of *Donald Winnicott Today*, 2013.

Andreas Giannakoulas, MD, is a psychiatrist, psychoanalyst, child and adolescent analyst. He is a Full Member in the British Psychoanalytical Society and the International Psychoanalytical Association; and a Full Member and Training Analyst of the Italian Psychoanalytical Association. Andreas Giannakoulas was Past President of the Italian Psychoanalytical Association; as well as Scientific Director, Chairman and Honorary President of the Courses of Psycho-dynamic Training for the Associazione per lo Sviluppo delle Scienze Neuropsichiatriche dell'Età Evolutiva (ASNE) in Rome University La Sapienza. He is a visiting professor at the Universities of Rome, Naples, Bari, Milan and in different European and American Universities. He has published several papers and books on psychoanalysis.

Angela Joyce is a Training and Supervising Psychoanalyst of the British Psychoanalytical Society and a Child Psychoanalyst trained at the Anna Freud Centre London. After many years at the AFC, she now works fully in private practice and is an Honorary Senior Lecturer at University College London. She is Chairperson of the Winnicott Trust and a Trustee of the Squiggle Foundation. Her book, edited with Lesley Caldwell, *Reading Winnicott* was published in the New Library of Psychoanalysis Teaching Series in January 2011.

Anna Maria Nicolò is a child psychiatrist, training and supervising analyst of the Italian Psychoanalytical Society. Child and adolescent psychoanalyst, Anna Maria Nicolò, is a former scientific secretary of the Roman Psychoanalytic Centre and chair of the Forum for adolescence of the European Psychoanalytical Federation (FEP), and currently a member of the FEP Adolescent Forum Committee. She served as a member of the Italian Committee for Child and Adolescent Psychoanalysis and in 2011 was elected Regional Representative (for Europe) to the Board of Representatives of the International

Psychoanalytical Association (IPA). Founder member of the Society for Psychoanalytic Psychotherapy for Children and Adolescents (SIPsIA) and Scientific Secretary of the Istituto Winnicott (ASNE-SIPsIA) the Course of Psychoanalytic Psychotherapy for Child, Adolescents and Couple, in Rome. She is supervisor of a therapeutic community for young psychotics. She is also co-editor of the book collection *Contemporary Psychoanalysis: Developments and Perspectives* (Franco Angeli) and Editor-in-Chief of the journal *Interazioni*. She has authored many papers and books in Italian, English, Spanish and French.

Wilfrid Reid, psychiatrist and psychoanalyst, is a member of the Canadian Psychoanalytic Society (Montreal French Branch) and of the Canadian Psychoanalytic Institute (Montreal French Branch). He works part-time in psychoanalytic private practice and part-time in psychiatric practice at the Pavillon Albert-Prévost, Hôpital du Sacré-Cœur de Montréal. In 1998, he won the Miguel Prados Prize of the Canadian Psychoanalytic Society for a paper entitled: "Plaidoyer pour la monadologie freudienne ou pour en finir avec la légende d'un Winnicott anti-sexuel", *Revue Française de Psychanalyse*, 4, 1997, pp. 1315–1342.

Maria Rhode is Emeritus Professor of Child Psychotherapy at the Tavistock Clinic and University of East London; a member of the Association of Child Psychotherapists and the Tavistock Society of Psychotherapists; and Honorary Associate of the British Psycho-Analytical Society. She works as Honorary Consultant Child Psychotherapist at the Tavistock Clinic, where she formerly co-convened the autism workshop. She has a particular interest in autism, language development and infant observation and is co-editor of *Psychotic States in Children*, as well as *The Many Faces of Asperger's Syndrome*, and *Invisible Boundaries: Psychosis and Autism in Children and Adolescents*.

Denys Ribas is a child psychiatrist, training psychoanalyst and member of the Paris Psychoanalytical Society. He was Director of the children's Day Hospital clinic at Entraide Universitaire in Paris for 30 years. He has written three books, two on childhood autism in 1997 and 2004—the second translated in English: *Autism: Debates and Testimonies* (Free Association Books, 2006) and one on D. W. W. Winnicott (2003, Presses Universitaires de France) as well as some articles in *Revue française de Psychanalyse* and "Autism as the defusion of drives" (translated by P. Slotkin), *International Journal of Psycho-Analysis*, 79(3), 1998, pp. 529–538.

René Roussillon is Training and Supervising Analyst of the Paris Psychoanalytical Society and of the Lyon Group of the SPP. He is Professor of Clinical Psychology and Psychopathology at the University of Lyon 2, where he is Director of the Department of Clinical Psychology. He is also Director of the Research Group on borderline pathology, and Director of the clinical "psycho-hub" of the Rhône-Alpes region in France.

Gabriel Sapisochin, MD, was originally trained as a Psychiatrist and he lives and work in Madrid. He is a Full Member and Training Analyst of Madrid Psychoanalytic Association (IPA). He is actual Editor of *Revista de Psicoanálisis de Madrid*.

Virginia Ungar, MD, is a Full Member and Training Analyst at the Buenos Aires Psychoanalytical Association. She is a specialist on Child and Adolescent Psychoanalysis, former Chair and current consultant on the Committee of Child and Adolescent Psychoanalysis of the IPA (COCAP). She is also Chair of the IPA Integrated Training Committee and member of the Latin American Board of the IJPA. She has published numerous papers in journals and chapters in books. She is a candidate to the IPA Presidency for 2017–2019.

Massimo Vigna-Taglianti, MD, is a Child Neuropsychiatrist, and a Full Member of Italian Psychoanalytical Society and International Psychoanalytical Association. He is Adjunct Professor of Child and Adult Psychiatry in Aosta University, and also works as psycho-analyst with children, adolescents and adults in his private practice. He is particularly interested in his clinical work and in his writings in transference/countertransference dynamics and above all in role-reversal phenomena, as well as in meaning of actions and play in psychoanalysis.

Laurie Wilson earned her undergraduate degree in art history from Wellesley College; her master's degree in Fine Arts and Fine Arts Education from Columbia University; and her PhD in Art History from City University of New York. She received psychoanalytic training at The NYU Psychoanalytic Institute where she is on the faculty as Clinical Associate Professor of Psychiatry at the Psychoanalytic Institute affiliated with NYU Medical Centre, and she practices in New York City. She directed the Graduate Art Therapy Program at New York University for 23 years and is Professor Emerita there. She has published extensively in three fields—art therapy, art history, and psychoanalysis and art therapy. Her book *Alberto Giacometti: Myth Magic and the Man* was published by Yale University Press in 2003.

Raquel Zak de Goldstein, MD of the University of Buenos Aires and Psychoanalyst, is a Full Member of the Argentinian Psychoanalitical Association (APA), and of the International Psychoanalytical Association (IPA), and has participated as Chair of the IPA Committee on Relations Between Psychoanalysis and Contemporary Science, and as Global Representative for Latin America to the Board during 2003–2007. She is Full Professor of the Institute of Psychoanalysis at APA, and participates in diverse Congresses, giving seminars and lectures in Latin America, Europe and the United States. She is the founder and Chair of the "Latin American Encounters on Winnicott's Thought", which have been held annually since 1992, as well as of the "Winnicott Space" in APA and creator and current Editor-in-Chief of the Journal *Encuentros*, published by the "Winnicott Space". She has published numerous scientific works, author of books such as *De la Erótica* and *And Then … Why Lacan?*, and co-author.

Introduction*

Christian Seulin

Playing and Reality was the last of D. W. Winnicott's books to be published during his lifetime. It is also undoubtedly the best known of his works, with its readership going far beyond psychoanalytical circles as such.

In it, with his own lively and inimitable sense of humour, Winnicott explores a whole series of innovative concepts that contemporary psychoanalysts have come to see as indispensable. These concepts have their roots in a highly subtle clinical approach that Winnicott shares with us unreservedly, so that it becomes possible for us also to have access to situations that take psychoanalysis to its limits, given their connection with the earliest stages of individual development as Winnicott tries to reconstruct them.

To a highly significant degree, he develops Freud's clinical approach and metapsychology, while at the same time avoiding the somewhat laborious dullness that often accompanies theoretical discourse.

---

* Translated by David Alcorn.

What is perhaps most remarkable is the attention that Winnicott gives to processual matters, to what is actually taking place, being played out, happening, developing . . . That attention goes beyond simply focusing on content and concentrates on the links and relationships between things much more than on the things themselves. Winnicott, of course, did say that there is no such thing as a baby, and the way in which he approaches creativity and culture in this book is based to a considerable extent on the facilitating role of the environment. He explores not only how one becomes a human being, but also the birth of representation and of the object, as well as all the processes that enable individual growth to take place.

His conception of psychoanalytical treatment is revolutionary in that he is very much on his guard with respect to interpretation and its inhibiting and anti-creative potential—and this all the more so when an interpretation is a clever one. He defines his work as a psychoanalyst in a way that merits our full attention.

In describing the task of therapy, he writes,

> It is a complex derivative of the face that reflects what is there to be seen. I like to think of my work this way, and to think that if I do this well enough the patient will find his or her own self, and will be able to exist and to feel real. (Winnicott, 1971, p. 117)

There are two major issues that go to the very heart of the book: being oneself, and tolerating loss.

Being oneself is, indeed, a core issue for the patients whom he describes in it. One has to be, to exist, before doing; being, in his view, has to do with the pure female element, while doing is, by its nature, male. Being lies at the root of creativity and of the very first creation. In a very subtle way, Winnicott pleads in favour of formlessness: formlessness is essential if a form is to be created. If formlessness proves impossible to experience, one of the consequences is the risk of being locked into fantasying, which Winnicott contrasts with dreaming and with life itself. While Bion was exploring the evacuative potentiality of dreams, Winnicott was drawing a picture of a deadly and inflexible fantasy world opposed to any kind of psychical development.

In the birth of the self, the mirror role of the mother's face is an essential element. Thanks to the quality of the mother's sensitive adaptation (in her handling, holding and object-presenting), her face reflects back to her infant his/her own image. In Winnicott's view, being oneself is primarily a matter of taking support from the environment, above all from the mother-as-mirror able to reflect her infant and, as it were, to identify him/her. Keeping in the background as a subject in her own right is a very important factor at first, one that fades away only gradually; it is fundamental in enabling the infant to perceive him/herself and to find what he/she created (or to create what he/she finds). This is where Winnicott shows just how much he owes to Freud who, in one of his final papers, "Constructions in analysis" (1937d), brought together hallucinatory creation and perception. It is interesting to observe the extent to which Winnicott's ideas can throw light on the active dimension in perception. Beyond that, he enables us to emphasise the processual dependence of perception on the modalities of its structuring in the primary object-related environment (Seulin, 2009). I would like also to underline the fact that in the extract about the work of therapy that I have just quoted, Winnicott says that he is there to reflect "what is there to be seen". Not everything is there to be seen.

Tolerating loss—and this is a stroke of genius on Winnicott's part—is possible only if there exists a potential space between mother and child; this space will become that of culture, and its best-known primary illustration, one that met with universal success, is the transitional object. That space both negates separation and is simultaneously the fruit of it, thereby setting up a paradox that does not have to be resolved or called into question. In his writings, Freud himself alludes to the idea of the impossibility of giving something up and of loss, but he does not explore the subject to any great extent. In "Creative writers and day-dreaming" (1908e), he writes, "Actually, we can never give anything up; we only exchange one thing for another. What appears to be a renunciation is really the formation of a substitute or surrogate" (p. 145) Winnicott shows us in great detail how effective the work of symbol formation is in developing and in having access to a creative capacity that enables us to experience loss and separation. The primary domain of the work of symbol formation is that of play, of play in movement, in a creative act that awaits a response from the environment.

Being oneself and tolerating loss implies also going from the subjective object—the object that is not yet acknowledged as being not-me—to the objective object acknowledged as being another subject, thus enabling it to be used. This gradual and delicate phase—

which perhaps goes on unfolding all through life—can be gone through only if the illusion of having created the object has been experienced; it takes place step by step, via the disillusionments that the individual is able to tolerate. This difficult task is accomplished through the destruction, in fantasy, of the object while seeing that, in reality, it still exists and is not retaliating: it can then be made use of. With potential space comes some degree of internal development, thanks to the possibility of having access to representation, differentiating it from the object in external reality and thereby strengthening the individual-as-subject, as a self. I would tend here to see something to do with "doing", that is, with the pure male element in action, to adopt Winnicott's own term.

In painting this picture of growth and development, which he saw as pre-programmed in human beings and which would be carried out as long as the environment is facilitating, Winnicott was also very much in tune with his work as a clinical psychoanalyst confronted with non-being, with emptiness, and with the negative dimension, as André Green would later describe it. What happens when nothing takes place, even though the environment ought to have enabled something to occur? When it has proved impossible to inscribe a traumatic experience within some subjective psychical locus? How can some subjective appropriation of these traces be carried out? The role of a therapeutic space is, above all, to be a locus in which something that has been lacking can at last be put into words or expressed in some other way. We can see how essential to Winnicott's work as a psychoanalyst was his sensitivity, patience, and creativity. I shall simply mention two examples of this. There is, first of all, the woman patient who said, "All I have got is what I have not got", adding, "And what will you do about it?" As Winnicott remained silent, she said, "Oh, I see." Thereupon, Winnicott made a comment full of humanity and humility: "I am silent because I don't know what to say." There is also the male patient talking about penis envy, to whom Winnicott said, "I am listening to a girl." Taking fully on board his maternal countertransference, Winnicott acknowledged that he, the analyst, was the one who was hearing a girl talk, adding, "The mad person is *myself*." Here we can see Winnicott at work, thinking, imagining, and dreaming in the service of his patients, with a remarkable degree of tact and plasticity.

In this book, the aim of which is to take another look, some forty years on, at that wonderful piece of work *Playing and Reality*, thirteen highly talented colleagues, all of whom have been influenced by Winnicott's fundamental contribution, discuss from their own personal and contemporary perspective his major developments as they appear in that book. Playing, transitional phenomena and objects, creativity, the use of the object, cultural experience, mirroring, and adolescence are the sources from which the present authors have drawn their inspiration.

References

Freud, S. (1908e). Creative writers and day-dreaming. *S. E., 9*: 143–153. London: Hogarth.

Freud, S. (1937d). Constructions in analysis. *S. E., 23*: 257–269. London: Hogarth.

Seulin, C. (2009). Trace manquante, inachèvement du traçage pulsionnel et destructivité. *Revue Française de Psychanalyse, LXXIII*(5): 1697–1704.

Winnicott, D. W. (1971). *Playing and Reality*. London: Tavistock.

CHAPTER ONE

Illusion in the origins of transitional phenomena and transitional objects[1]

Raquel Zak de Goldstein

> "The transitional phenomena represent the early stages of the use of illusion, without which there is no meaning for the human being in the idea of a relationship with an object that is perceived by others as external to that being"
>
> (Winnicott, 1971, p. 11)

> "Transitional objects and transitional phenomena belong to the realm of illusion which is at the basis of initiation of experience. ... the mother's special capacity for making adaptation to the needs of her infant, thus allowing the infant the illusion that what the infant creates really exists"
>
> (Winnicott, 1971, p. 14)

> "It will rightly be objected that an organization which was a slave to the pleasure principle and neglected the reality of the external World could not maintain itself alive for the shortest time, so that it could not have come into existence at all. The employment of a *fiction* like this is, however, justified when one considers that the infant – provided one includes with it the

care it receives from its mother – does almost realize a psychical system of this kind. It probably hallucinates the fulfilment of its internal needs; it betrays its unpleasure . . . by the motor discharge of screaming and beating about with its arms and legs, and it then experiences the satisfaction it has hallucinated"

(Freud, 1911b, p. 220)

Introduction

The aim of this presentation is to establish and focus on the questions that lead us to consider once again, first, the details—either favourable or pathogenic and susceptible of historicisation—of those factors that guarantee the intrinsic relationship between transitional phenomena and the transitional object (an observable pivot) and their functions in the constitution of the subject, and, second, the relevance of those factors to the field of the cure.

Alterations of the ego

The early "revelation" experienced by Winnicott on observing the function of transitional objects in infants led him to pay particular attention to the initial aspects of upbringing and the dialectics of its failings. Winnicott, who by then had read Freud, confirmed the validity of the ideas proposed in the psychoanalytic treatment of children at the British Society. At the same time, he began to consider with this fresh look, as it were, some hypotheses on the genesis of the psychotic anxieties underlying those failings in upbringing and consequent damage to the ego, reconsidering this through his daily practice with children and borderline patients.

The clear effect of his interventions with the patients he treated at what he called "my psychiatric snack bar" (Paddington Green Children's Hospital) led him to consolidate those hypotheses regarding early damage.

In *An Outline of Psycho-Analysis* (1940a), Freud writes,

> The neuroses are, as we know, disorders of the ego; and it is not to be wondered at if the ego, so long as it is feeble, immature and incapable

> of resistance, fails to deal with tasks which it could cope with later on with the utmost ease. In these circumstances instinctual demands from within, no less than excitations from the external world, operate as "traumas", particularly if they are met halfway by certain innate dispositions. The helpless ego fends them off by means of attempts at flight (repressions), which later turn out to be inefficient and which involve permanent restrictions on further development. The damage inflicted on the ego by its first experiences gives us the appearance of being disproportionately great; but we have only to take as an analogy the differences in the results produced by the prick of a needle into a mass of cells in the act of cell division (as in Roux's experiments) . . . [and] bear in mind the part played by this biological characteristic of the human species – the prolonged period of its childhood dependence – in the aetiology of the neuroses. (pp. 184–185)

These are the earliest environmental misfits that, like Roux's needle prick, constitute observable evidence. Noticeable, too, are their long-term effects on the constitution of personality, its symptoms, and the subject's way of suffering and making others suffer.

Freud, facing the "impossible pact" with those "un-analysable" cases, was already calling for a technical device that could prove more adequate, as expressed in the following text, as a legacy of his maturity:

> If the patient's ego is to be a useful ally in our common work, it must, however hard it may be pressed by the hostile powers, have retained a certain amount of coherence and some fragment of understanding for the demands of reality. But this is not to be expected of the ego of a psychotic; it cannot observe a pact of this kind, indeed it can scarcely enter into one. . . . Thus we discover that we must renounce the idea of trying our plan of cure upon psychotics – renounce it perhaps forever or perhaps only for the time being, till we have found some other plan better adapted for them.
>
> There is, however, another class of psychical patients who clearly resemble the psychotics very closely – the vast number of people suffering severely from neuroses. The determinants of their illness as well as its pathogenic mechanisms must be the same or at least very similar. But their ego has proved more resistant and has become less disorganized. Many of them, in spite of their maladies and the inadequacies resulting from them, have been able to maintain themselves in real life. These neurotics may show themselves ready

to accept our help. We will confine our interest to them and see how far and by what methods we are able to "cure" them. (pp. 173–174)

The function of the transitional object

In my view, and following Winnicott, the transitional object is a possession and the primary protective anti-trauma support. When misfits take place between the constitution and the function of the transitional object, the latter, which is already damaged and scarcely effective, turns into a "malevolent fetish", or a talisman lacking warmth and protection. This state of affairs obscures things, as it were. The terror of the abhorrent and resisted absolute dependence appears as a dependence that, in cases such as these, is "malignant", to put it in Balint's words (1967). This leads to a development of a resistance to the transference with the analyst. These cases of what I would term the psychopathology of survival already involve damage to the constitution of normal narcissism, and states of "ripped boundaries in the definitive reality Ego", which, in turn, give rise to "depressions, dissociations and encapsulation". A state of "subject in suspense" is thus determined (André, 1999; Rassial, 1999), a subject between frontiers, overwhelmed by those unthinkable anxieties that Winnnicott had already defined as "the stuff of the psychotic anxieties" (Winnicott, 1960). In this state, we witness the demand, impossible to achieve, that the analyst should provide relief and freedom.

As far as a possible cure goes, there is none yet. However, these persons consult an analyst and expect something. The fields outlined by classic Freudian psychopathology are transference neuroses and narcissistic neuroses, neither of which caters for these challenges presented to us. The function of the transitional object, which should have supported the purified pleasure ego until the investment of "the other" could begin, has failed. It is in that place, that "other" non-place, that the position of the analyst is possible and awaiting us. It is that volatile, unhinged, unstable third field that is constantly inhabited by the impossible demand.

The initial ego, "a system of neurons constantly cathexed" (Freud, 1950a) is endowed with a symbolic matrix and the *infans*, albeit prematurely, knows "how to fly". In a human "neuro-scopic" instant, as I would term it, which has been activated since the beginning of life because the *infans* has already experienced, for a brief period, a magical scopic power that corresponds to an equally "brief period of normal madness" in the mother (Green, 1986), the child is definitely involved in the phenomenon of being in love and hypnosis (Freud, 1921c, pp. 111–116), an instant of alienation, which is, as we know, the state of identification, because I is another (*"Car Je est un autre"*; Rimbaud, 1871).

From then on, seeing what he sees, the eye that gazes, Winnicott's eye, is changed, and this leads him to reconsider the dynamics of psychopathology based on what he has seen. This observable field is a complex context where mothers, according to Winnicott, know what to do. The transitional object, and the transitional phenomena that create and give life to it, are the most important supports of a specific quality of mental life, reconfigured within a founding context (Zak de Goldstein, 1992). And the "good enough mother", to whom Winnicott makes reference, is the one providing external help as "the prehistoric, unforgettable other" (Freud, 1896), who also helps the *infans* through the mirror phase (Lacan, 1949).

The good enough mother is enough because, in her partial withdrawal, which is led, in turn, by her own desiring sexuality, she gives rise to the oscillation between illusion and disillusionment. It is through this oscillation that she moves and gradually ceases to support "His Majesty the Baby" (Freud, 1914c).

This withdrawal, in turn, allows the *infans* to develop and experience his own dreams and desires. By virtue of this dynamic scene the child can float, like the motto of the city of Paris *"fluctuat nec mergitur"*, protected, in particular, from the risks of an endogenous or primary depression, held by his transitional object. In addition, the good-enough mother knows how to carry out what Winnicott has described as "holding, handling and object presentation", essential for personalisation, until illusion, which is already creating the traits of the transitional phenomena (Winnicott, 1971), thanks to its persistence, gives rise to the future transitional object, which will appear now as a stable and favourite object.

In this context of being in love and hypnosis, the effects of which constitute the image within the mirror phase (Lacan, 1949) between the ages of six and eighteen months, the mother, as the beautiful and erotic object that she is for her child (Freud, 1940a), also transfers desire of desire, sexual identity and transgenerational identity. If there is anything in this complexity (i.e., the aforementioned complex context) that fails, there is also terror (*Schreck*) as a result, which, in the Freudian texts, refers to the uncanny, the encounter with sightless eyes. This is the tragic fate of Narcissus and the fountain, which is illustrated in Oscar Wilde's poem "The Disciple" (1991) as the great maternal flaw. The mother, not good enough by virtue, perhaps, of her narcissistic unstableness, is driven mainly to look for herself (moody, unfeeling) in the eyes of Narcissus, devastated and tormented by Echo.

In my view, the hallucination of desire (Freud, 1950a) and its heir, illusion, support each other and support, in turn, the first passes of the transitional phenomenon. However, if the illusion should shatter, as in the case of "The Disciple", due to failures in the essential gaze of recognition (following Hegel's ideas), in the good-enough facilitation, dissociations would appear, along with a certain kind of "affective anaesthesia" (alexithymia, according to Sifneos, 1973), which could determine the fearful and dumb "experience of futility" in the future. If the normal complex function we are describing collapsed due to these failures, a certain kind of death of the transitional object would then take place. And the transitional object, deprived of the vitality granted by what Freud termed as "fiction" (see epigraph) becomes some sort of fetish, such as the case of the string described by Winnicott (1971, Chapter One).

Under these conditions, the ego, still premature and lacking an effective transitional object, obviously becomes distorted and resorts to primary masochism. Even more: this leads the child to go back to the expectation of a brief and essential absolute dependence. Later on, he will become, at best, the child described by Ferenczi (1949), with his look of "wise child" who, in a movement of reversion, offers anti-depressant functions in order to support the narcissistic deprivation of his parents. We are faced with the "early damages" which also affect the constitution of the definitive reality ego, which, in turn, involves damages to trophic narcissism, to the bodily ego, to the ego as a great erotogenic zone. In contrast, in healthy enough conditions, the ego has at its disposal an essential capacity to invest while playing and to create a field along with the other; the open-ended squiggle is there, as a possibility.

A challenge

In my opinion, the perspective of this investigation involves a challenge, introduced by Winnicott's thought. How can the analyst position himself in a field that is characterised by the almost impossible analysability of these "other kinds" of suffering? As we know, because of the abundance of therapeutic failures, the response to this question is connected to the confidence and hope we analysts manage to build while we listen to Winnicott's ideas on the distortion of the ego, on the perspectives of psychoanalysis (Zak de Goldstein, 2002), and on the helplessness anxiety and the terror of dependence involved in these cases, about which Winnicott spoke as early as 1955, in "Metapsychological and clinical aspects of regression within the psycho-analytical set-up".

These are some of the challenges to what I have called the dynamics of the cure: some invisible micro-Stendhal syndromes, following Maghierini's ideas (1989), and several "supernumerary catastrophes" have affected those times of "constitutive failures" which, in addition, develop a visible impossibility of inclusion within the social bonds and the culture, with its comforts and discontents.

In "Clinical varieties of transference", Winnicott (1956) outlines some metapsychological suggestions which had ample repercussions for this clinical approach. For example: when the analyst, attentive to the analytic field, realises that some "mistakes" have taken place, he should know that this could be a wonderful occasion to make visible, in the field, something of the prehistoric mismatches that, according to Winnicott's understanding, are the ones producing this early pathology, to which Freud referred in "Analysis terminable and interminable" (1937c). I am following Bleger's approach (1967) to that kind of essential micro re-edition of trauma in the transference, a "fortunate mistake". The analyst then tries to capture this brief, precious instant of the unfreezing of that anger, and refers this anger to something. This is an outline of those constructions of what became lost in that (past) context, and is now already susceptible to historicisation, and proves to be essential, although it can be achieved only gradually. We should stress here the absolute centrality of these types of constructions (Freud, 1937d), which are part of the repetition within a "furious and passionate transference" of something from the personal "history of traumas", traumas that we know unbind and deconstruct. This perspective was widely supported by Willy Baranger (Baranger & Baranger, 1969) in his clinical teachings, and proved that, in most cases, traumas could be dated.

In his clinical follow-up of families, and studying the use each of the children made of the transitional object and its vicissitudes, Winnicott builds the approach included in the text we are revisiting, that is, *Playing and Reality*, and which constitutes a model of a specific follow-up.

Premature and almost irreversible, the damage in the oscillation and the display of illusion–disillusionment impair the work of the transitional and of playing, guarantors of mental continuity. We should point out that the playing we wish to recover is not only different from *the game*—the difference between them has several consequences—in that it lacks pre-established regulations and rules, but also frequently comes to replace *playing*. The painless pain, the absence of *signal anxiety* (Freud, 1916), and accompanying insatiability that cannot be felt or quenched, all of these permeate forms of survival that account for the presence of those sufferings in a wide range of society, in particular in present-day society. This leads people to consult analysts, without commitment, but certainly with suffering. The lack of a thinkable register of something that is only felt, but not yet thought about, results in their seeming to be looking for someone to *listen*. Let us see what we can do so that the analyst, even in his "impossible" position within this oscillating, elusive, blurred, intermediate field, can say something about "that piece of something heard there": short constructions, gradually undertaken.

The dynamics of a certain possible cure

By reading and understanding the works of Winnicott, it might be possible for both the analyst and the person asking for help to gain access to this field, which is like a stage where pieces of the former states might be seen enacted. These half-opened zones, new versions of what Winnicott termed "frozen experiences", relative to catastrophes and breakdowns that had no meaning whatsoever at the time, might even lend themselves to being put into words, and, therefore, we might have access to brief moments of "transference neurosis" (McDougall, 1982). In the clinical stages we were describing, the non-analysand makes different attempts at reproducing the madness he has been subjected to and, in addition, tries to madden the analyst with his condition (Searles, 1979). The theoretical and technical advances made by García Badaracco (1986) and his conception of the "maddening object" have significant resonances with what we have described as the most current challenges for psychoanalysis.

Taking the perspective I have proposed as a starting point, some of these states—perhaps even in clinical practice with neuroses—can be traced back to their traumatic origins. They constitute the profound effects of an invisible "shattered illusion". I would like to suggest that these states, the object of our study, are at the core of forms of endogenous depressions, or endogenous or primary melancholy, which are so perplexing. These clinical states, with their transgenerational, intergenerational connections, as well as their connection to the particular time that they take place, point to the possible origins, which become more visible during adolescence and youth, of a persistent and extended social feeling that latently oscillates between boredom and a feeling of futility and disorientation, and also tends towards impulsive behaviour and the growing phenomena of hostility and social and school violence, such as the newly rediscovered bullying, among others. Moreover, these states appear to be connected to an underlying inhibition of originality and creative activity.

From another perspective, Winnicott traces back the failed effects of the good-enough mother. In my own view, this is the essential variable: when and how the illusion was shattered due to those failed effects.

Struggling with its subordinate relationships and faced with demanding powers, the ego distorts and, at the same time, prevents the occurrence of a definitive implosion. The struggle of the ego is possible so long as the conditions, which are discussed so thoroughly in the works of Winnicott, are sufficient to allow the initial ego to gain the consistency of pleasure in acting, which is basic and necessary for survival (see Freud's observations about the Fort-Da game in *Beyond the Pleasure Principle*, 1920g).

Freud and Winnicott share the idea that the existence of illusion, and of the "resting place" (Winnicott, 1971) or "nature reserve" (Freud, 1911b) where the subject enters in order to preserve the illusion, is necessary (Freud, 1927c). The former constitutes, precisely, the transitional space.

Following Winnicott, we could say that if the *self* is false, it is false with regard to the patient himself. He has betrayed himself in order to stay alive and to experience in some way the old entropic desire of carefree day-dreaming that, due to the lack of transitional resources, he was unable to preserve adequately. A possible alternative, which appeared when facing the horror (*Schreck*), has him teetering on the edge of the tragic experience of helplessness and at risk of prematurely discovering that, perhaps, there is no one out there, no someone he can call in order to stay calm, depend upon, and day-dream, practising the privacy and the capacity to be alone, but no longer with that feeling of helplessness we call loneliness.

That someone, that "experienced person" (Freud, 1950a), whom Winnicott called both the "good enough mother" and the "facilitating environment" experiences a "brief period of normal madness", according to Green (1986), and lovingly offers herself for a short time to an experience of an "as if situation for two". She is the provider of external help that grants sufficient stability and trust. In this way, she gains the power to produce fiction in a paradoxical state (Roussillon, 2012): the illusion, the paradox of thinking, disillusionment and transitionality, in an inextricable sequence, as a whole, in a net of psychosexual inscriptions and transcriptions (Freud, 1896), with the erotogenic oral zone. In *An Outline of Psychoanalysis*, Freud writes,

> A child's first erotic object is the mother's breast that nourishes it; love has its origin in attachment to the satisfied need for nourishment. There is no doubt that, to begin with, the child does not distinguish between the breast and his own body; when the breast has to be separated from the body and sifted to the "outside" because the child so often finds it absent, it carries with it as an "object" a part of the original narcissistic libidinal cathexis. This first object is later completed into the person of the child's mother. . . . By her care of the child's body she becomes its first seducer. In these two relations lies the root of a mother's importance, unique, without parallel, established unalterably for a whole lifetime as the first and strongest love object and as the prototype of all later love-relations – for both sexes . . . And for however long it is fed at its mother's breast, [the child] will always be left with a conviction after it has been weaned that its feeding was too short and too little. (1940a, pp. 188–189)

Within the topography of illusion–hallucination, the transitional, in the coming and going of the effects of the transitions of the transitional neuro-optical effects (typical of the human species endowed with articulate language) are transported. Topographic–dynamic–structural inflections and torsions appear, they traverse the endless "magic" of the Möbius strip which reflects itself and duplicates, perhaps in an endless spiral, the grace that grants life, brightness, and seduction to that piece of the Real and succeeds in forming a topography, an economy, and a dynamic (Freud, 1940a, p. 145), generating the effect of "something alive", *aliveness*.

Perhaps Bachelard's *Poetics of Reverie* (1971) and *Poetics of Space* (1994) are fortunate titles that facilitate these metaphors in perspectives of tri-dimensional time and space, and they encourage the revisiting of "On narcissism: an introduction" (Freud, 1914c), for instance, along with the topography of specular phenomena.

Between the illusion, the hallucination, and the disillusionment, the rescuing limit appears. The transitional object—a piece of the Real—supports that limit, and thirdness embodies the "adult other" of upbringing that forces the *infans* to start thinking, to put it in Laplanche's words (1990). Later on, the analyst will have to think about what has been lost, what has not yet been thought about.

What have we gained for our psychoanalytic understanding, and to face and carry forward the difficult clinical practice? We have learnt to avoid, for instance, the drift of psychoanalytic thought towards the inadmissible reductionist Procustism, and to defend psychoanalysis from the disorientation affecting the analyst when he faces the "impossible" clinical practice with the tragic vicissitudes connected to early failures.

Illusion and nostalgia

If *nostos* is going back home and *algos* is the pain accompanying it, this feeling (nostalgia) appears to be essential in order to bear the coming and going of the drive when it threads together, in a psychosomatic way, affect and representation, image and word, and stabilises "psychic work as an original paradoxical thought". This challenges certainties and (it is important to insist on this point) it constitutes the essential support in order to try to "sew up" those alterations of the ego.

Let us remember one of Winnicott's most characteristic statements: "Home is where we start from". Perhaps it would not be superfluous to recall that "Two worlds" is the title of the first chapter of Hermann Hesse's novel, *Demian* (1948). Also, in the article on "The 'uncanny'" (1919h), we see Freud dealing with the relationship between the familiar and the other, the "uncanny".

In the extreme tension where the human being ends up, between rationality and primary creativity, which alludes to the tensions between the primary and the secondary processes, and between the pleasure principle and the reality principle, the familiarity of the place where we live broadens only if the so called "nature reserve" (Freud, 1911b) coexists with it. *The warmth of home*. We emerge from a tension "between Aha-Erlebnis (of identification) and the state of helplessness" (Lacan, 1949), looking for the familiar to give us shelter.

The initial psychic work of metaphorisation, sheltered by these processes, revolves around pleasure and reality, and stabilises the process of thought, which always seems to oscillate between two or more logics. I would call the activity of thought that we are discussing here a paradox emerging from a stabilised oscillation at the core of "tertiary processes", which grants us a surprising gift: "paradoxical thought".

Re-reading Winnicott's text

Inspired by the text "Transitional objects and transitional phenomena", I have attempted to point out what I recognise as the presence of certain elements involved in the origins, as well as the establishment, and functions of transitional phenomena and transitional objects, emphasising the importance of these processes for the constitution of the subject, which are originated in a "phenomenology" of the transitionality, locus of qualities which constitute the possibility of a human existence, the gift of *living a life*.

In the first place, we have stressed the importance attached by Winnicott to illusion, in close connection to the "hallucination of desire" in Freud's thought, which configures what I like to call "the first psychic act", the first reaction to endogenous tension that returns when there is frustration. This process gives rise to a production that turns a "hallucinated construct" into a transitional object.

This very original production of the *infans*, which emerges from the work between transitional phenomena and the first future transitional object, leads us to ask: is it possible to build upon the effects of a lack? Is it possible to produce from pain? Pain is trauma and causes shock to the psyche and the soma. Therefore, does this building take place from a lack whose remains become "a pearl"? The mental capacity of the *infans* can produce infinite meanings—nacre layers, as it were—to what remains of that pain, and looks for that *something*, that sparkle, that reminds him he once was His Majesty the Baby to the mother's eyes. Despite the fact that he knows that this is only an agalmatic object, the wish sparkling in his mother's eyes, this, nevertheless, is how he secures the dream of living. Touched by the parallel effects of the processes of illusion and disillusionment involved in these complex phenomena, and the original product (an illusion), Winnicott's transitional object, which is neither external nor internal, emerges and succeeds also in supporting—as a barrier against trauma—the constitution and the consistence of the beginning of mental work. Thus, the child succeeds in pursuing the enchantment of Proustian time, *A la recherche du temps perdue* (1908–1922) and goes back once more to the times of Arcadia (Goldstein, 2005).

In the second place, we are surprised by the new metapsychological location, according to Winnicott, of the paradox, the paradoxical thought (a specific form of the tertiary processes in human thought) that accompanies this sequence, and the display of the tertiary process, from which playing, humour, and the metaphoric work involved in the essential "as if" emerges, in the folds of life, away from pathology.

Last, the development of the investigation I am presenting encourages analysts to consider in particular those "crucial times" where serious or repeated failures cause alterations of the ego, to which Freud refers in "Analysis terminable and interminable" (1937c). Hence their importance for clinical practice: because we find in borderline patients and in other patients, which until now were considered unanalysable, certain details that help us think about damage that takes place in very early stages and the possibility of their historicisation in the transference, when they are re-edited within an analytic situation, that is "impossible" by definition, even though it goes on . . .

Within this new impossible specific field, this third field between transference neurosis and narcissistic neurosis, sudden and brief new editions appear, new editions which are almost acted out, through which the analyst is anachronically accused and considered, briefly, as his failed transitional object. Working through is recalled and different answers are available for discursive constructions, which can be historicised and captured, piece by piece, by repression. This is how the dynamics of cure progresses.

Illusion and dreams in a personal script

"We are such stuff as dreams are made on . . ." (Shakespeare, 1611, Act 4, Scene 1).

> Life's but a walking shadow, a poor player
> That struts and frets his hour upon the stage
> And then is heard no more. It is a tale
> Told by an idiot, full of sound and fury,
> Signifying nothing.
>
> (Shakespeare, 1623, Act 5, Scene 5)

And this is what we are: dreamers creating sparkles and light and, helped by illusion, we start to move, fulfilling the Freudian formula (1923) *Wo Es war, soll Ich werden:* "Where id [it] was, there ego [I] shall be".

This is what the child who plays does, and this is what this is about: creating shapes and, with art, endowing them with life, putting them in motion, thus training the "tender drive" and the drive for mastery, while the pleasure gain of playing is a promise. *Ars poetica.*

"Should we not look for the first traces of imaginative activity as early as in childhood?" asks Freud.

> Might we not say that every child at play behaves like a creative writer, in that he creates a world of his own, or, rather, re-arranges the things of his world in a new way which pleases him? . . . he takes his play very seriously and he expends large amounts of emotion on it. The opposite of play is not what is serious but what is real. (Freud, 1908e, pp. 143–144)

Then he will "day-dream and dream" both asleep and awake (Ogden, 2010). He knits the Shakespearean fabric and prompts the work of the symbolic machine and the thickness of the preconscious. The initial lack of meaning to which Macbeth refers begins to acquire a meaning of oneself. Time intertwines time and personal desire, as Borges describes in his poem "Chess" (1960). We can see there the beginning, the mythic aspect of time for a human being:

> They know not that the player's selected
> Hand governs their destiny,
> They know not that a rigor adamantine
> Subjects their will and rules their day.
>
> The player also is a prisoner
> (The saying is Omar's) of another board
> Of black nights and of white days.
>
> God moves the player, and he, the piece.
> Which god behind God begets the plot
> Of dust and time and dream and agonies?

Throughout this text, I have tried to show that what supports and makes it possible for the plot to begin, between dreams and agonies, and accounts for the fact that "the player also is a prisoner of another board".

Conclusion

I began by focusing on the transitional phenomenon and the transitional object to show their specificity as support of subjective experiences. None of these is objectifiable or observable. What can be observed is the use made of them, their function and the enigma of their origins and intrinsic power. The transitional phenomenon is a specific phenomenon: a first psychic phenomenon, perhaps. The transitional phenomenon and the transitional object, in a very specific interaction, maybe as a first psychic act, generate and use a *fiction*: hallucination as the wishful activation of the mnemonic image of the object, producing the same thing as a perception (Freud (1950a, p. 319).

If the necessary dimension of uncertainty were not yet stabilised, or if it were frankly unstable and feared, it would threaten dissolution. The beginning and the stabilisation of "personalisation" are guarded by the presence of the transitional object, which, with its availability, welcomes demands and offers support with a malleability that objective reality cannot offer in equal measure.

The cure, which is perhaps our major objective on revisiting these concepts, paves the way for a need of lucidity expected from the analyst's position, who, with his own experience with certain "border phenomena", succeeds in making contact, by means of "reverie" (Bion, 1962), with those aspects important for the analysand within this "impossible cure".

The neutral and kind consideration of the effects of mismatches and failures that occur allow the analyst to go through those moments of "blind" repetition, which are inevitable in every analysis and, in particular, in these kinds of cure, walking in those zones where the dark dimension of confusion lives on, in order to work for the recovery of feared ambiguity and uncertainty involved in healthy paradoxical thought.

Winnicott's work reveals a powerful rearranging of psychopathology, due to the genealogy of the damage to the ego and its prehistoric or mythic origins. These primitive times are exposed to the quality of the psychosexual state of both parents. This will also depend on how the parents handle the symbolic movements and actions and their effective inscription in the *infans*. The period of the oedipal complex leads the *infans* to undergo a process by virtue of which he emerges sexualised and endowed with desire, capable of having the gift of "living alive".

Scientific innovation allows progress in psychoanalysis because we are open to *cross-fertilisation*, and we are aware that we sustain our "uncertainty", in our renewed challenge of becoming psychoanalysts, on a basis: the Freudian corpus and its undiluted development, which is our *common ground*.

Note

1. In memory of J. Outeiral.

References

André, J. (Ed.) (1999). *Les états limites. Nouveau paradigme pour la psychanalyse?* Paris: PUF.

Bachelard, G. (1971). *The Poetics of Reverie: Childhood, Language, and the Cosmos*. Boston, MA: Beacon Press.

Bachelard, G. (1994). *The Poetics of Space.* New York: Orion Press.

Balint, M. (1967). *The Basic Fault: Therapeutic Aspects of Regression.* London: Tavistock, 1968.

Baranger, M., & Baranger, W. (1969). *Problemas del campo psicoanalítico.* Buenos Aires: Kargieman.

Bion, W. R. (1962). *Learning from Experience.* London: Karnac.

Bleger, J. (1967). Psycho-analysis of the psycho-analytic frame. *International Journal of Psychoanalysis, 48*(4): 511–519.

Borges, J. L. (1960). The Game of Chess. In: *Dreamtigers* (p. 59). Austin, TX: University of Texas Press.

Ferenczi, S. (1949). Confusion of tongues between adults and the child. *International Journal of Psychoanalysis, 30*(4): 225–230.

Freud, S. (1896). Letter 52. *S. E., 1*: 233–239. London: Hogarth.

Freud, S. (1908e). Creative writers and day-dreaming. *S. E., 9*: 141–154. London: Hogarth.

Freud, S. (1911b). Formulations on the two principles of mental functioning. *S. E., 12*: 218–255. London: Hogarth.

Freud, S. (1914c). On narcissism: an introduction. *S. E., 14*: 73–101. London: Hogarth.

Freud, S. (1916). Introductory lectures on psychoanalysis (Part III). *S. E., 16*: 395. London: Hogarth.

Freud, S. (1919h). The "uncanny". *S. E., 17*: 217–251. London: Hogarth.

Freud, S. (1920g). *Beyond the Pleasure Principle. S. E., 18*: 7–64. London: Hogarth.

Freud, S. (1921c). *Group Psychology and the Analysis of the Ego. S. E., 18*: 67–143. London: Hogarth.

Freud, S. (1923). *The Ego and the Id. S. E., 19*: 12–66. London: Hogarth.

Freud, S. (1927c). *The Future of an Illusion. S. E., 21*: 5–55. London: Hogarth.

Freud, S. (1937c). Analysis terminable and interminable. *S. E., 23*: 216–253. London: Hogarth.

Freud, S. (1937d). Constructions in analysis. *S. E., 23*: 255–269. London: Hogarth.

Freud, S. (1940a). *An Outline of Psycho-Analysis. S. E., 23*: 144–207. London: Hogarth.

Freud, S. (1950a). *Project for a Scientific Psychology. S. E., 1*: 295–394. London: Hogarth.

García Badaracco, J. (1986). Identification and its vicissitudes in the psychoses: the importance of the concept of the 'maddening object'. *International Journal of Psychoanalysis, 67*(2): 133–146.

Goldstein, G. (2005). La experiencia estética: escritos sobre psicoanálisis y arte. Buenos Aires: Del Estante.

Green, A. (1986). *On Private Madness*. New York: International Universities Press.

Hesse, H. (1948). *Demian*. New York: Henry Holt.

Lacan, J. (1949). Le stade du miroir comme formateur de la fonction du je telle qu'elle nous est révélée dans l'expérience psychanalytique. In: *Ecrits* (pp. 93–100). París: Seuil, 1966.

Laplanche, J. (1990). *Nouveaux fondements pour la psychanalyse: la séduction originaire*. Paris: Presses Universitaires de France.

Maghierini, G. (1989). *La síndrome di Stendhal*. Florence: Feltrinelli.

McDougall, J. (1982). *Plaidoyer pour une certaine anormalité*. Paris: Gallimard.

Ogden, T. H. (2010). On three forms of thinking: magical thinking, dream thinking, and transformative thinking. *Psychoanalytic Quarterly, LXXIX*(2): 317–347.

Rassial, J. J. (1999). *Le sujet en état limite*. Paris: Denoël.

Rimbaud, A. (1871). Je est un autre. Letter from Arthur Rimbaud to Paul Demeny, in Charleville, 15 May.

Roussillon, R. (2012). Actualidade de Winnicott. In: A. Clancier & J. Kalmanovitch (Eds.), *O Paradoxo de Winnicott* (pp. 1–23). Porto Alegre: Maresfield.

Searles, H. (1979). The dedicated physician in psychotherapy and psychoanalysis. In: *Countertransference and Related Subjects: Selected Papers* (pp. 71–88). New York: International Universities Press.

Shakespeare, W. (1611). *The Tempest*. In: *The Complete Works* (pp. 148–158). Oxford: Clarendon Press, 2005.

Shakespeare, W. (1623). *Macbeth*. In: *The Complete Works* (pp. 280–287). Oxford: Clarendon Press, 2005.

Sifneos, P. E. (1973). The prevalence of alexithymic characteristics in psychosomatic patients. *Psychotherapy and Psychosomatics, 22*(2–6): 255–253.

Wilde, O. (1991). The Disciple. In: *The Complete Works of Oscar Wilde* (p. 901). London: Collins.

Winnicott, D. W. (1955). Metapsychological and clinical aspects of regression within the psycho-analytical set-up. *International Journal of Psychoanalysis, 36*(1): 16–26.

Winnicott, D. W. (1956). Clinical varieties of transference. In: *On Transference. International Journal of Psychoanalysis, 37*: 4–5: 386–388.

Winnicott, D. W. (1960). Ego distortion in terms of true and false self. In: *The Maturational Processes and the Facilitating Environment: Studies in the Theory of Emotional Development* (pp. 140–153). New York: International Universities Press, 1966.

Winnicott, D. W. (1971). *Playing and Reality*. New York: Basic Books.

Zak de Goldstein, R. (1992). Entre el júbilo identificatorio y el estado de desamparo. Presentado en el XIX Congreso Latinoamericano de Psicoanálisis, FEPAL, Montevideo 1–7 agosto.

Zak de Goldstein, R. (2002). *Encuadre y analizabilidad. Encuadre, cura y desidentificación*. Paris: Soc. Psych. Paris (SPP).

CHAPTER TWO

Playing

Anna Maria Nicolò

Introduction

Winnicott is one of the authors with the largest influence on the psychoanalysis of today, seemingly an easy read, yet with every re-reading we get the feeling that however much we might have taken for granted at the beginning, there are other hidden meanings that have managed to escape us.

That this should be so is due to many reasons, foremost among which are the revolutionary implications of some of his discoveries, but also his use of language. Over the past years, many authors (Abram, 1996; Bonaminio, 1991; Ogden, 2013) have pointed out that Winnicott invented a new language, one that is simple, direct, not usual, not intellectual, and one in which he even made up his own words. To me it seems that all of this derives from his enormous clinical experience, which kept him continuously in touch with a very large variety of patients, as well as from the fact that he progressively perfected his discoveries and refined his ideas. He did this in a manner so that, within himself, he kept the psychoanalytical theories of his time in conflict with the data of what he had himself observed. This new language of his was born out of the necessity to describe new concepts, for which the theoretical and philosophical context of the time did not provide him with any adequate instruments. Like many precursors, he made himself the bearer and protagonist of a conceptual revolution, carrying with it a multitude of implications. However, he did not craft it into an organised and organic theory; rather, it was born out of his clinical examples and the commentary that he furnished them with.

Today, at a time when we are increasingly often confronted with patients with ever more severe problems in the course of our work and when we are in need of tools to treat them with, we turn to Winnicott, or Bion, for directions and answers. I believe this to be the reason for the spread of his thought in our day. Each day we learn to recognise more of him in his pioneering discoveries. Winnicott in particular has enabled us to open ourselves for the study of the relations between the internal world and the environment in which we live. None the less, we are sometimes left confused over certain statements that can seem contradictory in the course of time. We must not forget that what he wrote was effectively born out of his paediatric experience and an enormous amount of observations of newborns and healthy as well as suffering children. Perhaps this is his primary lesson: that we should always stick close to our observations of our patients, whether they behave normally or are in situations of distress. The clinical and the psychoanalytic child are kept in a balance within him, and we manage to get a look at this in his works, in his letters that we have access to thanks to Rodman's biography (2003), and in some commentaries on his work. All of these characteristics contribute to create a very particular situation. Winnicott is often interpreted by different analysts in ways that seem to be opposed to each other. Thus, every reader has their own Winnicott: I, for example, will have my version of him and show this to you in the text that follows, also because, as Ogden tells us (2013), Winnicott's writing is not synthesisable and cannot be paraphrased. We can only observe within ourselves the effect that it produces, the experiences we have upon reading, rethinking, forgetting, and then re-encountering it in our observations. Perhaps we can also hypothesise, as Ogden says, that he wrote "to create experiences in reading that are inseparable from the ideas he is presenting, or more accurately, the ideas he is playing with" (Ogden, 2013, p. 213).

A natural corollary of this is to ask oneself how much commentary it is possible to make on such an author, given that in doing so, we already feel that we reflect only palely on his discoveries and that we even run the risk of taking away that particular presence that characterises Winnicott's writings.

This is another important aspect of Winnicott's work: it is impossible to dissociate his writings from his personal being and mode of living, according to what we have been told by many of those that knew him, first and foremost among them his wife, Clare.

A short historical incursion

Clare Winnicott wrote about her husband that the ability to play "was part of his way of putting himself into and being in relations" and "of his entire way of living" (Winnicott, 1958a, p. 2). She also quotes the following statement by him: "playing is an experience, always a creative experience, and it is an experience in the space–time continuum, a basic form of living" (Winnicott, 1971d, p. 50). *Playing and Reality* (1971a) was published posthumously, as many will know, but his theory of playing had long been in preparation over the course of his life. In the Foreword, Winnicott stated that it represented a continuation of his work published under the title "Transitional objects and transitional phenomena" (1958b), and in the chapter "Playing: a theoretical statement" (1971d, p. 48) he also recalls some of his other work in which he had begun to develop this idea. But as we know and are reminded by Abram (1996), the author of a most accurate and valuable commentary on Winnicott's work, he had already laid the groundwork for his later observations in "Why children play" (1942). Thus, we might well say that playing features in many of the topics of Winnicott's thinking from the beginning, even though, when looking at dates, important works on the topic itself stem only from around the 1960s. It is interesting to look at the subjects connected to his conception of playing (Abram, 2008, p. 102): fantasy, creativity, the exploration of the self, object use, the potential space, illusion, and cultural experience.

While those child analysts preceding him, such as Klein or Anna Freud, observed playing in its various meanings, but primarily as an expression or representation of the conflicts and unconscious fantasies of the infant, and used it as a channel for communication and interpretation (Schacht, 1999, p. 179), Winnicott stressed its nature of being a process, a transformation, a becoming. Looking at this attitude from another perspective, putting the emphasis not on the product but on the process of producing often led him to use verbs instead of nouns, for example, "fantasising", "going on being", and, consequently, "playing" instead of "play": playing, thus, became a motion, the experience of creating the self, an area consigned to potential space, a place of illusion, a space for the encounter with the other both inside and outside the self, a source of creativity. Ogden brings this perspective to a comparison of these aspects of Winnicott's thinking to that of Bion and asserts that the latter "moved the focus from the symbolic contents of thoughts to the process of thinking and from the symbolic content of dreams to the process of dreaming", and that in the same manner Winnicott moved the focus "from the play (as symbolic representation of the internal world of the child) to the experience of playing" (Ogden, 2009, p. 16).

Playing within the potential space

At the heart of playing lies the fact of its being consigned to potential space and its making use of transitional qualities. In this way, it combines intrapsychic experiences with input coming from the outside world, and uses whatever is provided by the interlocutor or external phenomena for internal re-elaborations. Schacht tells us that "it emerges in the intermediary space between the visible and invisible, between the mysterious and the evident, between the playful and the serious" (Schacht, 1999, p. 180). In my imagination, Winnicott encountered a dilemma during the course of his career. Unlike other analysts of his time, he noticed the importance of the environment in the development of the individual through his clinical consultations, and had observed the coexistence of two spaces, one internal, the other external. Thus, he became aware that there existed phenomena and experiences taking place in, and partaking of, both these spheres. He called the phenomena transitional because the child constantly commutes between the one sphere and the other. Taking as starting point this discovery of transitional objects and phenomena, Winnicott began to explore this particular area of the relation between child and mother, of the encounter and superposition of the self and the other, of reality and fantasy, of subjective objects and those that are objectively perceived, of what is found and what is created to signify this extraordinary experience that the infant has: of creating an object that the mother, for her part, allows him/her to find.

Transitional objects and phenomena are "not part of the infant's body yet are not fully recognized as belonging to external reality" (Winnicott, 1958a, p. 2).

Playing is also located in this area and it is to this that it owes its transformational capacities.

"This area of playing is not inner psychic reality. It is outside the individual, but it is not the external world" (Winnicott, 1971d, p. 51). The paradox of the existence of the potential space itself dissolves the dichotomy of the coexistence of these two spaces, internal and external. To this effect, Winnicott asserts that

> a description of the emotional development of the individual cannot be made entirely in terms of the individual, but that in certain areas, and this is one of them, perhaps the main one, the behaviour of the environment is part of the individual's own personal development and must therefore be included. (Winnicott, 1971e, p. 53)

If we read carefully into how many times he repeatedly took up writing about this, we cannot but be astonished at how controversial and debated these topics must have been within him.[1] This makes it easier to understand how it can be that today there are so many diverse authors interpreting Winnicott, all of them invoking him and naming models after him, and yet seeming to be opposed to each other. From this, we might be able to get a glimpse of the creative evolution of a theory or way of thinking. Winnicott planted evolution at the centre of his conceptualisations. He himself underwent an evolution in the concepts he theorised, the work on the use of the object representing the ultimate stage of his reflections, and he conceived of the growth of a person in the same way. For him, a growing and maturing individual recognises the object as external and distinct, and not as "a bundle of projections". In a sense, with these statements he created the foundations for the study of phenomena that run both between individuals and between an individual and his/her external world, incorporating the environment into the internal functioning of the individual from the beginning of his/her life. His discovery of the potential space as a third space and of its paradoxical nature that we can only live and accept is the solution that he proposed for the dilemma.

> Winnicott's insistence that neither the one-person model of the infant nor the two-person model which is dependent upon the awareness of another and its implications for psychic life contain all the factors that are basic to human development. (Caldwell & Joyce, 2011, p. 102)

Illusion and playing

The focal point of the experience of playing, built in the potential space, lies on what the infant will experience thanks to a sufficiently good mother, who is one that is capable of furnishing him/her with the illusions that "her breast is part of the infant" and that "there is an external reality that corresponds to the infant's own capacity to create" (Winnicott, 1958a, p. 12).

In this way, illusion becomes a point of intersection in Winnicott's conception, above all concerning the experience of playing and of creativity. He plants illusion at the root of symbolism and asserts that this makes it possible to "describe ... the infant's journey from the purely subjective to objectivity; and ... the transitional object ... is what we see of this journey of progress towards experiencing" (Winnicott, 1958a, p. 6).

To paraphrase Winnicott here, we might say that in physiological situations a tolerant mother will provide her child with a state of affairs in which they can live through an experience together as if two lines had joined from opposite directions, producing a moment of illusion that is an "interplay in the child's mind of that which is subjective (near-hallucination) and that which is objectively perceived (actual, or shared reality)" (Winnicott, 1971d, p. 52; see Ogden, 2001, p. 130 It. ed.). It is, therefore, a sufficient amount of illusion that the mother provides which allows the child to gain access to reality in order to experience its relations and also to have access to symbolism.

Thus, both symbolism and the creations of the transitional space are linked to the capacity of the mother–child couple to maintain a prolonged illusion for the time that it takes to come to terms with the approaching external reality. Kluzer Usuelli describes this phenomenon in a very clear fashion:

> Within this theory, in which the status of *reality* is that of *shared illusion*, everything that is representable is situated in the transitional space. This implies that it is included, at least virtually, in a network of meanings, based on the feeling that the object and the subject, the outside and the inside worlds, the "me and not-me", somehow correspond to each other, or even that the one exists as a function of the other. This feeling arises at the beginning of psychical life, simultaneously with the construction of the transitional space. It constitutes the prehistory of the subject (and of the object) and is what will allow the subject to make sense of experience. (Kluzer Usuelli, 1992, pp. 180–181)

Pathology is an inability to have access to illusion. It is generated by a rough and abrupt passage from a fusional state to reality, without a sufficient dose of illusion to allow for a more gradual encounter. Some people suffering from it will react to this by never leaving factual reality again. However, we may also observe the opposite happening: people who flee from reality, taking refuge in solitary constructions and sustaining their delusion, something that we must not confuse with an excess of illusion.

Here again, Winnicott's love for the paradox cannot be denied. In fact, he asserts that it is only by creating and recreating illusions that we are given access to reality and that the play-space opens for us. Illusion and disillusion will take turns in this process, as some authors suggest (Hernandez & Giannakoulas, 2003; Kluzer Usuelli, 1992). In this view, it becomes obvious why playing is equivalent to being free within our own minds. Having such an ability allows one to search and study within the self as well as with the other without impediments, to change levels of functioning during the session, moving from regression towards a more integrated functioning, to touch upon aspects of chaos and to tolerate inexplicable ones. With patients lacking this kind of experience, it is the duty of the analyst to let them experience it, or even to bring them to a state in which this becomes possible. However, playing is also "doing". In sessions with children, the child will do some things, and the analyst will, too. These actions, which in sessions with children "involve . . . the body" (Winnicott, 1971d, p. 52), relate to a language that communicates at several levels, one being that which analysts have always been inclined to interpret: the fantasies and conflicts inhabiting the internal world. There is also another level that finds its expression primarily through the body and through actions, and which we have today learnt to consider and evaluate as an "unthought known" (Bollas, 1987). It often has traumatic origins that are given an opportunity to manifest themselves through playing.

All of this allows us to understand why Winnicott stated that even playing can have a therapeutic and transformative effect. Playing actually arises from a capacity to experience an illusion where this had not been possible before.

Playing as a process

Giorgio is a boy aged eight, who was adopted at the age of three. His schoolteacher brings him to our attention because of his reclusive behaviour, restlessness, and aggression in his interactions with classmates. His parents, however, who are very caught up in their work, are not aware of anything being amiss and display both their incredulity and their concern.

Giorgio is normally in the care of his father, because his mother is often away from home. The father very much insists on rules and norms in his upbringing. He seems to be a fragile and sometimes childish man, worried about making mistakes with his son. He often takes him to football matches featuring his favourite team.

In the first session, taking place in the father's room (although he has to absent himself after a short time), Giorgio sits in his chair and responds monosyllabically. The therapist sits down on the floor and, after having invited the boy to play with her, she begins to rummage inside the toy box, taking out toy soldiers, little machines, and figurines of wild and domestic animals. Meanwhile, she asks the boy if he knows why they are here together, and if he knows who the therapist is. Giorgio answers that he knows that she is a doctor, but that he doesn't know why they are here, perhaps because he hasn't been such a good boy at school. The therapist asks him whether that is true. He says he doesn't know and withdraws. Thinking that it is more important to create an atmosphere of trust, and in order to avoid persecutory topics, the therapist turns back to the toys. Being invited to do so, Giorgio reluctantly moves to look inside the toy box and only brightens up for a moment when the therapist pulls out a dinosaur. It is still a difficult atmosphere, but Giorgio seems to be happy to see the winged dinosaur that she is holding. He has one of them, too. "We have a similar toy, but how is yours made?", the therapist asks, and he then describes it to her. The session concludes a little later, when the boy finally leaves with a smile, albeit timid.

The analyst did not make any interpretations, just a few comments. Above all, she showed that an activity is possible in which she explores the contents of the toy box, commenting on the toys and listening to the boy's opinion on them. The aim of the first session seems to have been to establish a relation of trust and of enjoying a shared activity, while a setting is building up.

The inhibitions that Giorgio shows towards playing in the first session dissolve quickly enough, at the same time that the boy gradually grows more comfortable in his relation with the analyst.

As Winnicott tells us (1971b, p. 101), a deprived child, having suffered from trauma and early loss, will not play and will develop a false sense of self. If contact with external reality was traumatic, so that it caused a dent in the protective shield, pathological dissociative processes of denial will be so massive that no space will be provided for dreaming, for fantasy, or for playing. The child presents morphologically as an adult, he or she is a wise baby, and the therapy will now consist of an attempt to reconstitute trust in the containing environment, and to rediscover the possibility of experiencing the realm of creative illusion, the potential space and the freedom of playing.

"In favourable circumstances the potential space becomes filled with the products of the baby's own creative imagination" (Winnicott, 1971b, p. 102). In unfavourable circumstances, when a premature disillusion has taken place, this potential space becomes "filled with what is injected into it from someone other than the baby" (Winnicott, 1971b, p. 102). Winnicott warns us that even the analyst can run a risk of causing such injections through his or her interpretations, because the potential danger exists that they might be merely fruits of the analyst's own imagination. Even if they are consistent with the child's history or internal functioning, these interpretative intrusions hinder the child from having autonomous activity in the process of playing. It is necessary for this activity to develop in order to let the child rediscover the pleasure of being active and of authorising himself to explore.

Some months later, Giorgio and his analyst seem to have established a good relation of mutual trust, and the boy enjoys going to the sessions. With increasing frequency, a certain repetitive game takes place during the sessions: Giorgio stages improvised surprise attacks on some of the toy animals with other animals or soldiers, or he builds towers or houses that he then suddenly lets collapse. After the destruction, however, the boy will suddenly and without delay engage in acts of reparation and reconstruction.

This game is extremely repetitive and hardly ever ceases. While engaged with the different building phases of the game, Giorgio seems very excited and withdrawn into himself. Initially, the analyst is called upon only to be the spectator of these events. Yet, over the course of the sessions, she is successively more involved, so that eventually she is made to witness the destruction of the toys she constructed at the invitation of the boy, or of the buildings she made from Lego or Play-Doh, while the role of their saviour always remains Giorgio's. He associates nothing with his repetitive game, and neither does he attribute it to anything that he can remember. In the game, the possibility for repeating a traumatic event that the boy can only remember through these actions seems to emerge. At a still later point in time, the game is shifted directly towards the person of the analyst. This shift is evidence of the boy's ever stronger investment in the analyst and the progressively increasing contact with his emotions.

I present an excerpt from a session.

> He arrives punctually with his nanny. The wooden toy blocks from last time are lying on the floor. He wants to play with the blocks, and asks the analyst to help him build a tower. The game consists of building a tower and then pulling out blocks piece by piece until it collapses. He definitely wants to win. He then asks the analyst not to watch, and after having built something, he suddenly gets ready to take it down by hurling animals at it. The analyst points out the repetitions in this game to him.
>
> Now Giorgio wants to play doctor. The analyst comments that maybe he would like to take care of that child that he destroyed a little. So Giorgio picks up a little suitcase and puts inside tape, scissors, some pieces of paper, and pencils. He writes "Doctor Lino" on a post-it note and sticks it on the suitcase.
>
> The analyst joins in the game and says, "Hello, are you the doctor Lino who is treating Giorgio?" He answers, "No, I'm the evil doctor who'll give you poison." He uses the pencil to inject the poison into the analyst's arm, and she pretends to faint and pleads for help.

> Giorgio then immediately changes tone and says "I'm the good doctor!"
>
> He asks the analyst to be both a sick girl as well as the mum. He treats the girl and interacts with the mother. As the end of the session is approaching, while they are still playing, Giorgio asks the analyst acting as the mother whether he can have dinner with her and the girl and then later sleep in their house as well, even though he left his wife and daughter at home.
>
> The analyst is very moved by this. Other than oedipal fantasies, Giorgio actualises very strong affections and relations in playing. Not only the fantasy of staying with the analyst, but there is also his feeling of being divided between two families, one of which is left behind, just like he was in the past.

In the following sessions, he will repeatedly die and let himself be saved by the analyst. Giorgio has progressively permitted himself to include the analyst in his playing, and has become sufficiently free and secure to be able to direct his attacks and aggressiveness towards her. The threat of death, as well as the attacks that he presumably had to suffer in his life in the orphanage before being adopted, still weigh upon him, but they are progressively staged in scenes and are being transformed.

Needless to say, in his behaviour both in school and at home, Giorgio calms down increasingly. He comes to enjoy the interactions with his classmates again and his academic performance is also improving.

In stressing the process dimension of this experience, we also highlight its transformational character. A child can acquire the ability to play even if he or she had lost it before or had never had it at all. This means overcoming the blockages and inhibitions that prevent him or her from playing, first of all mentally, and then in reality. However, is playing in one's mind not also a foundation for thinking? Winnicott voices his criticism of this proposal in an argument against those analysts who used to see only the game and not the process, saying, "in the total theory of the personality the psychoanalyst has been too busy using play content to look at the playing child" (Winnicott, 1971d, p. 40).

Not only the contents of a game are important, which so interest child analysts as communications about unconscious fantasies, but also the entire complex process by which a child or an adult transforms unconscious contents, brings them to fruition, renders them digestible and makes them partially or wholly conscious. In this sense, "playing is itself a therapy" (Winnicott, 1971d, p. 50).

Playing between novel experience and repetition

If we take a close look at the sessions with Giorgio, it becomes clear that playing means taking the liberty of exploring unknown areas of the self, and of confronting the unknown while at the same time being certain of the protection provided by the analyst's or the other's presence. On the one hand, this is indeed a liberty, but, on the other, a necessity, for when the boy finally reaches a stage at which he can allow himself to play, this playing then becomes repetitive for a certain period of time, in order to reproduce and revisit again and again the same scene of destruction with its subsequent reconstruction and repair. Giorgio seems to be compelled to repeat the game that he inaugurated. He has the liberty of doing so, but it is an inner necessity that urges him to repeat the same scene in search of a way out, an alternative solution he does not yet know the nature of. Regarding this very phenomenon, Schacht confirms that playing arises from an oscillation between the liberty to play and an inner necessity for doing so (Schacht, 1999, p. 202), and she reminds us also that

> this is preserved, even though it seems to disappear after childhood or adolescence, in a particular form within the sphere of creative life that is the realm of culture, in which novelty or artistic activity is generated out of an internal necessity.

Playing effectively takes different forms according to the stage of life one is in, even if the process of playing is the same whether with infants or with adults. Child analysts know this well. They are well prepared to use dolls, Lego, or Play-doh when playing with a child; later they bear the endless games of draughts or with pens that youngsters in the latency phase are fond of, and progressively these will shift ever further towards adolescent dramatisations when the patient becomes interested in games on the Internet, for example. Adults, eventually, come to play with their free associations, their paintings, their music, their theatre. Over the course of time, a progression takes place, a shift from concreteness, or from doing, towards the verbal or mental realm. All of these games are symbolic, but their means of expression are different.

Winnicott is quite explicit in this regard: "Whatever I say about children playing really applies to adults as well. . . . [With them, i]t manifests itself, for instance, in the choice of words, in the inflections of the voice, and indeed in the sense of humour" (Winnicott, 1971d, p. 40, see also the Winnicottian thinker (Giannakoulas, 2010; Green, 1975, 2003; Hernandez & Giannakoulas, 2003).

Winnicott considered the most important component of playing to be its creative moment. It is not remembering and understanding that is meant here, but, rather, experiencing anew. The extraordinary transformative and healing powers of playing are to be found not only in its capacity for highlighting hidden meanings, something which is also characteristic of playing, but above all in its capacity for a new creation of the self and of meaning, which can only happen in relation with the other, with the external world, the analyst, and within the particular space that Winnicott discovered and which he called "potential space".

There are two points I would like to draw attention to. The presence of the other in a relation, be it real or imagined, is necessary for the development of creative and playful activities. A child plays in relation with the other, whether it is another child, or an adult, or another self. Playing always presupposes the other: as witness, as guarantor, as playing companion, as the person at whom activity is directed, as a double and other of the self, who can both represent the self and the unknown with which to experiment.

Winnicott here speaks of the infant's acquisition of the ability of being alone in the presence of the other. Even if the ability of being alone is the endpoint of a long process of growth, it is in constant alternation with a state of being with the other. Especially in this regard, the presence of the other constitutes an unknown and "other" contribution, reassuring in the reconstruction of a relation of trust for the child, but also disturbing for being a representation of what is new. This process of continuous coming, staying, and going, of moving between different levels (reality–fantasy, internal–external, etc.) and different vectors (self–other, self–other internal to the self) ensures that transformation can take place. This is the process of playing. Behind the door of the room, behind the door of playing, we will find the reality that the child must learn to accept, not through adapting to it with a false self, but through a process of progressive disillusion. However, we also know that we will never cease to play during the course of our lives, and that this will provide us with a spool of creativity for various areas of our life, actually for our entire life itself.

Not only are unknown parts of the self brought back to our lives in this fashion, but new meanings are also acquired. This is the second point to reflect upon.

I am aware of how controversial this last point might be. In his work "Potential space in psychoanalysis", Green (1975, p. 200), for example, distances himself from the idea that new meanings could be created during sessions, and asserts instead, "I prefer to describe it as an absent meaning, a virtual sense which awaits its realization . . .". According to this proposal, both the relation with the analyst and that with the mother allow for a rendition of what seemed to be absent into something potential, and of what used to be potential into something actually existing.

To maintain that meanings become actualised in the relation with the therapist, where they had been potentially present already, presupposes a model (Green's) based on the idea of discovering something that the patient or the child carries within themselves. Just to give an example, this is a position different from that taken by Schacht in her work "Il gioco tra trauma e creatività" [Play between trauma and creativity] (1999, p. 181), where she asserts that

> it is likely that novel areas of experience of the self become conquered both in the child and in the therapist – including, not least, an expansion of the experience of the ability to play, the experience of an attitude, internally fluctuating, of opening up to what is new and unforeseen, and which is shared by both sides. (Translated for this edition)

These are areas of the self that also include the analyst and his or her own ability to play, as Winnicott has told us many times. Ferro (1999, p. 272) also underlines this aspect, maintaining that the child and the adult construct something new and that they invent new meanings when playing together, and that it is the presence of the other that is the matrix of creativity.

Playing as dreaming

"Let's play that you're Agata [the girl] and I'm Anna [the analyst]", my young patient Agata tells me. "Let's play that I'm the teacher and you're the student and I give you homework and you make mistakes everywhere and I write lots of blue marks on them."

"Let's play that . . ." is the constituting paradox of the setting itself, realm of dream and metaphor.

"Let's play that you're the mother who I need to fuse with, that you're the father I would like to tenderly seduce, that you're the little brother I would like to murder." The temporal limitation of the session can provide great reassurance that whatever may occur, however terrible or wonderful it might be, does not belong to the reality of the everyday world. Here it is impossible not to be reminded of what Freud said: "The opposite of play is not what is serious but what is real" (Freud, 1908e, p. 144).

"Let's play that" catapults us into a different space, one that is no less real than our everyday reality, but which constitutes a different reality. "Let's play that" presupposes a request by the child and the adaptation to his or her needs by the mother or the analyst. This is possible and permitted within the setting, in playing and in metaphor, in poetry and in film. As a creative experience of the self and a mode of mental functioning, making use of thoughts and free associations, we may encounter it also in metaphor, in drama, and in fables.

Allow me to explore this topic more deeply: what is the relation between the fiction of playing and the fiction of lying? Between acting in real life and acting on stage? They say that when being called a liar, Italian director Federico Fellini, hugely famous for *La Dolce Vita* and *Amarchord*, responded that he was not a liar, but that he created fictions. We know perfectly well how much a novel, drama, or film can correspond to conflicts or fantasies that each of us harbours within their internal world. Our internal worlds are also constructed based on worlds of fantasy. Hence, they are as real as our real world, just at another level and in a different fashion. We can recognise ourselves in a literary or dramatic character, or in a painted picture. Does it not happen occasionally that we define one of our patients as a Don Giovanni? Or another as a Madame Bovary? It is possible to recognise oneself in a character. In this process we re-cognise ourselves, in the sense that we get to know certain aspects of ourselves a second time.

This process is very much present in games played by adolescents: for example, in role-playing games on the Internet, in which they take on different personalities. Sometimes, they adopt another name, age, or gender, and explore different relations and identities in their fantasies and on the web. As an outcome, it might either happen that they remain entangled in identities that do not belong to them, or, instead, that after playing such interactive games on the Internet they are capable of transforming themselves and that they become better equipped for confronting everyday reality.

The paradoxical coexistence of two spaces, that of reality and that of the imagination, is a never-ceasing source of creativity and transformation.

This aspect seems to resemble the ideas of one of Winnicott's great contemporaries, Wilfred Bion. In fact, Winnicott asserts, "In playing, the child manipulates external phenomena in the service of the dream and invests chosen external phenomena with dream meaning and feeling" (1971d, p. 51).

Playing, therefore, partakes of the functioning of dreaming, even if only in part. We might speak of the frame of playing, just as of that of dreaming, as a frame provided in the game not only through the setting, but through the implicit or explicit agreement of the players. The confinements of playing allow us to explain the "Let's play that . . ." as well as the space of dreaming as a zone where the oniric process can be experienced (Khan, 1974, p. 301).

Even if it is in a non-explicit fashion, this point also reveals the proximity between Winnicott and Bion regarding their philosophy of intervention and the reconsideration of what we might consider pathological.

The paradoxical dimension of playing

"Let's play with the ball," Luigi says to me in the second session after the Christmas holidays. He is an eight-year-old boy suffering from encopresis. "You're in the goal first and later I'll go there. We're playing for points." I get ready to start playing, but after the first few shots I notice that his balls are all shot directly at me, intended to hit me. "I think you're angry with me today," I remark to him while trying to dodge his shots, but I don't stop returning the soft rubber ball to him that we are playing with. "Now I'm winning," Luigi replies, but he passes the ball back to me low on the floor. After a short time, however, he launches it violently towards my face again. He notices that he grazed me and grows anxious, and says, "But it's only a game! It's only a game!" The excitement that accompanied the game has blocked him, and caused a sudden throwback into reality. He then becomes anxious and aware that he really hit me. He needs the confinements of the game to be re-established, and so he cries, "It's only a game!"

Is his having hit me deliberately therefore not part of the game? Certainly, but not only that: in fact, Luigi is angry with me, but not in the game. But is the game not the best place, time, and way to express this, confined within a relationship of mutual trust with the analyst, without having to feel too anxious about his aggressiveness towards me as both his mother, who is often absent or distracted, and as the analyst who has taken his long Christmas holidays away from him?

Luigi and I are in the middle of the paradox of playing. Neither unconscious nor conscious, neither primary nor secondary process, neither reality nor fantasy, but all of these. The two spaces are not in conflict but, instead, interact in a dialogue, a sort of cross-fertilisation. Leaning too closely towards the one or the other would mean leaving the healing paradox of playing in the session. In these situations, the analyst is often confused and unsure what to do. Unable to continue suffering further blows, out of a need, first of all, to protect the patient, whom it would have hurt to feel and to be too destructive, the analyst at the same time cannot deny or pretend anything: Luigi is angry with the analyst in the transference. The paradoxical conviction "It's only a game" also allows verification of the survival of the object after its "destruction".

The object gets up after having been dead, and proclaims, "I am alive". In this way, the danger of destructiveness, the fragility of the object, and its resilience can be explored.

Technical revolution

> The principle is that psychotherapy takes place in the superposition of the child's playing space and that of the adult or the therapist. The squiggle game is an example for the way in which this mutual game can be facilitated. (Winnicott, 1989a, p. 317, see also Abram, 1996, p. 264)

With this formulation that he picks up again in further works, Winnicott summarises the most important of his viewpoints regarding a new model of clinical intervention. In a certain sense, we might take squiggling as an exemplification of this.

I provide a brief summary here of some of these characteristics and the way Winnicott defines them.

We must bid farewell to the preconceived notion that a patient will come to the therapeutic talk with a sense of confidence that he or she will receive help. In this situation, the analyst provides "a natural and freely moving human relationship within the professional setting" (Winnicott, 1989a, p. 299). The "role of the therapist is to supervise the setting, while being also bound up in playing".

With these short phrases, Winnicott revolutionised the way of thinking about psychoanalytic techniques. By stressing the crucial importance of the setting, as he has done repeatedly, which, as he says, for some patients does not represent as much as it actually is "the mother's embrace" (see references to the setting and regressive aspects), he shows us a mobile, human, and natural analyst who is committed to playing.

By affirming that the analysis must aim to provide the patient with an ability to play with him/herself or with the analyst (an ability which he maintains is an expression of a healthy mind), and to bring the patient to actually develop that creative and free mind-set that he attributed to the ability of playing, Winnicott set into motion a Copernican revolution, both at the level of analytic technique and at that of the self-conception of psychoanalysis.

As for the objectives of psychoanalytic treatment, these no longer consist in reaching the defensive position, or in the resolution of conflicts by making the unconscious conscious, or in making progress along a path towards subjectivisation. Instead, what becomes crucial is the quality, the meaning, and the fullness of life. Bollas (2008), one of the most original analysts inspired by Winnicott, pursues this angle further when asserting that the analysis must increase "the reach and depth of the unconscious thought processes". Enabling a process that in my view has a lot to do with internal playing, the analysis must reach a point at which the patient can lose him/herself in their free associations as "a sort of personal creativity", "without knowing which mental image will emerge at whatever day", in order to eventually reach what defines a kind of emotive talent, like a "form of creativity in being and relating oneself to others and to the world" (Bollas, 2008, p. 26). What we are talking about here is playing with the mind, with memories, associations, and images that come up when the patient permits him/herself this state of mind thanks to having forged a trustful relationship with the analyst. As Winnicott describes them, the means by which to reach these objectives have less to do with just the interpretation and rather more with several other factors that ultimately depend on the analyst's character and his/her position in the analytic process.

In this way, interpretation is dethroned as the ultimate instrument that bestows the power of knowing upon the analyst in the perspective of a psychoanalysis that aims to reveal and to make conscious what was unconscious. In fact, Winnicott says, "In this kind of work we know that even the right explanation is ineffectual. The person we are trying to help needs a new experience in a specialised setting" (Winnicott, 1971e, p. 55). While, for Freud, analysis is a talking cure, for Winnicott, interpretation is, especially with certain difficult patients, a way of expressing to the patient the cure, one's comprehension, and one's contact, "the willingness of the analyst to help, the analyst's capacity to identify with the patient" (see Winnicott 1965b, quoted in Phillips, 1988, p. 140). It is the patient who must develop and create the work that the analyst lets him/her find. If that is not the case, it is a case of indoctrination. There cannot be an interpretation that goes beyond what the transference's trust permits.

The position of the analyst in the analytical relation becomes crucial, in so far as it must remain asymmetrical. At this point, we must remember the great distance of this view from the humorous metaphor that Meltzer employed when he divided analysts into two groups, hunters and farmers. Those of the first group forge ahead to detect, ferret out, and catch their prey, while those of the second group plant a seedling and then wait for it to grow. In both options, the analyst holds the active role and takes the initiative, even if using different methods. On the other hand, the method that Winnicott suggests, and that he lets us experience from his books, makes use of the analyst, "uses the object" to revive creativity, to reinforce language, of all things, in a continuous search process for the unreachable true self. From this point of view, the resistance that, in my opinion, forms part, among other things, of the very nature of the analytic process "reflects an inability to play on the part of the analyst", as Phillips (1988, p. 142) reminds us.

I have asked myself many times whether Winnicott would often have been silent during sessions. There certainly exists a difference in his interventions during consultations and analyses with children to those in analyses with adults. Bollas (1995, p. 239) maintains that Winnicott "suspended standard interpretations and created an atmosphere of containment from silence and concentration and without expectations on behalf of the analyst". The possibility of creating a receptive holding, of giving things their right time (sometimes Winnicott would expand sessions for two or three hours) and of suspending interpretation allowed for "experiencing a formless state, sufficiently loose" (Bollas, 1995, p. 239). None the less, at other points in his work, he is critical of taciturn analysts who try to give the impression to their patients that they have understood everything (Winnicott, 1965a and elsewhere); it suffices here to read any one of his works. We might be astounded at his frequent interventions, especially during consultations. For example, in the Piggle we can witness a tight dialogue of his with the girl Gabriella and how he dramatises his interpretations, something that many child analysts also began to do after him. Also, in many treatments of adult patients, he would play with the interpretations and make use of many other types of interventions, often direct ones.

In the famous case reported in "The split-off male and female elements to be found in men and women" (1989b), we can see this clearly. In this case, Winnicott makes a direct and surprising comment to his patient: "I am listening to a girl. I know perfectly well that you are a man but I am listening to a girl and I am talking to a girl, and I am telling this girl, 'You are talking about penis envy'" (Winnicott, 1989b, p. 170).

Winnicott informs us about what effects this interpretation had on the patient: initially acceptance of it at an intellectual level as well as relief, and then longer-term effects. When the patient replied, after a pause, "If I were to tell someone about this girl I would be called mad" (Winnicott, 1989b, p. 171), Winnicott continued by saying (and noting in the article that he had done well to do so, as would be shown by what followed), ". . . it is I who see the girl and hear a girl talking, when actually there is a man on my couch", and then added, "The mad person is myself" (1989b, p. 171).

These interventions did not take the form of classical interpretations, but, rather, had the characteristics of being unforeseen and of conveying a certain urgency, not just on behalf of the patient (that we cannot know), but certainly on that of the analyst.

Without any need for making this explicit, these interventions brought into the light the particular type of relationship that had manifested in the here and now within the analytic consulting room, and which reproduced the primal relation that the patient had had with his mother, who had denied him in his masculine identity.

Boldly, the analyst informs us about his bewilderment at experiencing these emotions and at finding himself in this position, whereupon he makes two interventions that are of paradoxical quality, to say the least: the first is "I am listening to and speaking with a girl", and the second is "The mad person is *myself*". With the first intervention, Winnicott demonstrates his capacity to immediately enter into the imaginary space of illusion, and that he is able to play and to dramatise. With the second, he repositions himself with respect to the relation that the patient had been re-enacting within the consulting room. The analyst no longer remains the mother who traumatically denies the patient his proper identity, because Winnicott makes this explicit with the statement, "The mad person is *myself*". Freeing the patient from craziness, he reassigns it to the mother–analyst and simultaneously transforms it.

What Winnicott discusses here does not merely concern the content of interpretations, but, rather, a mental attitude on behalf of the analyst. Therefore, it is possible to say (with Winnicott, 1971d, p. 51) that only "When there is mutual playing, then interpretation according to accepted psychoanalytic principles can carry the therapeutic work forward".

What makes Winnicott different from most of his contemporary analysts does not concern aspects of technique as much as the analyst's position in the analytic session, his overall attitude (Bonaminio, 1991, p. 653), and the philosophy of the analysis itself, as well as that of the encounter with the patient.

If it is the case that analysis takes place in the superimposition of two playing spaces, that of the patient and that of the analyst, then the character of the analyst is crucial, but, in order to reach this mental state, we must be at a level of not "organi[sing] nonsense" (Winnicott, 1971e, p. 56), and instead permit ourselves "unrelated thought sequences which the analyst will do well to accept as such, not assuming the existence of a significant thread" (1971e, p. 55).

How much the analyst him/herself is capable of playing and of allowing the emergence of playing in the child or of its equivalent in the adult is a crucial topic, given that playing is born out of the potential space granted through a relation of trust with the mother or with the analyst in the setting. Evidently, the formula of the analyst being sufficiently devoted to solving the task is not enough for us, in so far as the question is, rather, whether he/she will be able to play in his/her mind and, in turn, enable the patient to play.

Undoubtedly, we must take into account the defensive use of our theories: to what degree do we allow ourselves to feel protected and well defended by our interpretations that we use as a shield against patients and against the emergence of the nonsensical, which so often dismays us much more than the patients. Is it possible to think that this might have something to with our training? Does it have to do with our personal analysis? Can we teach spontaneity, the ability to become engaged and improve oneself in discussion, the acceptance of the unknown, and the joy of playing?

In order to reach this objective, which is connected to a creative activity that consists of self-creation above all, we must allow ourselves to wait, to let ourselves be surprised and to discover the patient as well as our selves. "It is in playing and only in playing that the individual . . . is able to be creative . . ., and it is only in being creative that the individual discovers the self" (Winnicott, 1971e, p. 54).

Note

1. He writes, for example, in a 1952 letter to Money-Kyrle,

   > I think we must accept as fact that at the emotional level, there isn't a contribution by the individual to the environment and by the environment to the individual. The individual communicates only with a world that he/she has created him/herself and the people in the environment communicate with the individual only to the degree that they are able to create him/her. Altogether, in healthy conditions, here we find the illusion of contact and it is this that furnishes the spark of life and makes art the most important part of human experience. (Quoted in Chagas Bovet, 1997, p. 192)

   However, a few years later he writes,

> But in examining usage there is no escape: the analyst must take into account the nature of the object, not as a projection, but as a thing in itself . . . relating can be described in terms of the individual subject, and that usage cannot be described except in terms of acceptance of the object's independent existence, its property of having been there all the time. (Winnicott 1971c, p. 88)

References

Abram, J. (1996). *The Language of Winnicott. A Dictionary of Winnicott's Use of Words.* London: Karnac.

Abram, J. (2013). The evolution of Winnicott's theoretical matrix. In: J. Abram (Ed.), *Donald Winnicott Today* (pp. 73–112). Hove: Routledge.

Bollas, C. (1987). *The Shadow of the Object: Psychoanalysis of the Unthought Known.* London: Free Association Books.

Bollas, C. (1995). *Cracking Up: The Work of Unconscious Experience.* New York: Hill & Wang.

Bollas, C. (2008). *The Evocative Object World.* London: Routledge.

Bonaminio, V. (1991). D. W. Winnicott and the position of the analyst and the analysand in the psychoanalytic situation. *Rivista di Psicoanalisi, 37*: 626–666.

Caldwell, L., & Joyce, A. (2011). *Reading Winnicott.* New York: Routledge.

Chagas Bovet, A. M. (1997). Gioco ed eccitazione. *Richard e Piggle, 5*(2): 191–200.

Ferro, A. (1999). Discussione del lavoro di Johan Norman. *Richard e Piggle, 7*(3): 267–272.

Freud, S. (1908e). Creative writers and day-dreaming. *S. E., 9*: 141–154.

Giannakoulas, A. (2010). *La tradizione psicoanalitica britannica indipendente.* Rome: Borla.

Green, A. (1975). Potential space in psychoanalysis. The object in the setting. In: J. Abram (Ed.), *Donald Winnicott Today.* Hove: Routledge, 2013.

Green, A. (2003). L'intuizione del negative in *Gioco e realtà.* In: M. Bertolini, A. Giannakoulas, & M. Hernandez (Eds.), *La tradizione winnicottiana.* Rome: Borla.

Hernandez, M., & Giannakoulas, A. (2003). Sulla costruzione dello spazio potenziale. In: M. Bertolini, A. Giannakoulas, & M. Hernandez (Eds.), *La tradizione winnicottiana* (pp. 101–118). Rome: Borla.

Khan, M. M. R. (1974). The use and abuse of dream in psychic experience. In: *The Privacy of the Self.* London: Hogarth Press (reprinted London: Karnac, 1996).

Kluzer Usuelli, A. (1992). The significance of illusion in the work of Freud and Winnicott: a controversial issue. *International Review of Psycho-Analysis, 19*: 179–187.

Ogden, T. H. (2001). *Conversations at the Frontier of Dreaming*. Northvale, NJ: Jason Aronson.

Ogden, T. H. (2009). *Rediscovering Psychoanalysis*. London: Routledge.

Ogden, T. H. (2013). Reading Winnicott. In: J. Abram (Ed.), *Donald Winnicott Today* (pp. 213–234). London: Routledge.

Phillips, A. (1988). *Winnicott*. London: Penguin.

Rodman, F. R. (2003). *Winnicott: Life and Work*. Cambridge, MA: Perseus.

Schacht, L. (1999). Il gioco tra trauma e creatività [Play between trauma and creativity]. *Richard e Piggle, 7*(2): 179–203.

Winnicott, C. (1989). D.W.W: A Reflection. In: *Winnicott D.W., Psycho-Analytic Explorations*. London: The Winnicott Trust.

Winnicott, D. W. (1942). Why children play. In: *The Child, the Family and the Outside World* (pp. 143–146). London: Penguin, 1964.

Winnicott, D. W. (1958a). Transitional objects and transitional phenomena. In: *Playing and Reality* (pp. 1–25). London: Tavistock.

Winnicott, D. W. (1958b). Transitional objects and transitional phenomena. In: *Collected Papers: Through Paedriatrics to Psycho-analysis* (pp. 229–242). London: Tavistock.

Winnicott, D. W. (1965a). Child analysis in the latency period. In: *The Maturational Processes and the Facilitating Environment. Studies in the Theory of Emotional Development* (pp. 115–123). London: Hogarth Press.

Winnicott, D. W. (1965b). The aims of psycho-analytical treatment. In: *The Maturational Processes and the Facilitating Environment. Studies in the Theory of Emotional Development* (pp. 166–170). London: Hogarth Press.

Winnicott, D. W. (1971a). *Playing and Reality*. London: Tavistock.

Winnicott, D. W. (1971b). The location of cultural experience. In: *Playing and Reality* (pp. 95–103). London: Tavistock

Winnicott, D. W. (1971c). The use of an object and relating through identifications. In: *Playing and Reality* (pp. 86–94). London: Tavistock.

Winnicott, D. W. (1971d). Playing: a theoretical statement. In: *Playing and Reality* (pp. 38–52). London: Tavistock.

Winnicott, D. W. (1971e). Playing: creative activity and the search for the self. In: *Playing and Reality* (pp. 53–64). London: Tavistock.

Winnicott, D. W. (1989a). The squiggle game. In: D. W. Winnicott, C. Winnicott, R. Shepherd, & M. Davis (Eds.), *Psycho-Analytic Explorations* (pp. 299–317). Harvard, CT: Harvard University Press.

Winnicott, D. W. (1989b). The split-off male and female elements to be found in men and women. In: C. Winnicott, R. Shepherd, & M. Davis (Eds.), *Psycho-Analytic Explorations* (pp. 169–183). London: Karnac.

CHAPTER THREE

Playing: listening to the enacted dimension of the analytic process*

*Gabriel Sapisochin***

Introduction

It will be recalled that when Freud (1914g) introduced the concept denoted by the German word *Agieren*,[1] he was implicitly foreshadowing a new model of the unconscious, which was to be made conceptually explicit some years later in what became known as the metapsychological turning point of the 1920s. He had in mind unconscious contents that were recorded, and expressed, in dramatic form, whereas the unconscious of the topographical model was more closely related to the narrative function of the ego.

In this chapter, I postulate that Winnicott revived this Freudian tradition, which, with some exceptions, had not been accepted by the post-Freudians: it is my belief that his concept of playing (Winnicott, 1971) constitutes a link between Freud's notion of *Agieren* (1914g) and the present-day concept of enactment.

For this reason, the argument presented in this chapter will inevitably be concerned with the place of the notion of playing in the

* This paper was delivered to the Editors in September 2013.
** Translated by Philip A. Slotkin, MA Cantab. MITI.

psychoanalytic process, as well as in the processes of symbolisation whereby the absent past becomes accessible as an object of analytic listening.

I shall suggest that the analysand uses the analyst, moulding him[2] as if he were an object from his past, to enact an unconscious script that cannot be expressed in words owing to the specific form of its recording in ideopictographic images—a form that I call a verbally unthought psychic gesture.

Acting out, playing, and enacting

It is well known that Winnicott described the process of symbolic exchanges between patient and analyst in terms of the "*overlap of the two play areas, that of the patient and that of the therapist*" (1971, p. 54, original italics). With regard to the analyst's function, he considered that if "the therapist cannot play, then he is not suitable for the work" (1971, p. 54).

Concretely, the playing to which Winnicott refers seems to concern the specificity of the analyst's task—that is, the capacity (or otherwise) to play the part of a guest actor invited to participate in the analysand's psychic drama production that unfolds on the analytic stage (Argelander, 2013; Bleger, 2012; Loewald, 1975; McDougall, 1986; Sandler & Rosenblatt, 1962). This could, in my view, almost be one of the criteria for admission to analytic training.

It is interesting to note that, many years before, in the context of a consideration of the recovery of memories in analytic treatment, Freud (1914g, p. 150, my emphasis) had written, ". . . we may say that the patient does not remember anything . . . but *acts* it *out*. He reproduces it not as a memory but as an action . . . and in the end we understand that this is his way of remembering". Freud's innovative hypothesis here is that a patient does not remember his absent past through verbal narration, but acts it out (*agieren*) on the stage of the transference, as if it were happening in the here and now of the session.

In this context, Freud uses the German word *Agieren*, which was initially translated by Richard Sterba in the English version of his *Handwörterbuch der Psychoanalyse* as "acting out"; this rendering seems to have been approved by Freud (1936b) and was used by Strachey in the *Standard Edition*.

However, it is important to note that, at least in his explicit conceptualisation, Freud held that this way of remembering through *Agieren* concerned only the transference. Owing to his resistance to theorising about the phenomenon of the countertransference, he was unable to conceive that the acted-out transference always calls forth an *ad hoc* countertransference position. After all, the staging of the transference is not a monologue, but is always a dialogue with another who plays a complementary part (Racker, 1948; Sandler, 1976).

This, I believe, was a brilliant clinical insight on Winnicott's part, when he proposed that the function of the analyst in the analytic process was to allow himself to *be used* by the patient. But how? In a discussion of the patient's way of expressing archaic levels of his psyche through action, Winnicott (1975, p. 289, my emphasis) wrote that in the patient's acting out "*the analyst will find it necessary to play a part*, although usually in token form". It is clearly stated that playing a part in the transference is always accompanied by corresponding countertransference manifestations, for which the analyst is recruited as second lead, cast in the role of a character in the analysand's psychic theatre with whom he is linked by a specific psychic gesture: for instance, "you are eating me up and I must run away"; "I control the other, who is my slave"; "you humiliate me and I feel ashamed"; and so on and so forth.

For this reason, in my *a posteriori* (*nachträglich*) reading of Freud's text, I thought it appropriate to expand the concept of *Agieren* by including in it the ineluctable involvement of the analyst's countertransference (Sapisochin, 2007, 2011, 2013). I also recommend that Freud's notion of *Agieren* be rendered in English by *enactment*[3] rather than *acting out*. This is, first, to emphasise that the unconscious of both patient and analyst inevitably plays an active part in enactment, thus giving rise to a specific transference–countertransference configuration that becomes the object of analytic listening. A further reason is that the concept of acting out belongs within a process model in which the analyst is a non-participating observer of the field in which only the patient is presumed to be active. This view has resulted in a slippage of meaning in the psychoanalytic literature whereby the term "acting out" has come to be used in an extended sense to denote impulsive psychopathic behaviour with the aim of evacuative relief of unbearable economic levels of psychic pressure, rather than for the purposes of working through.

My own view, however, is that in asserting that the patient has asked for help because he is unable to play, Winnicott is implicitly assuming that the treatment outcome will depend on whether or not he learns to play with the reality inevitably presented to him by the analyst—in other words, on whether the analyst is or is not able to generate a situation of ambiguity sufficient for his professional attitude (Winnicott, 1960, p. 160) to be suspended and relegated to the backstage area while playing as an invited actor the part of a certain character transferred by the analysand. But then the analyst must return to the stage and, like the narrator in Greek tragedy, transform the scene he has witnessed between himself and his patient into a "narrative fiction" (Sapisochin, 1999, p. 756). Through his interpretation, he can then return to the patient the conviction that what has been enacted belongs to the patient's own history.

It is, therefore, my belief that the characterisation of enactment as resistance, inherent in the twentieth-century term "acting out" and taken for granted by several generations of analysts, conceals the analyst's inability to produce a fantasy capable of assigning meaning to the meeting of minds that is taking place, as it were, live and on camera.

By this assumption of pathological acting out implicit in his listening, the analyst encodes the reality of the encounter by attributing his incapacity for symbolisation to the analysand, who is then seen as resisting the process of working through in order to remain ignorant of himself.

The analyst, thereby, forgets that the analysand has ultimately asked for help so as to recover his ability to *play*. So, Winnicott's thesis, in my view, encourages the analyst to take up the challenge of performing the countertransference role in which he has been cast in the encounter—that is, by temporarily ceasing to be who he is and turning himself into someone else who he is not, as with all good actors.

After all, when Winnicott composed "Hate in the counter-transference" in 1947 (Winnicott, 1975a), at almost the same time as the publication of the relevant contributions of Racker (1948[1988]) and Heimann (1950), the paradigm of the positions of the analytic couple throughout the process—the combination of the patient's free associations and the analyst's evenly suspended attention—expanded to include not only the patient's associations, but also the effects of his verbal communications on the analyst's subjective position in the analytic process. The innovation was the creation of conceptual tools for determining the analyst's position in the encounter, on the basis of which he could gain insight into the texture of the transference object with which he had been identified by the patient. In other words, analytic listening was now to proceed via the detour of the countertransference and was no longer confined to the semantic content of the words spoken.

Yet, the matter is not so simple. This is because, encouraged by instrumental use of the countertransference, analysts came to forget that both the transference and its inevitable counterpart, the countertransference, are unconscious by definition. They represent a bond that both members of the analytic couple unconsciously repeat because the unconscious is repetition in action and not a specific content.[4]

So, if both the transference and the countertransference are unconscious and cannot be known by introspection, the need is to conceptualise how the analyst can use the activation of his unconscious in this meeting of minds for the purpose of analytic listening. I contend that the countertransference will be knowable only *a posteriori*—that is, *after* an enactment, which makes it visible and objectively accessible to the speaking ego. That is the sense in which I understand Winnicott's notion of playing.

Considered in these terms, the analytic process comprises a constant alternation of, on the one hand, the combination of the patient's free associations and the analyst's evenly suspended attention and, on the other, its interruption by enactments, whose function is the imaginary staging of the unconscious emotional states stemming from the transference and the countertransference.

This is the principle that usually, although not always, allows the analyst to resume his evenly suspended attention and his task of verbal interpretation pending another enactment, and so on and so forth. That is why Winnicott (1975b, p. 289) stresses that the playing of the different positions of the patient and the analyst is not an end in itself, but "only the beginning, however, and there must always follow a putting into words of the new bit of understanding".

Hence, the analytic process could be described as the staging and de-staging by verbal interpretation of infinite scenarios of emotional playing involving the patient and the analyst to differing degrees.

Playing and symbolisation

A re-reading of *Playing and Reality* shows that it transcends the issue of analytic technique, in that, as stated earlier, it renders the transference and countertransference objectively accessible, because Winnicott is also concerned to rethink the human psyche's processes of symbolisation, understood as the capacity to generate subjective experience in the encounter with reality represented by the other in the present.

It will, no doubt, be recalled that, from the very beginnings of psychoanalytic conceptualisation, the metapsychological status of subjective experience was burdened by Freud's idea of affect as a phenomenon of discharge, which was either pleasurable or unpleasurable but not recorded in the psyche, as formulated in his first topography.

In this context, I see Winnicott's notion of playing with reality as a model for conceptualising the manner in which the subject can succeed in representing and knowing his emotional states in the encounter with reality. The proposed model is the mirror function of the primary (m)other's face in the early stages of emotional development (Winnicott, 1971, p. 111).

Winnicott writes (1971, pp. 112, 114),

> What does the baby see when he or she looks at the mother's face? I am suggesting that, ordinarily, what the baby sees is himself or herself. . . . I am . . . postulating a historical process (in the individual) which depends on being seen: When I look I am seen, so I exist . . .

It follows that, for Winnicott, the genesis of representation of the self in an intersubjective field corresponds to an early stage of maturation.

However, Winnicott's thesis, as a developmental model, transcends this stage of maturation because it implicitly addresses the philosophical problem of the attribution of meaning in the encounter with reality. For he postulates that, in adult life, this mirror function is performed by real-world objects, which the subject moulds as if they were made of plasticine into characters from his internal world whereby a given subjective state finds expression. This subjective state arises in the space between what the subject has expressed, on the one hand, and what the object receives and inevitably changes with his own subjectivity, on the other.

Winnicott, in fact, belongs, together with Bion, Lacan, Kohut, and others, within the psychoanalytic trend of the 1960s that was dialectically opposed to a solipsistic idea of the psyche according to which the genesis of subjective meaning takes place in isolation from, and outside of, social interaction.

Beyond the specificity of any theoretical development within its particular cultural context, the innovative thesis that unites all these approaches is the idea that subjectivity tends to be transformed into objectivity by way of external events that symbolise them and render them visible. The psyche's motivation comes to be seen as an unceasing search for self-representation in the encounter with reality, the intersubjective space being used as the locus of representation. In the context of my rereading of Freud, it was interesting to see that he uses the word "playground" (Freud, 1914g, p. 153) for the space of the meeting with the other, thus emphasising the idea of an area, or perhaps a stage, for representing the internal drama. Milner (1952, pp. 182, 184, my italics) describes this as follows:

> . . . the internal necessity for inner organization, pattern, coherence, the basic need to discover identity in difference without which experience becomes chaos . . . moments when the original "poet" in each of us created the outside world . . . *by finding the familiar in the unfamiliar.*

This constitutes a specific way of assigning meaning to the encounter with the real, which has become a preconception and stems from the relational tools internalised in the past with the primary objects. It could be seen as a relational script recorded in the psyche as a psychic gesture.[5]

The importance of this approach to conceptualising symbolisation is that it represents a way of seeing an emotional state invisible to the subject performed in an external production that renders it visible to the psyche as a precondition for it to be thought in words. Ogden (2007, p. 354) has recently called this "a process of turning experience inside out"—a way of recalling the absent past as represented in the present.

When such events occur in the analytic process, they are called enactments owing to the involvement of both the transference and the countertransference. Enactment thus becomes the symbol that represents and communicates the unconscious emotion which links the members of the analytic pair. In other words, it allows an unconscious emotional state to be rendered conscious by making it perceptible in the form of drama and, hence, susceptible to narration in words created by the ego.

Enacting: representing psychic gestures dramatically

Besides the developmental or phenomenological and philosophical explanation mentioned above, the presence of the other as a precondition for the symbolisation of subjective experience has a metapsychological explanation which Winnicott failed to pursue further.

My metapsychological hypothesis is that, owing to the very structure of the psychic recording of emotional experience, intersubjective performances are required for it to be expressed and known by the subject. In the following, I explore this type of non-verbal recordings, which are knowable only by way of the detour of playing with reality.

I have postulated elsewhere (Sapisochin, 2007, 2011, 2013) that, in addition to the recording in the psyche of experiences that were once the subject of verbal thought, which Freud called the repressed unconscious in terms of the metapsychology of his first topography, there is an unconscious that archives experiences which have never been thought by the speaking ego, which Freud (1923b, p. 18) conceived as an unconscious "which is not repressed".

The non-repressed unconscious records emotional experiences that are not represented in the same way as those once recorded in words. These are non-verbal recordings, which I have called psychic gestures and which I see as a sequence of ideopictographic images like film trailers that record in each subject's mind the quality of the emotion that links the subject to the object.[6]

It is because of this form of emotional representation between the subject and its objects that intersubjective productions are needed for the expression of this unconscious relational script, which belongs to the area of intrasubjective idiosyncratic experience that can be expressed and known only through experience with others.

Thus, we have a system of ideopictographic recording of emotion that can be inferred only after the event from the way the object, the analyst in the analytic situation, senses that he has been positioned by the patient in the encounter—that is, when his countertransference becomes accessible to introspection following an enactment (*nachträglich*). Considered in these terms, my proposal describes the manner in which this type of non-verbal material presents itself in the analytic process solely through the imaginary staging known technically as enactment, whereby a psychic gesture of the analysand becomes a psychic gesture of the analytic couple.[7]

This metapsychological hypothesis could, in my view, account for some authors' claim that knowledge of the countertransference is always achieved subsequently to an enactment (Renik, 1993).

Such a conception of the processes of symbolic recording, which can be made explicit only by way of an intersubjective detour, is consistent with present-day research on memory: the mnemic registers are currently thought to store not replicas of experience, but categories or modes of connection with reality, which require a specific event in order to find expression (Modell, 1994; Sandler & Sandler, 1984). For this reason, it is experience sought with objects of current reality that is thought to impart visibility and objective accessibility to this emotional category, which is recorded as a psychic gesture and is invisible to the verbal logic of the ego.

In my view, both Freud's assertion in 1914 that acting out is the patient's way of remembering and Winnicott's concept of playing constitute implicit acknowledgement of the inadequacy of the psychoanalytic method, based on the combination of the patient's free associations and the analyst's evenly suspended attention, for the purpose of listening to the manifestations of the psychic aspects that are expressed via the detour of the enacted countertransference.

After all, in maintaining that a patient remembers very early experiences only by playing them out in the present on the analytic stage, Freud is subverting his own theory of analytic listening by implicitly raising the problem of the impossibility of recalling all of the past in words. Again, the idea of *remembering through playing* signifies that the analytic method becomes an analytic process, since the focus of listening shifts away from verbal communication to the symbolic exchanges between analysand and analyst considered in diachronic terms. Klein (1957, p. 180, n. 1) called this mode of recall "memories in feelings" in order to emphasise that the experience of an emotional state is remembered in performances on the analytic stage in the present. This is a conception of the work of remembering in which what is absent, in becoming a present event in the here-and-now of the analytic process, subsequently (*nachträglich*) acquires the status of a memory.

That is why, nowadays, we work with the theoretical assumption that the past we shall come to know will always be a past which is re-created *a posteriori* (on the basis of *Nachträglichkeit*). So, the analyst is seen as analogous to the day's residue of a dream that confers presence and visibility on the unconscious recorded mnemically as a potential memory.

In noting that the task of analysis calls for playing, Winnicott is, thus, reminding us that it is not a matter of choosing between interpretation of the past and interpretation of the present, because, given the structure and functioning of stored memories, any interpretation of the played-out present is implicitly a construction of the absent past, a past recorded as a psychic gesture.

Playing the script of a little girl feeding a starving mother

The following vignette of a supervision is given solely as an example of my view of how the interplay of transference and countertransference becomes established in the analytic process and—as less often reported in the literature—of how these interpsychic emotional exchanges are reflected in the communication that takes place in the supervision process (Searles, 1955[8]). My aim is to demonstrate the power and inertia of playing within the processes of both analysis and supervision.

Some time ago, I was consulted by Dr T, a talented colleague with substantial clinical experience, about the analysis of a woman he had been treating for about four years that had, in his view, reached an impasse. She was a famous scientist, Professor C, who had come to him shortly after the end of an over-long course of psychotherapy with quite a lax setting. Dr T felt that this treatment had exacerbated certain narcissistic characteropathic defences.

From his very first descriptions of the process, I was struck by the pleasure my colleague took in treating such a famous patient. At one point, he joked that he had sometimes imagined that he himself might also become famous as the progenitor of such a brilliant creature.

On the other hand, Dr T's description of his analytic technique, which seemed correct in terms of timing and content, left me cold as a psychoanalyst of a psychoanalysis (Arlow, 1963, p. 583)—that is, I could not hear anything entirely new and potentially surprising. I just found it easy to anticipate the interventions of the analyst, who was always in the position of a third party and narrator of the events of Professor C's psychic life, the patient, as reported by Dr T, always being in a state of surpassing creativity and well-being. This was not readily comprehensible, given that she has sought analytic help. However, I could see that this state pandered to my colleague's expectation of receiving from Professor C the keys to understanding how the epistemophilic processes develop in a scientist's mind.

It gradually became clear to me that Dr T's technique avoided any work on the transference–countertransference situation, in which I felt I could glimpse the presence of a psychically quite helpless little girl, who was largely overlooked in Dr T's manner of interpretation.

Ten months into the supervision process, the element of abandonment emerged in the patient, which Dr T linked in his interpretations to the prolonged periods she had spent as a girl in a Swiss boarding school and to her resentment towards her mother of infancy. This emotional state was inconsistent with the affectionate, caring relationship she currently had with her mother, as if a split had arisen between past and present. This situation was manifestly being repeated in the analytic process, because both Professor C and the analyst were seemingly inhabiting an area free of transference–countertransference conflicts.

After a year and a few months or so of supervision, Dr T began to bring material in which he remarked that Professor C was referring some close friends of hers to him as patients.

I recall having mentioned a paper I had read many years before about an analytic process in which the analysand sent a vast number of patients to his analyst, as if he had an inexhaustible supply. I tried to enquire whether the treatment of so many of Professor C's acquaintances did not present a technical or ethical conflict to Dr T, but noted that this was ego-syntonic, because the meaning of this situation in Professor C's analytic process had not been explored. I avoided making any comment that might represent an interference with Dr T's vision of the process.

The important point, however, is that I began to see that this communication by Dr T, united with his *provider patient*, put me in the position of a third party, excluded from the fame and glamour and containing all the feelings of poverty, impotence, and infantile helplessness. I connected this with the fantasy of becoming famous through Professor C and recalled the plot of a film about the close relationship between a pop star and her mother of humble origins who moved up the social ladder through her daughter. Adopting a playful tone so as not to undermine Dr T's professional self-esteem, I therefore conveyed this impression to him and suggested a possible identification with the poor mother of a rich daughter who fed her.

A few weeks later, Dr T arrived for his supervision appointment in great anxiety, saying that he felt uncomfortable with me on account of his shame at expressing his experiences. Seeing that I was prepared to listen to him, he said he was afraid of the use I might make of my supervision notes because he had a fantasy of writing a paper on the psychology of a scientist and feared that I might steal his idea and publish before him.

I was very surprised at this "narrative fiction" (Sapisochin, 1999, p. 756) that was being concocted with my participation as a guest actor, and suggested that he think about it. In his next supervision session, Dr T told me that he himself had wondered about this, triggering a self-analysis which had indicated that a current personal situation involving himself might have been the psychic "hook" (Baranger, 1979, pp. 27, 29) which had enabled a certain psychic gesture of helplessness in the patient to find a possible means of representation. I later learnt from Dr T that he was deeply concerned about his daughter, who was seriously ill, thus predisposing him to take part himself in this scene of a bond, supporting a daughter in an idealised role.

Work on the bond between the analyst, cast in the character of a starving mother, and a daughter in the role of an inexhaustible food-provider object, made it possible to understand *a posteriori* (*nachträglich*) how the chronic depression of Professor C's mother had facilitated the manic reversal, in Professor C's infancy, of her helpless, starving aspects. In this context, I was called upon, in my role as supervisor, to play the part of a third object that threatened this symbiotic fusion of the daughter with the mother represented by Dr T.

In this way, if the imaginary scene of the mother-fed-by-the-daughter, as chronically repeated by Professor C in various extra-analytic contexts,[9] could be transformed into a verbal narrative, she would potentially be able to work through her pregenital conflicts and character defences.

Conclusions

My aim throughout this theoretico–clinical presentation has been to show that in this model of analytic listening, the analysand's unconscious lies neither underneath nor behind his manifest communications, as in the topographic model, but within the space of emotional intersection that unites him with, and separates him from, his analyst. This is the space of playing in which the *objects-of-analytic-listening* are created through the recruitment of the analyst as an actor invited to take part in an unconscious script recorded in the patient as a psychic gesture (Sapisochin, 2007, 2011, 2013). The above vignette illustrates the psychic gesture of a daughter feeding a starving mother, which leaves no space for the emergence of anything new.

It is usually the analyst who, from a third-party position, creates a *narrative fiction* that describes by a verbal thought the various identifications of the analytic couple that symbolically represent a given psychic gesture of the analysand's. In other cases, as in the vignette with Dr T, it is the supervisor who is required to compose the narrative fiction of this *folie à trois*.

However, the need is principally to identify the conditions for the generation of this neo-reality that emerges in the interpsychic encounter, given that there is not normally a motor act, but only an exchange of words. The phenomenon can be conceptualised in a variety of ways, depending on each analyst's theoretical model. I personally find it useful to regard the verbal communication as constituting an "act of language". Words, when spoken in a given context with a given prosody, have the secret property of arousing a certain subjective response in the other, as part of a process in which *saying is doing* (Alvarez de Toledo, 1996; Austin, 1962; Loewald, 1975).

Close examination of the transference phenomenon shows that, at certain points of heightened significance in the analytic process, the transference is expressed in a certain event that always requires the analyst to embody the role of the enigmatic transferred object.

The analyst's neutral posture is, thus, demolished, either temporarily or permanently, when he is forced to identify with the object preconceived as present. At such times in the process, the analyst ceases to be, for the patient, an intrasubjective representation of the past, which is alluded to metaphorically in dreams or verbal communication, but has, on the contrary, become the *a posteriori* re-creation of the past in the analytic situation.

The transference, as an entity beyond the intrapsychic process of actualisation, is expanded to include the patient's unconscious attempts to generate a given preconceived identificatory position in the analyst's psyche. Grotstein (2005) called this situation projective trans-identification, so as to stress the projecting subject's intersubjective pressure on the recipient to identify with the role assigned to him.

At these times of heightened significance, the important aspect of the verbal communications is not so much their semantic content as their ability to summon up in the analyst an emotional experience that cannot be described in words because it is expressed in the archaic register of psychic gestures dating from time immemorial, before words were available to name emotions.

In claiming that there could be no analytic process without playing, Winnicott was, in my view, implicitly asserting that the transference and its inevitable counterpart, the countertransference, rested on a *false connection* (Freud, 1895d, p. 302, original italics) that should not be severed. On the contrary, he encouraged us maintain this transference connection, which finds expression through playing, as a part of the therapeutic regression that permits transformative working through.

The reason is that, in stressing the therapeutic importance of the emergence in the analytic process of the entity in his model, which he calls the true self, Winnicott is presupposing that the patient's psyche is saturated with certain relational scripts formed in the encounter with objects of the past which, having become preconceptions, he compulsively repeats in every intersubjective encounter in the present. Because these scripts occupy excessive space in the self, they prevent the emergence of new, original, and idiosyncratic modes of assigning meaning to the encounter with reality.

It is in this sense that playing becomes the royal road for the reception on the analytic stage of a particular psychic script of the analysand's which, thereby, achieves *dramatic representation* (Sapisochin, 2007): seeing is believing. In order to be "published" by the ego of verbal narration, the emotional experience requires a conviction, and this can be furnished only by an event, in the form of a specific transference–countertransference realisation.

Winnicott was aware that a patient could be treated only if the analyst could playfully maintain what he called the therapeutic regression. I see this as meaning that it was necessary to create the conditions of ambiguity whereby the archaic, presenting itself as a verbally unthought psychic gesture, could be expressed in dramatic form within the confines of the setting. Only then can the compulsively repeated past cease to be an ongoing present and be transformed into the history that the subject can narrate about himself and his ancestors.

Notes

1. Translator's note: The word is spelt with an upper case initial letter when used as a noun, and with a lower case initial letter when used as a verb.
2. Translator's note: For convenience, the masculine form is used for both sexes throughout this translation.
3. This term is used by Loewald (1975) and Sandler (1976). The Spanish equivalent would be *puesta en acto* and the French *agir*.
4. This is, in my view, important because the term "countertransference" has undergone a slippage of meaning that, for me, has unacceptable implications for technique. In particular, I reject the familiar notion that the analyst can gain access to the countertransference by preconscious introspection. The reader will recall case histories from, for instance, the 1960s to the 1980s purporting to show the analyst acquainting himself with his countertransference position by introspection during the session.
5. In cases of pathology, this notion of an internalised script also facilitates conceptualisation of the compulsion to repeat that results from the subject's historical vicissitudes in terms of the repetition of a fixed relational plot.
6. A psychic gesture must not be confused with its physical counterpart, which is one of the normal channels for the expression of affectivity and emotion, because the former involves the non-verbal representation of a certain form of emotional connection between two subjects—that is, the image of a psychic gesture that links the patient to another object.
7. From this point of view, there would no longer be any difference between *acting in* and *acting out* (Paniagua, 1998; Zeligs, 1957), since the unconscious represented as a psychic gesture would always be expressed through the detour of intersubjective enactments. There would, indeed, be no distinction between enactments outside and inside the analytic situation, because, as Joseph (1985) writes, transference is a "total situation"—expressed outside an analytic session through enacted lateral transferences and inside it through transference–countertransference

enactments. Deciding where to place the focus of an interpretation—that is, whether it relates to configurations within or outside the session—is a matter of analytic listening and of timing.

8. Harold Searles (1955) was the first analyst to conceptualise what he called the "reflective process". This denotes the power of certain aspects of the patient's non-verbal unconscious that are expressed in the analytic situation by enactment, whereby the supervisee's communications about the relevant analytic process are mediated more by his actions, as seen "live and on camera" in the supervision process, than by his spoken words about his patient.
9. Subsequently to this enactment (*nachträglich*), this scene also came to represent Professor C's manic position, which was now ego-dystonic and placed in the service of the therapeutic alliance.

References

Alvarez de Toledo, L. de (1996). The analysis of "associating", "interpreting" and "words". *International Journal of Psychoanalysis, 77*: 291–317.

Argelander, H. (2013). The scenic function of the ego and its role in symptom and character formation. *International Journal of Psychoanalysis, 94*: 337–354.

Arlow, J. (1963). The supervisory situation. *Journal of the American Psychoanalytic Association, 11*: 576–594.

Austin, J. (1962). *How to Do Things with Words* (2nd edn). Oxford: Oxford University Press, 1976.

Baranger, W. (1979). Proceso en espiral y campo dinámico [Spiral process and dynamic field]. *Revista Uruguaya de Psicoanálisis, 59*: 17–32.

Bleger, J. (2012). Theory and practice in psychoanalysis: psychoanalytic praxis. *International Journal of Psychoanalysis, 93*: 993–1003.

Freud, S. (with Breuer, J.) (1895d). *Studies on Hysteria* . *S. E.*, 2. London: Hogarth.

Freud, S. (1914g). Remembering, repeating and working-through. *S. E., 12*: 147–156. London: Hogarth.

Freud, S. (1923b). *The Ego and the Id*. *S. E., 19*: 1–66. London: Hogarth.

Freud, S. (1936b). Preface to Richard Sterba's *Dictionary of Psycho-Analysis*. *S. E., 22*: 253. London: Hogarth.

Grotstein, J. S. (2005). 'Projective transidentification': an extension of the concept of projective identification. *International Journal of Psychoanalysis, 86*: 1051–1069.

Heimann, P. (1950). On counter-transference. *International Journal of Psychoanalysis, 31*: 81–84.

Joseph, B. (1985). Transference: the total situation. *International Journal of Psychoanalysis, 66*: 447–454.

Klein, M. (1957). Envy and gratitude. In: *Envy and Gratitude and Other Works 1946–1963* (pp. 176–235). London: Hogarth,.

Loewald, H. (1975). Psychoanalysis as an art and the fantasy character of the psychoanalytic situation. *Journal of the American Psychoanalytic Association, 23*: 277–299.

McDougall, J. (1986). *Theatres of the Mind: Illusion and Truth on the Psychoanalytic Stage*. London: Free Association Books.

Milner, M. (1952). Aspects of symbolism in comprehension of the not-self. *International Journal of Psychoanalysis, 33*: 181–194.

Modell, A. H. (1994). Memory and the psychoanalytic cure. *Canadian Journal of Psychoanalysis, 2*: 89–101.

Ogden, T. H. (2007). Reading Harold Searles. *International Journal of Psychoanalysis, 88*: 353–369.

Paniagua, C. (1998). Acting in revisited. *International Journal of Psychoanalysis, 79*: 499–512.

Racker, H. (1988)[1948]. The countertransference neurosis. In: *Transference and Countertransference* (pp. 105–126). London: Hogarth.

Renik, O. (1993). Analytic interaction: conceptualizing technique in light of the analyst's irreducible subjectivity. *Psychoanalytic Quarterly, 62*: 553–571.

Sandler, J. (1976). Countertransference and role-responsiveness. *International Review of Psycho-Analysis, 3*: 43–47.

Sandler, J., & Rosenblatt, B. (1962). The concept of the representational world. *Psychoanalytic Study of the Child, 17*: 128–145.

Sandler, J., & Sandler, A. (1984). The past unconscious, the present unconscious, and interpretation of the transference. *Psychoanalytic Inquiry, 4*: 367–399.

Sapisochin, G. (1999). My heart belongs to Daddy: some reflections on the difference between generations as the organiser of the triangular structure of the mind. *International Journal of Psychoanalysis, 80*: 755–767.

Sapisochin, G. (2007). Variaciones post-freudianas de *Agieren*: Sobre la escucha de lo puesto en acto [Post-Freudian variations on *Agieren*: On listening to enactment]. *Rev Psicoanál APM, 50*: 73–102.

Sapisochin, G. (2011). La escucha de la regresión en el proceso analítico [Listening to regression in the analytic process]. *Rev Psicoanál APM, 62*: 39–85. [Also published in Italian as *'L'ascolto della regressione nel processo psicoanalitico'. Psicoanalisi, 15*: 29–73.]

Sapisochin, G. (2013). Second thoughts on *Agieren*: listening to the enacted. *International Journal of Psychoanalysis, 94*: 967–991.

Searles, H. (1955). The informational value of the supervisor's emotional experiences. *Psychiatry, 18*: 135–146.

Winnicott, D. W. (1960). Counter-transference. In: *The Maturational Processes and the Holding Environment* (pp. 158–165). London: Hogarth, 1965.

Winnicott, D. W. (1971). *Playing and Reality*. London: Tavistock.

Winnicott, D. W. (1975a). Hate in the counter-transference. In: *Through Paediatrics to Psychoanalysis* (pp. 194–203). London: Hogarth.

Winnicott, D. W. (1975b). Metapsychological and clinical aspects of regression within the psycho-analytical set-up. In: *Through Paediatrics to Psychoanalysis* (pp. 278–294). London: Hogarth.

Zeligs, M. A. (1957). Acting-in: a contribution to the meaning of some postural attitudes observed during analysis. *Journal of the American Psychoanalytic Association, 5*: 685–706.

CHAPTER FOUR

Creative processes and artistic creation

Andreas Giannakoulas

In the unlimited potential space of science, alternative paths are constantly opened for exploration, both brand new and very old, modes and forms, appearances and realities that can deeply change our fantasies and actualities, influence our creativity and modify the individual and collective image, and even the quality and *continuity* of our being.

It has been observed that nowadays every branch of science seems to demonstrate that the world is based on very thin entities such as quarks, DNA messages, and some original neurons that determine the individual destiny from the very start of its life and conception.

Deprived of his own unconscious, robbed of his psyche, of his own experience, and of his imaginative and personal self, the Oedipus of neuroscience ceases his quest for *himself and for whom brought him into the world* (Aristofane Grammatico, third century BC).

Yet, poets teach us that it is from the encounter of man with himself and the significant other that, through the centuries, flow the most fertile and imaginative forces of our culture, and it is well known that poets and artists were the ones who infused into the passions and vicissitudes of the individual the human dimension of the psychic and the tragic.

The term *tragedy* includes for me both the Greek meaning and the psychoanalytical one: indeed, since the ancient times, the known truths on the natural world, on the course of history, and on the variety of human behaviour have been creatively translated into mythological stories, tragic works, poetic constructions, and symbolical, oneiric creations.

Ascribing to the individual the property of the symbolic creation of his own dream, at the beginning of the twentieth century, in the *Interpretation of Dreams* (1900a), Freud acknowledged the creator in us all and transformed deeply the quality of human awareness and experience, marking the onset of true personalisation.

It is in the therapeutic setting invented by Freud that the patient can even find his own personal history, containing an immemorial intimacy with his native idiom, anchored in time and space to his roots, his country, his family environment: we could say, the essence of the themes and images around which originates and crystallises the self.

Referring to the origin of an artwork, Heidegger (1889–1976) wrote,

> With the term "origin" we intend that from which and through which *something is what it is and the way it is*. . . . The origin of something is the source of its nature. The question about the origin of the *artwork* concerns *the source of its nature*. Usually the work emerges from and through the activity of the artist. The artist is the origin of the artwork. *Nobody is anything without the other*. (Heidegger, 1950, my italics)

Towards the end of the seventeenth century, the English philosopher John Locke (1632–1704) noted that all that is known—both externally and internally—comes to us through our senses: art critics, in fact, think that nothing visible can be understood by the sense of sight other than light and colours.

It is really extraordinary that Albert Einstein (1879–1955), wrote,

> The eyes of the scientist are focused on the phenomena which are accessible to observation at the moment of their apperception and scientific formulation. In the attempt to acquire a conceptual formulation of the bulk of the observable data, so bewilderingly immense, the scientist uses a *whole arsenal of concepts that he absorbed virtually with his mother's milk*. (Einstein, 1954)

According to Helmholtz,[1] one of Freud's teachers, perceptions are then based on unconscious inferences which make it possible to find the usual in the unusual, the familiar in the new.

For Marion Milner

> the *perception* of the external world is in itself a creative act, an act of imagination . . . *without imagination, in fact, we would not be able to see what is there to be seen* . . . it is a state that we all experience in certain stages of our infancy, and then is often lost in growing up. But we can find it again in art and in one's creativity . . . (Milner, 1950)

The cosmos as we know it through our senses is the "only creation" of man as Demiurge.

Following Rycroft, I use the word *imagination* for the processes of working through, organisation, and configuration of the imagined, processes that require effort and an executive capacity of the ego (Rycroft, 1973).

In this sense, imagination is a fundamental human faculty, through which more or less fruitful activities and functions flourish in different persons and in different social and cultural environments.

We could say that the image created by the dream is the fertile, unthought-of, repressed, or dissociated aspects of the self that the imagination of waking life has not foreseen.

In his paper, "Creative writers and day-dreaming" (1908e), Freud underlines the similarity between the poet (who daydreams) and the child (who plays): the continuity between art and the usual psychic functioning in daily life emerges.

Donald Winnicott, a consummate poet of human nature (Nina Farhi), represents a prevailing British attitude in enhancing both the theoretical and clinical foundations and those related to the empirical knowledge and creativity. At the same time, he adopted pre-Socratic wisdom in appreciating the freedom and spontaneity of thought and experience in creation.

Forty years after the paper "Creative writers and day-dreaming" (Freud, 1908e), with *Playing and Reality* (1971a), Winnicott works out Freud's contributions and observes that the relationship between playing and creating "stretches beyond the whole intermediate field between the internal psychic activity and the external world . . .", that is, it encloses the whole cultural field: "In order to study to play and then the cultural life of the individual one must study the fate of the potential space between any one baby and his mother who is essentially adaptive because of love".

In this way, Winnicott stressed the vital dialectic relationship between what the world offers and what the individual creates.

According to him, in normality, the mother makes possible for the child to have the illusion that the breast he is imagining is the same breast she is offering to him: the paradox lies in the fact that the created object is, at the same time, the found object.

We owe to Winnicott the concept of illusion as a non-pathological process differing from delusion because it does not give way to the problem of what is believed, it never becomes a dogma, and it is also different from hallucination, intended as a wrong interpretation of the real experience.

According to Freud, the illusion of transference as a false connection and the imagination of transference as a remaking were progressively seen not as a mistake to be rectified, but as a metaphorical representation of the psychic reality (Rycroft, 1973; Pontalis, 1981; and others).

Milner also regarded transference—without pathological connotations—as a creative illusion.

Potential space is the general term used by Winnicott to refer to the intermediate area of experience placed between illusion and reality; transitional in the double meaning of "placed between" and "mediating between" inner psychic reality and external reality. In fact, in his book *Frontiers in Psychoanalysis: Between Dream and Pain* (1981), Pontalis states that "The area of transitional phenomena constitutes a psychic space between the outside and the inside, a virtual, potential space where Winnicott places the *origin of* [my italics] *creativity*" (p. 139, original italics).

In *Therapeutic Consultations in Child Psychiatry* (1971b), Winnicott metaphorically underlines that, deep down, the core structuring the wide issue of the "consultation" is that intense participation of the patient in the free creation of his own space: a space through which transit significant objects, gestures, needs, wishes, and, of course, personal secrets.

In his paper "Unheimlich" ("The 'uncanny'", 1919h), Freud introduces a particularly fruitful intuition that is the relationship between the invisible secret of the artwork (hidden meaning) and the artwork itself (absent meaning):[2] "*Unheimlich*" ('uncanny') is that kind of dreadful that goes back to what we have known for a long time and to what is familiar to us".

The German term *unheimlich* is, from the semantic point of view, the opposite of *heimlich* (from *heim*, "home") which means "private, known, reliable, intimate, familiar".

Un-heimlich (with a privative *Un-*) means, therefore, "unusual, strange, and unfamiliar"; in the Dictionary of the German language by Daniel Sanders (1974), it is also "kept inside, hidden", but trying to come to light.

The uncanny, then, comes into being when, in an object or a situation, features of strangeness and familiarity come together in an affective emotional dualism of sorts.

In falling in love—the perturbing experience *par excellence*—the uncertainty, hesitation, wonder, trepidation, and the onset of the unexpected seem to be, partly as in a dream, inherent and consubstantial to this state of mind, in which there is an ongoing metaphorical search for the familiar in the strange, in the hope that something—often vague and archaic—present in the ego as an internal image could not only be projected, but also re-discovered as an external perception recreated as something totally original and new.

In adolescence (and not only then), the stage of flirting and falling in love by which a couple's relationship is set off, can be seen as an impelling and passionate exchange, a sequence of echoes and reverberations not only for the eye and the ear, but for all the senses and feelings and for the soul in general: indeed, it is a play of constant mirroring between two persons and their individual and shared imaginations in an absolutely dreaming attitude, sustained by unconscious inferences and loaded with deeply creative evocations. The wealth of potential in this state of mind is well expressed by art, which has always chosen falling in love as one of its elected objects.

We could say that when partners, in the phase of falling in love, create and find themselves in each other, subjectivising each other, a creative dynamism comes into being between them. In this case, the metaphor is, as it is in art, mainly a way to know, to explore and to communicate.

In the third chapter of *Three Essays on the Theory of Sexuality*, Freud said, "There are thus good reasons why a child sucking at his mother's breast has become the prototype of every relation of love. The finding of an object is in fact a *refinding* of it . . ." (Freud, 1905d, pp. 222–231). In this sense, the refinding of the object (Freud) gives the latter a distinctive potential and emanates a sort of energy whose content is not declared, felt, and recorded, as if it had never before met, encountered, and experienced.

In adolescence, on the other hand, the free play of intimate experiences and recent shared memories are immensely more explicit and present than in any available vocabulary and gives an unmistakable strength to what is experienced as actual—in the here and now; in this sense, the elements of the play, the inner imaginative world and the external reality, can get along together creatively.

The potential of the area of the illusion sustained and shared by partners, therefore, lies in the possibilities of the endlessly variable exchange of playing and of the intimacy in which sexual fantasies, words and silences, phrases, truths, and carnal images, kept for occasions of intimacy and full initiation, can be dramatised: "It is in playing and only in playing that the individual, be a child or an adult, is able to be creative and to make use of his own personality, and only by being creative that the individual discovers the Self" (Winnicott, 1971a).

Art and poetry, therefore, have something magic, just like play and love, where dream enters reality and reality enters the dream (Winnicott, 1971a).

In other terms, in intimacy the experience is allusive, allegoric, enigmatic, radically playful, transitory, and, most of all, creative (see Milner, 1950; Rycroft, 1973; and others).

Paraphrasing Freud, the experience of the child's intimacy with his mother "takes the function of *organizing* the sexuality" and, undoubtedly, his entire psychic life.

I think that this could be the very psychological base of the process of creative metaphorisation and symbolisation (as Milner says in the chapter headed "The role of illusion in symbol-formation", 1987, pp. 83–113): "to gather, to catch the unknown through the known and to let – reciprocally – the known represent the unknown to us".

In this sense, the metaphor (like the symbolic creation) poses itself as a complex mediation between the transcendent and the idiosyncratic world of sensations, sentiments, and subjective emotions on the one hand, and the constant, steady world of schemes and patterns of the socially codified meanings on the other.

As is well known, in Freud's writings, creativity was the sublimation of infantile sexuality and aggressivity, although Freud never described the true nature of the sublimating creative activity in a really convincing way.

For Melanie Klein, on the other hand, art *was* essentially reparative and was consequent to the destructiveness and the sense of guilt, as testified by the child in the depressive position (Segal).

Winnicott, in his "The depressive position in normal emotional development" (1955) did not appear to be satisfied with Kleinian aesthetics: he writes, indeed, that a sense of guilt and the ensuing wish to repair were "[a] source of strength, of social contribution, and of artistic performances but not of art itself, that has its *roots in a deeper level*" (p. 270, my italics).

For Winnicott, "there were other roots for creativeness but reparation provides an important link between the creative impulse and the life the patient leads" (1955, p. 91). For him, therefore, the earliest developmental stages are inherently creative and the child creates through his own wish the mother who is ready to be found, so that the subjectively conceived object is, at the same time, the objectively found object.

Winnicott writes that "The world is created anew by every human being and this task begins at least at the moment of birth and of the first theoretical feed" (1955, p. 163), and adds that "We know that the world was there before the child, but he doesn't know it and at the beginning he has the illusion that what he finds was created by him" (1955, p. 163).

We must admit that these concepts present the deepest analytical challenges.

Naturally, the development of new hypotheses and different references gave new impetus to this interesting debate.

Particularly towards the end of his life, Winnicott clearly asserted that creativity is linked to the capacity of being aggressive: for him, aggressiveness occupies a prominent position in development and in the processes of separation–individuation, besides the necessity of making oneself and the others real, and also because it induces one to explore a somewhat remote area of what exists outside and inside the self.

In his well-known essay "Hamlet and Freud" (1989), Starobinski stressed that "the unconscious is not only a language; it is dramaturgy.

It is word as a theatrical work, as a spoken action stretched between the two extremes of clamour and silence" (1989, p. 156). His conclusion—"nothing is beyond Oedipus, because Oedipus is already *depth* by himself" (1989, p. 156)—has an aspect of burning topicality, a *depth* that we risk to lose or deny (Pontalis, 1981; and others).

It was Marion Milner, with her significant contribution at the Congress on the "Change of the use of dreams in the psychoanalytical practice" (London, July 1975), who referred to the world of art. She actually quotes Maritain, who talks of creative subjectivity as an experience on the edge of dreaming and says that many people totally erased it from themselves, and refers to Ehrenzweig

> who, after studying art and Freud for a long time, came to the conclusion that . . . the mind, in its deepest part, fulfils *tasks of* [creative] *integration* that greatly overcome the capacities of the conscious mental superficial activity. (1987, pp. 193–194, my italics)

Milner, finally, referring to the artist in all of us while we dream, and to the integrative functions of art, deems "Fundamental, [in dreaming like in art], the impulse to get into touch with the Self, to know not only bits of the Self, but its totality" (1987, pp. 194).

In conclusion, we must consider that, in terms of transference, all this means that the analyst and the patient are part of a total process wider than the analytical setting, in which one is created and found by the other.

The aesthetical but also clinical parallel is, according to Plato, very close: "if the soul is to know itself, it must look into a soul".

Notes

1. Hermann Ludwig Ferdinand von Helmholtz (Potsdam 1821–Berlin-Charlottenburg 1894) was a German physician and physicist who made significant contributions to several widely varied areas of modern science.
2. Masud Khan and André Green.

References

Einstein, A. (1954). Foreword. In: M. Jammer, *Concepts of Space* (pp. xiii–xvii). Cambridge: Harvard University Press.

Freud, S. (1900a). *Interpretation of Dreams. S. E., 4–5*. London: Hogarth.
Freud, S. (1905d). *Three Essays on the Theory of Sexuality* (1905), *S. E., 7*: 125–245. London: Hogarth.
Freud, S. (1908e). Creative writers and day-dreaming. *S. E., 9*: 143–153. London: Hogarth.
Freud, S. (1919h). The "uncanny". *S. E., 17*: 219–256. London: Hogarth.
Heidegger, M. (1950). The origin of the work of art. In: *Off the Beaten Track* (pp. 1–56). Cambridge: Cambridge University Press.
Milner, M. (1950). *On Not Being Able to Paint*. London: Hogarth.
Milner, M. (1987). *The Suppressed Madness of Sane Men*. London: Tavistock Publications Ltd.
Plato, *Alcibiades*, 133 B.
Pontalis, J.-B. (1981). *Frontiers in Psychoanalysis: Between Dream and Pain*. London: Hogarth.
Rycroft, C. (1973). *Imagination and Reality*. London: Hogarth.
Sanders, D. (1974). *Wörterbuch der deutschen Sprache/mit einer Einführung und Bibliographie von Werner Betz*. Hildesheim: G. Olms Verlagsbuchhandlung.
Starobinski, J. (1989). Hamlet and Freud. In: J. Starobinski, *The Living Eye* (p. 156). Cambridge: Harvard University Press.
Winnicott, D. W. (1955). The depressive position in normal emotional development. *British Journal of Medical Psychology, 28*(2–3): 89–100.
Winnicott, D. W. (1971a). *Playing and Reality*. London: Tavistock Publications Ltd.
Winnicott, D. W. (1971b). *Therapeutic Consultations in Child Psychiatry*. London: Hogarth.

CHAPTER FIVE

Genesis, primal scene, and self-engenderment*

Denys Ribas

Genesis

A young woman remembered her rebellion as a child at the religious teaching of the creation of the world. She found the idea of submissively having to surrender any logic in her own thinking unacceptable. How could God create the world "in the beginning", and the days and the nights on the first day? She stopped believing in the religious dogma that very day, and went on believing in herself!

It is easy to imagine that Winnicott might have appreciated this childhood insubordination at the temporal illogicality: "how it is possible to claim to create time one day?", as the young woman explained she had wondered. Yet, as life holds surprises in store, my admiration for her youthful lucidity had to reckon with two challenges to the dismissal of the religious doctrine of the world's creation. First, astrophysicists, in discovering a strange aspect of the nature of time that is more intrinsically linked to the space of our universe, have

* Translated by Sophie Leighton.

hypothesised an original big bang that is equally surprising. More unexpectedly, however, Winnicott has revealed to us how the child creates the world he discovers in a temporal paradox made possible by his union with the mother's psyche, by clearly explaining that a union can exist between the mother and the child without the idea of union. On the basis that it describes the psychic genesis of over ten billion former little gods that inhabit the planet, genesis becomes rather Winnicottian.

In an exacting modern translation of Genesis, such as André Chouraqui's (www.levangile.com/Bible-CHU-1-1-1-complet-Contexte-oui.htm), this is how it begins:

1 ENTÊTE Elohîms créait les ciels et la terre,

2 la terre était tohu-et-bohu, une ténèbre sur les faces de l'abîme, mais le souffle d'Elohîms planait sur les faces des eaux.

3 Elohîms dit: "Une lumière sera". Et c'est une lumière.

4 Elohîms voit la lumière: quel bien! Elohîms sépare la lumière de la ténèbre.

5 Elohîms crie à la lumière: "Jour". À la ténèbre il avait crié: "Nuit". Et c'est un soir et c'est un matin: jour un.

1 FIRST God created the heavens and the earth

2 the earth was all confusion, a darkness on the faces of the abyss, but the breath of God hovered over the faces of the waters.

3 God says: "There will be light." And there is light.

4 God sees the light: what a good thing! God separates the light from the darkness.

5 God calls the light: "Day". The darkness he calls: "Night". And there is an evening and there is a morning: day one.

A more classical translation reads as follows:

1 Au commencement Dieu créa le ciel et la terre.

2 La terre était informe et vide; les ténèbres couvraient l'abîme, et l'Esprit de Dieu se mouvait au-dessus des eaux.

3 Dieu dit: "Que la lumière soit!" et la lumière fut.

4 Et Dieu vit que la lumière était bonne; et Dieu sépara la lumière et les ténèbres.

5 Dieu appela la lumière jour, et les ténèbres Nuit. Et il y eut un soir, et il y eut un matin; ce fut le premier jour.

1 In the beginning God created the sky and the earth.

2 The earth was formless and empty; darkness covered the abyss, and the Spirit of God moved over the waters.

3 God said: "Let there be light" and there was light.

4 And God saw that the light was good; and God separated the light and the darkness.

5 God called the light Day and the darkness Night. And there was an evening, and there was a morning; this was the first day.

The formlessness and the darkness on the face of the abyss, but with the protection of a shielding breath and a creative naming process are highly evocative of psychic birth. One of Winnicott's major contributions was the concept of primary unintegration. He thereby challenged the postulate of a self constituted from the beginning and threatened by a fear of disintegration.[1] He always considered that genuine creativity entailed maintaining some proximity to this.

It is also worth noting that the succession of the days and nights is born in the genesis of their separation: the first organising splitting.

I shall say little about Adam and about Eve born from his side, except to consider that this can be seen as a metaphor of giving birth: the man (Chouraqui's "le glébeux", the glebous one) can exclaim, "She . . . is the flesh of my flesh."

It seems very apposite, therefore, to suppose that the earliest experiences of being do, in fact, belong to the primary identification with the mother in Freudian terms, as suggested by Winnicott himself in his text, but they are the outcome of the mother's psychic elaboration of the child's protopsychic materials in a communion unknown to the child. Bion, of course, concurs, I think, with the version conceptualised by Esther Bick as adhesive identification, preferring the term adhesive identity in her later works. Didier Anzieu's skin-ego concept is broadly similar.

It is through the temporal dimension that these beginnings of the ego gradually become beginnings of the self—the English term (used in French) actually implying, I believe, a temporal continuity—through the confluence of these affective and sensory experiences. With Winnicott, we recognise the importance of a secure environment for the continuity of being to be woven.

In "The location of cultural experience" (1971, pp. 95–103), the author introduces the objective time of the mother's disappearance and the child's resulting emotions in the experience of deprivation during "x + y + z". It is not topographical disintegration that is the most primitive anxiety here but, quite differently, an unthinkable anxiety connected with a break in the continuity of his existence.

Concerning childhood autism, Tustin's (1972) suggestions, which accord with this Winnicottian conception, have been criticised with the same adultomorphic common sense: how could a child outside time possibly experience agonistic anxiety when he has no concept of death? Of course, it is not a matter of thinking about death, but a sense of annihilation, and, in the absence of time, an endless agony.

Although, towards the end of his life, Winnicott revisited his concept of pure femininity less affirmatively in discussions with his colleagues, he remained faithful to this fundamental idea of a transmission of the experience of being between the mother and her children of either sex. This is affirmed in his posthumous autobiography that was to be entitled *Not Less Than Everything*,[2] in which, according to Clare Winnicott (1977), he reaffirms his standpoint after having described the sadness experienced by a man in dying "when he has not had a son to kill him in his imagination and survive him—which provides the only continuity that men know. Women, in contrast, *are* continuous" (translated for this edition).

André Green, a great admirer of Winnicott who contributed enormously to increasing awareness of the depth of his thought in France, wondered at the end of his life (2011), following Rodman (2003), whether the ultra-famous clinical case of creativity and its origins might not have been Winnicott himself.[3]

Whatever the case might be, we can see the importance attached by Winnicott to this conception of psychic birth that privileges the earliest foundations of narcissism and makes this an essential issue in human health. This aspect of his work has been fully recognised by psychoanalysts, but beyond this consensus and leaving aside theoretical axiomatics, a genuine question arises in treating narcissistic fragilities, with their severity and difficulties that are an issue for all psychoanalysts: how far is omnipotence the ally or the enemy of change?

For Winnicott, it is clear that the child's initial god-like position and the fact that his mother protects this illusion prepares for the recognition of reality. The subjective object leads the way to the object recognised as separate. The solidity of the foundations of being prepares for the capacity to create the object, to cathect it with drives.

How does this relate to the adult treatment? Winnicott's confidence in the therapeutic potential of regression requires him to take a bold and subversive standpoint towards this intimate sphere of omnipotence that he considers especially important not to shatter, as in his view it contains the hope of acceding to a more authentic integration of the self. Therefore, he makes it the ally of the struggle against the denials and splittings that afflict the self by making it "false", but this requires him to avoid any attack on the infantile illusion.

Although Winnicott's position is infinitely hopeful and avoids a nosographic designation that deprives some psychotic or perverse patients of any capacity to benefit from a psychoanalysis, does it not also lead to the risk of complicity with denial?

The perversion of transitionality

In *Playing and Reality* (1971), Winnicott's meditation on psychoanalysis and the human being at the end of his life, this question appears implicitly: when he returned to "Transitional objects and transitional phenomena", some changes occurred between the 1951 and the 1975 versions. These relate specifically to fetishism. Winnicott deletes his criticism of Wulff's "fetish object" at the end of the article. His criticism related to the use of a pathological term:

> he has taken back to infancy something that belongs in ordinary theory to the sexual perversions. I am not able to find in his article sufficient room for the consideration of the child's transitional object as a healthy early experience. (1975, p. 241)

Nevertheless, he completes his text in *Playing and Reality* with two clinical cases: the second describes the woman getting lost in fantasying, for whom the negative is paramount: "all I have got is what I have not got" (1971, p. 24). This relates to the questions raised in "Fear of breakdown" (1974).

However, the first case is, in fact, the boy who was using a piece of string. He describes a perverse development of transitionality, after a hope of overcoming the symptom by interpreting its meaning—the denial of separation—to the child's mother and by the fact that she openly broaches this question with him. But the return of the symptom one year later, when the mother had to undergo an operation, or during a new depressive episode, was also accompanied by a major alteration: the function of the string changed "from communication into a *denial of separation*" (1971, p. 19). Winnicott also describes the emergence of a perversity when the child pretends to have hanged himself in order to terrify his parents. The string that represented the bond therefore mimics suicide. Winnicott himself recognises that "This case therefore is of special interest if it makes possible the observation of the development of a perversion" (1971, p. 19).

Origin and the primal scene

The primal scene is obviously a retrospective construction. If Freud was fascinated by the question of the direct observation of the parents' intercourse, as the case of the Wolf Man shows, this might contribute to the structuring of a primal fantasy for Freud. Its importance is fundamental for identity in establishing a filiation and, above all, in organising and articulating sexual and generational difference. Aulagnier (1984, p. 200) illustrates this retroactive construction of the origin, T0 time—birth of the *infans*, the child who does not yet speak—with a perforated loop that leads him there retrospectively from the accession of the I, T1 time, whereas, from this accession, a series of identificatory modifications, T2, contributes to the historicisation of the human subject (Figure 5.1).

Of course, we know about Melanie Klein's commitment to early interpretation in processing the primal scene from the very first session for Dick and for Richard. Winnicott, therefore, asserts his independence by emphasising the opposite standpoint. We know that this does not mean he is unaware of the importance of sexuality or is overlooking it. He thinks about women's menstrual periods when the very young Piggle draws some red on the electric light bulb that she has

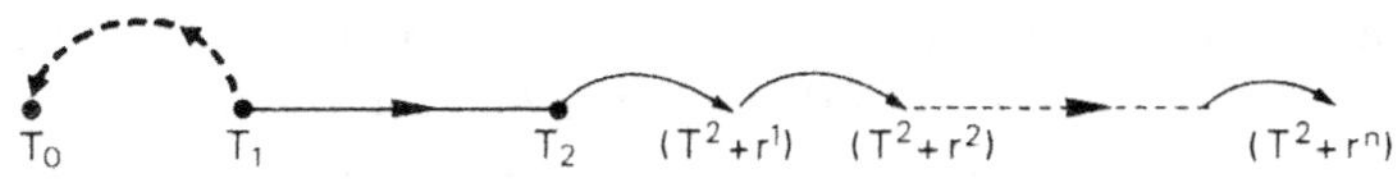

Figure 5.1. The retroactive construction of origin.

made into a character and asks Sarah about this matter (1971, in "Interrelating"), or is delighted that a girl patient can look at her parents as spouses.

He interprets the aggression that stems from the primal scene.

However, it is shortly after "Creativity and its origins" that the "Location of cultural experience" appears in *Playing and Reality* with the beautiful Tagore quotation: "on the seashore of endless worlds, children play" as its epigraph. Winnicott still has a precise memory of having been moved by it without understanding what it meant, which is reminiscent of the enigmatic sexual signifiers for the child emphasised by Jean Laplanche.

He then brings in the primal scene with his caustic humour:

> When I first became a Freudian I knew what it meant. The sea and the shore represented endless intercourse between man and woman, and the child emerged from this union to have a brief moment before becoming in turn adult or parent.

But he immediately continues and amends as follows:

> Then, as a student of unconscious symbolism, I *knew* (one always *knows*) that the sea is the mother, and onto the sea-shore the child is born. Babies come up out of the sea and are spewed out upon the land, like Jonah from the whale. So now the sea-shore was the mother's body, after the child is born and the mother and the now viable baby are getting to know each other. (1971, pp. 95–96).

Undoubtedly, women are continuous . . .

Self-engenderment

In France, the emphasis placed by Lacan on the paternal function and its foreclosure in psychosis drew attention from psychoanalysts and Aulagnier has developed a convincing theorisation of this by redefining the psychic apparatus as diachronic. Among Freudian analysts, we are indebted to Racamier (1992) for a major work on the psychoanalysis of the psychoses. In particular, he strongly emphasised in his work with schizophrenics the importance of the denial of the primal scene and the self-engendering fantasy that accompanies it.[4] Thus, he developed a negative version of this fantasy that aids the understanding of some suicide attempts: the fantasy of self-disengenderment. As shown by the Russian roulette player, the person who brings about his death negatively reappropriates his life and, if he survives it, this ordeal gives him a new birth. What could be more aggressive and denying of any parental ownership of oneself and one's life than to act like the child with the string: to hang oneself in front of one's parents! I think that this might explain some adolescent suicides, as anorexia nervosa undermines the living proof of the parents' bodily intercourse: the body of the child they have engendered.

Bion remains faithful to Klein, but in an existential mode and in a highly Winnicottian interpretative formulation with his patient who has been saying for six months in his sessions: "I don't know what I want to say . . ." He interprets to him that, in fact, the patient wants his analyst, in seeing a man stretched out on his couch, to understand that a man and a woman have made love! The interpretation of the denial of the primal scene also encompasses the analyst's place and psyche here.

Winnicott, who committed himself to understanding the marasmus of adolescence, once again with the demand to allow time for the patient before designating a pathology, has well described this temporal immobility, while telling us that (external) time will resolve this crisis if nothing fatal has occurred.

An adopted young man of African origin who was being treated in psychodrama because of his difficulties in thinking and his inhibition gave me a useful lesson a few years ago. He was exhausting himself after school by repetitive physical activities, seeking their self-soothing effect.[5] This had led to him being offered a psychodrama, a form of play using acting that includes some elements reminiscent of the squiggle: the patient is treated individually by several analysts who can play in the scenes he suggests, as indicated by the play leader, who does not play directly himself. Their play demands particular creativity from the psychodramatists, assuming a quality of representation and interpretation. A fairly transitional realm allows shared psychic processes in which the patient experiments in the space of the psychodrama with more neurotic psychic modes, supported by the therapists' psyches. Finally, some motricity is brought into play by the movements in the room.

Notwithstanding that, the sessions were rather dull until one day I found our patient reading a time-based science fiction book while he was waiting for us. I directed the play for him and, drawing on a shared interest in this literature, I suggested that he choose a scene on this subject. For his first scene, he chose the role of Ravaillac, bringing about a regicide. Then he imagined a place where all the creatures of all times would be united. I signalled to two colleagues, a man and a woman, to enter the play, and they introduced themselves to him as his biological parents. This was something fairly violent for him: he began to tell them about the suffering that his life was because of them, which he had never expressed in sessions. Then while we were feeling rather moved by his affects, something different happened; he suddenly stopped dead and said, "No! Don't change anything; otherwise I won't be myself!"

We were fairly overwhelmed to have witnessed this boy authorising his biological parents to engender him and accepting his adoption by his current parents, with the preceding abandonment that this had entailed.

On reflection, it seems to me that this patient not only sheds light on some issues specific to adoption, such as the difficulty of playing with the family romance, but also on the need that we all have to create the parents who engender us.

The neurotic's original fantasy of the primal scene has an undeniable masochistic basis: my parents are excluding me from their pleasure in order to make me suffer. I am, therefore, the beneficiary of the relationship and have always been present. One of my adult patients exclaimed one day, in discovering his feelings towards his parents who had gone away for a few days on a romantic break during his childhood, "It's *my* pleasure that they're taking!"

The neurotic is no more realistic than the schizophrenic about the intolerable contingency and chance that preside over birth.

But I have only postponed the question: when does the omnipotence allowed by the treatment—the psychodrama made my young patient the master of time, clearly a divine prerogative—enable the patient to emerge from the deadlock and when does it risk imprisoning him in it with the analyst's complicity?

On the one hand, it is not possible to match Winnicott's own genius in being right, but, on the other hand, he too sometimes fails, as with Masud Khan, who was Winnicott's patient while Wynne Godley's treatment with Masud Khan was taking place, with transgressions of the setting and narcissistic abuses, if the patient's criticisms are to be believed (Godley, 2001). Winnicott also thanks Masud Khan, who is not only his patient, but also his editor, at the beginning of *Playing and Reality*.

Recourse to the superego

Two authors in the past few years, Laurence Kahn (2004) and Martine Girard (2010), have paid great tribute to Winnicott's work. Kahn also devotes a chapter of her remarkable book *Cures d'enfance* to the superego, as if implicitly complementing Winnicott's contribution. Girard, who reassesses transitionality most opportunely, particularly in the institutional treatment of the psychoses, as the concept had been trivialised by its success, seemed to me also to be moving away from Winnicott in the importance accorded to observing the setting and the therapeutic contract, as if it were a key element of the treatment to provide a limit to the omnipotence of chronic psychotic patients. The French psychotherapeutic tradition in psychiatry uses the way in which the patient attacks, or refrains from attacking, the setting and institutional rules as material that is accessible to interpretation and adaptations.

While Winnicott is inflexible with regard to the secondary benefits, he nevertheless seems to me to be clearly committed to the accompaniment in regression as a therapeutic hope and he refuses to shatter the protective illusion. My question, therefore, relates to the pertinence of the trend that assigns to Winnicott's contribution a reference to the superego that he himself almost never makes. Is this taking the best of Winnicott to add to it our own convictions, and so much the better, or is it distorting his postulate and should we be assessing the consequences of that? I would raise the question.

Despite his own regret that his father left him a little too much alone with "his three mothers" (his mother and his two sisters), did

Winnicott not accept the submission inherent in the establishment of the superego? This can only result from an introjection of the prohibition. Everyone is cowardly before his superego.

However, the analyst today more often wonders how to foster the establishment of a superego, in particular among young patients, than how to reduce its excessive severity.

In his personal life, Winnicott seems to have been driven by an ego ideal that required freedom, which made it necessary for him to put forward his opinions, including to the national authorities, or against his colleagues, as is demonstrated by the highly enjoyable *Selected Letters* (1987). It is like an ideal of insubordination.

Winnicott and Bion

It is unfortunate that we have no traces of any deep discussions between Winnicott and Bion about their standpoints. That two such creative contemporaries were not able to have such a discussion is truly frustrating if we consider their points in common and their psychoanalytic genius.

Both had been deeply affected by the First World War, Winnicott as a nurse on a destroyer without a doctor and always feeling accountable for a portion of the life of his friends who had vanished so early, Bion having experienced finding his men mutilated in the debris of their tanks in northern France. It is well known how Freud's sense of powerlessness while his sons were at the front before the murderous insanity that had gripped civilised Europe also had an impact on his reflections and his works.

Winnicott and Bion also shared a similar epistemological viewpoint: describing psychic birth in the processes involving the two psyches of the mother and the child while considering Klein's postulates as unsupported by evidence. This also fundamentally differentiates them from Freud's intrapsychic perspective, which founds psychoanalysis but leads to an aporia concerning the description of the internal situation before the separation occurs between inside and outside.

Perhaps the fidelity and allegiance or otherwise to Klein was too sensitive an issue at the time. Perhaps, also, Winnicott, the "isolated phenomenon" in English psychoanalysis (child analyst, paediatrician, and man) and the solitary figure of Bion both wanted to remain so. In any case, we find a different place being accorded to the primal scene in the same consideration of the mother–child dyad: Bion adds the male and female signs to the terms container–contained.

The drives

Winnicott's objection to the death drive is well known (this is another issue of allegiance in the psychoanalytic context of the time), considering it as a religious scoria and an avatar of original sin. It is also known how much his work fuelled the work of psychoanalysts who draw on the second theory of the drives to take an interest in *Beyond the Pleasure Principle* (Freud, 1920g) and, therefore, in the issues that threaten existence and the sense of being.

Both *Playing and Reality* and "Fear of breakdown" show the doubts and uncertainties of a Winnicott who knows the burden of negativity and decathexis. It is the poets that he entrusts with conveying this, as when the forty-year-old single patient appeals to Gerard Manley Hopkins to explain that "she was completely at the mercy of some power like gravity, drifting, with no control over anything" (1971, p. 135).

> I am soft sift
> In an hourglass – at the wall
> Fast, but mined with a motion, a drift
> And it crowds and it combs to the fall;
> I steady as a water in a well, to a poise, to pane,
> But roped with, always, all the way down from the tall
> Fells or flanks of the voel, a vein . . .

This inertia would make a perfect representation of the entropic quality that seems to me to characterise the Freudian death drive aimed at the individual himself and the return to the inanimate. But I would particularly emphasise the hourglass that summons time, which has served me as a guiding thread in my reflection, and which I find provides the death drive with the energy that it intriguingly lacks for many analysts. It is that of physical time, the entropy that is exercised over the living being.

Winnicott's resolute opposition to the death drive probably conceals his implicit alliance with the life drive, less often emphasised because of the general confidence of English psychoanalysis in the psyche's capacities for growth and integration, as when Winnicott states that the manic defence is also life. Green defined the death drive as disobjectalising. This is to emphasise that the life drive supports cathexis. Lebovici explained that "the object is cathected before it is perceived". With creativity, Winnicott goes further and writes, "Everything physical is imaginatively elaborated, is invested with a first-time-ever quality. Can I say that this is the meaning intended for the word 'cathect'?" in "The location of cultural experience" (1971, p. 101).

Hiatus in the found, intensification of the created

Creative people who come to consult a psychoanalyst fear that the treatment will take away from them the painful but fertile nutrient of their creation by alleviating their suffering. Usually, this is not the case, and the gain over the inhibition frees their creativity. However, injuries and sufferings are often important in those who create and, without making it a rule, the hypothesis that survival mechanisms have subsequently fuelled the creative capacity in the artistic sense merits our attention.

I have wondered if deficiencies in the *found* have not therefore been compensated by an intensification of the *created*.

Winnicott himself, and his exceptional creativity, might be testimony to this, if we think of the poem "The tree", which he wrote at the age of sixty-seven, in hoping never to relive this experience, as we learn from Phillips (1988, p. 29):

> Mother below is weeping
> Weeping
> Weeping
> Thus I knew her
>
> Once, stretched out on her lap
> as now on a dead tree
> I learned to make her smile
> to stem her tears
> to undo her guilt
> to cure her inward death
> To enliven her was my living.

Notes

1. This concept has since been highly valuable in understanding childhood autism.
2. T. S. Eliot's line from the poem *Little Gidding*, the last poem in *The Four Quartets*, which introduces a circularity of time in life, "The end is where we start from" appeared as an epigraph.
3. "A man of mature years, married, who had been successful in an established profession . . . and father of a family", Winnicott explains.
4. Discovering psychiatry as a nurse during my medical studies—Winnicott had had this experience with medicine and was glad to have done so—and having a large beard at that time, I entered for the first time a ward of mental patients, women, who were having their meal. A schizophrenic woman suddenly stood up and shouted at me, "Joseph the cuckold!"
5. A willing slave in the sense described by Gérard Szwec (1992) in developing an idea of Michel Fain's with Claude Smadja.

References

Aulagnier, P. (1984). *L'apprenti-historien et le maître-sorcier* [The apprentice historian and the master sorcerer]. Paris: PUF.

Freud, S. (1920g). *Beyond the Pleasure Principle. S. E., 18*: 7–64. London: Hogarth.

Girard, M. (2010). Winnicott's foundation for the basic concepts of Freud's metapsychology? *International Journal of Psychoanalysis, 91*(2): 305–324.

Godley, W. (2001). Saving Masud Khan. *London Review of Books, 23*(4): 3–7.

Green, A. (2011). Origines et vicissitudes de l'Être dans l'œuvre de Winnicott [Origins and vicissitudes of Being in Winnicott's works]. *Revue française de psychanalyse, LXXV*(4): 1151–1170.

Kahn, L. (2004). *Cures d'enfance* [Treating children]. Paris: Gallimard.

Phillips, A. (1988). *Winnicott*. London: Fontana Press.

Racamier, P.-C. (1992). Le génie des origines [The spirit of the origins]. Paris: Payot.

Rodman, F. R. (2003). *Winnicott, Life and Work*. Cambridge, MA: Perseus.

Szwec, G. (1992). *Les galériens volontaires* [The willing slaves]. Paris: PUF, 1998.

Tustin, F. (1972). *Autism and Childhood Psychosis*. London: Hogarth.

Winnicott, C. (1977). Donald Winnicott en personne [Donald Winnicott in person]. *L'Arc, 69*: 28–38.

Winnicott, D. W. (1971). *Playing and Reality*. London: Tavistock.
Winnicott, D. W. (1974). Fear of breakdown. *International Review of Psychoanalysis, 1*: 103–107.
Winnicott, D. W. (1975). *Through Paediatrics to Psycho-Analysis*. London: Hogarth Press.
Winnicott, D. W. (1987). *The Spontaneous Gesture: Selected Letters*. London: Karnac.

CHAPTER SIX

Creativity: a new paradigm for Freudian psychoanalysis

René Roussillon

Introduction

Before I deal with the main points of this presentation of, and commentary on, the question of creativity in Winnicott's book that we are being asked to analyse, I feel it necessary to say a few words about the state of mind that lies behind this analysis and structures it. I would like to begin by emphasising something that is true of all authors, but even more so of Winnicott: every "reading" of his work is an interpretation of the text and, as such, involves not only the reader's own particular parameters, but also those of the period in which that particular reading is taking place. The value of any book to which several authors have contributed lies in the fact that it offers not only several "points of entry" into the reading of it, but also different points of view, different "interpretations" of the chapters of which it is made up.

I would like to begin by emphasising the fact that, although Winnicott's book contains papers which were all written before 1970—that is, more than forty years ago now—and even if the reader attempts to reconstruct the metapsychological context in which they were written, he/she remains, none the less, influenced by the situation of the questions raised in it at the time when the book and its impact on current thinking are being analysed.

That is one difficulty, and, in my view, another must be added to it: the necessity for any analysis that is being put forward to respect the "spirit" of the author whose work is being examined. That requirement has, for me, several implications. First of all, we cannot attempt to analyse the question of creativity by doing what Winnicott himself saw as a kind of plagiarism or paraphrasing of his work; that would amount to a form of betrayal. It was never Winnicott's intention to "acquire a following", and, in my view, what he wanted above all to hand down to us was the absolute necessity to be creative ourselves when reading or commenting upon his work—in other words, to go on developing whatever contribution he had made. We must, therefore, think not only "with" Winnicott, but also "beyond" Winnicott, to make use of his writings and of what inspired them as a springboard in order to think, in the present time, about the issues that he raised.

Winnicott emphasised, too, that we can be original in our thinking only in so far as we are also part of a tradition. In psychoanalysis, that tradition is, first and foremost, Freud's metapsychology and clinical contributions. I have the impression that there is room for a "reading" of Winnicott's work that would attempt to show how closely its more significant aspects relate to Freud's metapsychology. Obviously, no one could argue that Winnicott's thinking lies outside of that metapsychology; he was very familiar with Freud's work and took care to link his own ideas with those of the inventor of psychoanalysis, although it was never Winnicott's intention to try to establish any particularly strong metapsychological connection between them.

There were several reasons for that. The first is linked to the traditional way of thinking in Britain, a tradition to which he belonged; the feeling one has is that this approach gives pride of place to clinical aspects without going too deeply into the mysteries of Freudian metapsychology, which, in its detail, is often highly complex. For example, although Winnicott put forward a theory of process and processing (hence the frequent use of the present participle/gerund in his writings), he never linked it in any very specific way to Freud's theory of mental processes: primary and secondary. It is quite true, of course, that such a perspective was never completely absent from his thinking, but the way in which he developed it never reached the degree of sophistication that can be found in the French or German tradition, to mention only those that are European.

However, that factor in itself does not tell us everything about why Winnicott was so undoubtedly hesitant with regard to a more determined metapsychological approach. My impression is that we can find in the very object of his explorations another source of that disinclination. I mention this because it seems to me that it has to do with the threat that hangs over every attempt to link his contributions too closely to the Freudian tradition *stricto sensu*. Winnicott explored—and insisted that psychoanalysis explore—what human beings actually experience, and that perspective is not a core concept in Freud's thinking, even though it is not completely foreign to it: "I am the breast" are Freud's own words, expressed towards the end of his life in his description of the infant's earliest identifications. Any metapsychology of what people actually "experience" undoubtedly runs the risk of diminishing the intensity of the new developments and proposals that emerged from his research.

The unique qualities of Winnicott's approach have often been emphasised: it adapted itself quite remarkably to its object, and, in itself, it contained the essence of what he was contributing to the clinical work of psychoanalysis. He agreed completely with Buffon's famous remark, according to which "the style is the man himself"; I am tempted to paraphrase that comment and say that "Winnicott's style is his work itself", because, in my view, his style of writing tells us just as much as the actual content of what he was helping us discover. In his writing, Winnicott's style bears witness to a step-by-step approach, which, in itself, expresses a clinical standpoint at the same time as he is describing it. Although that deceptively simple style of writing—it would be a mistake were we to let ourselves be taken in by what appears to be simple and perfectly clear—is undoubtedly one of the keys to his success, it is also—the price of fame—a kind of writing that does not fit in well with the rough and even, at times, "arduous" character of Freudian metapsychology.

Freud had his own style, the sheer quality of which earned him the Goethe prize; his art lay in creating a style of writing that was both elegant and compatible with the rigour of his metapsychology. Winnicott's style was not on the same scale: his aim was to create a kind of "atmosphere of being", with the idea of taking on board experiences which, most of the time, are buried in the depths of mental life and which cannot become manifest unless certain very specific conditions are met.

The metapsychological perspective does not offer that kind of condition; issues concerning being and the paradoxes inherent in transitional processes are more a matter of formulations that are potentially paradoxical, or even "shocking", than of clear and explanatory rationality. In order for thinking to offer a space in which formlessness and the eventuality of "what has not yet come to fruition" can find accommodation, a place in which they can feel at home, there needs to be the kind of security offered by tolerance of paradoxes, putting completely on hold any judgements that involve knowledge of manifest concrete reality.

That said, more than forty years after some decisive ideas put forward by Winnicott—and this is one of the points that I intend to emphasise—brought about a new and paradigmatic shift in psychoanalytical clinical thinking, the time has perhaps come to take the risk of losing some of the substance and poetry of his contribution in an attempt to relate it more closely to the fundamentals of Freudian metapsychology. Some of Winnicott's critics—and, indeed, some of those who praise him highly, because they all find themselves in this respect in complete agreement with him—are tempted, first, to argue that he led psychoanalysis to a point far removed from the direction in which Freud had propelled it, and, second, to ignore the epistemological developments and evolution that Winnicott brought to contemporary psychoanalytical thinking. It is only by doing our best to show how his thinking is, in fact, an extension of Freud's, while at the same time preserving all of its richness, that we have any hope of convincing people that it cannot be divorced or cut off from that tradition first set up by Freud.

I am now in a position to explore what seems to me to be fundamental concerning the question of creativity in Winnicott's work; I would argue that it amounts to a paradigmatic development in psychoanalytical thinking.

Creativity, the drives, and the sexual dimension

The first question that we come up against is that of the articulation between creativity, the sexual dimension, and sublimation of the drives in Freud's thinking. Winnicott goes out of his way to emphasise that his thoughts on creativity do not correspond to what Freud described as a process of sublimation involving the drives. It is true that, in Freud's theory, sublimation is one possible outcome in the life of the drives, whereas, for Winnicott, creativity represents an absolutely fundamental aspect of mental life. Obviously, these two processes do not take place on the same level: one of them appears to be "regional", as it were, involving only part of mental functioning, while the other could be seen as lying at the very heart of the structure of the psyche, defining the relationship between the individual and his/her internal and external worlds.

Therein lies one of the difficulties that we encounter in attempting to relate Winnicott's ideas to Freud's metapsychology, a difficulty that cannot be ignored. On several occasions, Winnicott emphasised that, in his view, the processes involved in the creative impulse have nothing to do with drive-related urges or the sexual dimension as such.

For Freud, the fundamental touchstone of psychoanalysis lies in the role it gives to the sexual dimension in the individual's unconscious mental life—it is one of the "shibboleths" which he defined as contributing to the very identity of psychoanalytical theory. For Winnicott, it is creativity that plays that fundamental role, so that the question of the relationship between creativity and the sexual dimension must be examined if we are to see Winnicott's thinking as part of "traditional" psychoanalysis. However, in this particular instance, Winnicott's position is much less clear than it would seem to be at first sight. He often argued that there is no drive-related activity in transitional phenomena, in playing, or in the process of creativity. Yet, at other times, he spoke in this context of hallucinatory processes and even of a kind of "ego orgasm", the sexual connotation of which cannot be denied. How, then, are we to understand Winnicott's desire to draw a distinction between what he was trying to define and the theory of the drives? I would interpret that reluctance in terms of the "theory of the drives" to which he himself subscribed.

Winnicott's writings and developments belong to an epistemological context in which the drive is taken to be a kind of excitation that is more or less overwhelming and disruptive; in other words, something that is unbound and unintegrated, "attacking" the ego in order to find a place for itself in the ego, a place which, hitherto, it has not been allotted. For example, when Winnicott speaks of playing and of the presence of the drives in that activity, he sees the drive as disrupting play, not as its mainspring. In that way of looking at it, the drive is not "introjected" into what the individual is doing and is not conducive to it—it is seen as being "out of play", "offside", as it were. The question of the driving force behind play and playing is not taken into account in terms of an activity arising from the need to integrate the drive. In Freudian terms, we could say that Winnicott sees drives only in terms of the id, not as being integrated to, and within, the ego. Does creativity therefore depend on the drive being brought into the ego, introjected and placed in the service of the ego?

One major element involved in the introduction of the concept of narcissism in Freud's metapsychology has to do with the relationship between the drives and the ego, and the manner in which they cathect the ego: either the drive takes the ego as its object—the classic way of looking at narcissism—or it integrates with the ego, in such a way that it is transformed by and through that integration and becomes structured by it.

In *Playing and Reality* (1971), Winnicott seems at times to be referring to drives which are not integrated and which, therefore, pose a threat to playing and creative activity, while at other times what he says seems to imply a momentum integrated with the ego and working at its behest. Yet, he says nothing about the nature of the impulse that incites someone to make use of his/her creativity—how is this to be thought of independently of the life of the drives? From what other elements could the creative process derive support?

Winnicott was perfectly correct when he argued that unrestrained and overwhelming drive-related excitation is a threat to creativity, to playing, and to transitional processes. However, the epistemological context in which he was developing his ideas did not enable him to imagine that drives and the sexual dimension are not merely disruptive; if they are in the service of the ego, they can also be the source of a creative impulse. Drives that are overwhelming and disruptive have never been able to be bound by the ego's activity, they have never succeeded in being integrated and introjected, and, therefore, they appear to be foreign bodies that must either be expelled or brought under control.

On that basis, I would argue that the momentum that is required for any creative activity to occur must be looked for in the integration of the drives within the ego, in their introjection. There is another key argument that I shall explore later, when I discuss the process that governs the found/created element, the key process in transitionality: hallucination.

This initial overview has led us to the question of drive integration; this, in turn, quite naturally leads to that of how such integration comes about, and opens on to another major issue when we explore the connection between Winnicott's thinking and Freud's metapsychology: that of the role and place of the object.

Creativity and the object

One of Freud's fundamental endeavours was to try to free psychoanalysis and psychoanalytical theory of the threat that the accusation of "suggestion" could have represented for its epistemological and therapeutic significance. That threat was present from the outset, and psychoanalysis was created in such a way as to differentiate it from therapeutic procedures based on suggestion. The threat was still present in 1937, when Freud was writing "Constructions in analysis" (1937d), through the accusation that psychoanalysis was a matter of "Heads I win, tails you lose". Initially, Freud led psychoanalysis towards a theorisation of the individual as such, looked upon simply in terms of his/her intrapsychical functioning, outside of any external influence or suggestion; more than play or artistic activity, dreams seemed to him to be the model *par excellence* on which to base his metapsychology.

Dreams are "narcissistic" and appear to be immune to all external influence. It was only quite late in his work, in the aftermath of his paper "On narcissism: an introduction" (1914c), that Freud came really to acknowledge the fact that, in human beings, psychology is also a "group psychology" (Freud, 1921c). He was, by then, sufficiently reassured as to the coherence of the psychoanalytical approach that he could, without too much apprehension, confront the issue of the influence that individuals have on one another. However, the idea of taking into account the fact that the object of a drive is also a subject in his/her own right, with his/her own wishes and impulses, never became for him a major theme of his theorisation, even though the issues that thereby arose were never neglected in his actual clinical work (cf. the idea of seduction and, more generally, questions involving traumatism and narcissistic disappointments). For such an important place to be given to that aspect in his metapsychology, it would have to have been linked to a fundamental theme in metapsychology, that of hallucination. It was only in 1937, towards the end of his life, that Freud began to realise that hallucination and perception are not mutually exclusive—indeed, they may accompany each other and combine together as in, for example, a delusion.

From the very outset in Winnicott's thinking (the first article that attracted a great deal of attention had as its subject matter manic defences and the denial of both internal and external reality), the role of external reality and its connection with psychical reality were seen to be important elements. However, as soon as he set out the problem, it took on a more complex aspect because of what he saw as an intermediate state that mixed together psychical reality and external reality and, therefore, hallucination and perception. In that sense, Winnicott's thinking is completely in line with Freud's ultimate idea concerning the structures that superimpose perception and hallucination. What Winnicott called the found–created process—a key element, and I shall come back later to that fundamental point—implies that the "created" breast (and how could it be created other than through some kind of hallucinatory process?) is simultaneously placed by the mother at the very spot where her infant creates it. The infant can, therefore, find, through perception, an external object sufficiently similar to the one that he/she was able to create in a hallucinatory way.

The key issue here—without which Winnicott's contribution would be inconceivable—is to identify the necessary conditions under which the adjustment between what the infant creates and what he/she finds in the relationship with the mother is good enough, to the extent that the infant can have the illusion of having created what he/she finds. It is also the necessary condition for the infant to be able to integrate—through primary "omnipotence", as Winnicott would say—what is found. The intermediate structure that brings together the created object and the one that is found, in creating a third mental category, also sets up a bridge and an element of continuity between internal and external reality, thereby avoiding what, in Winnicott's view, was the fundamental danger in all development: that of dissociation.

Indeed, the found–created process must operate in both directions: the infant has to find what he/she is able to create, and be able to create what he/she finds. This implies a properly constructed environment, one that does not confront the infant with the impossibility of integrating what he/she finds. That is precisely what is involved in the traumatism of failed creativity: being faced with a situation that cannot be integrated, a situation *per se*, "in itself", that cannot be turned into one experienced as "for oneself". The failure of that process will result in an increase in destructiveness, the intensity of which appears to be a direct consequence of the traumatic character of the failure. On that point, Winnicott crossed swords with the concept of primary envy put forward by Melanie Klein; in Winnicott's view, envy and envious attacks are a reaction to early trauma, and are directly related to a failure in the processes of integration to which they bear witness and, therefore, to an inadequate mothering environment.

In Winnicott's thinking, setting up the found–created process is initially made possible through the mother's perfect adaptation to the situation, thanks to that fundamental kind of primary maternal empathy that he called the "primary maternal preoccupation". Later, a gradual gap between what is created and what is found becomes tolerable in so far as the infant is able to accomplish the work required to narrow that gap while continuing to maintain the creative illusion. At that point, the infant will be able to create what he/she finds, as long as what is found is sufficiently adapted. The found–created dimension is thus preserved throughout the entire process of development, thanks initially to the mother's adapting herself to her infant's needs and then to the child's own psychical work when he/she becomes able to carry it out.

Before attempting to take a look step by step at what is involved in the process that underlies creative activity, I would like to mention two elements that will help me to do so: hallucination and the malleable medium.

Two complementary elements: hallucination and the malleable medium

The first comment that I would like to make has to do with hallucination and its relationship to the sexual dimension and creativity. I mentioned earlier the nature of the process through which the "breast" is created, and I shall come back later to the complex issues to which this process gives rise as far as theorisation is concerned. For the moment, I would like to emphasise the fact that, in "traditional" psychoanalytical thinking, that process becomes intelligible only when it is related to hallucination. That is why the connection between creativity and the sexual dimension, with which I began this exploration, is so fundamental. Hallucinatory satisfaction of a wish—which, in my view, is brought into play in the "created" process as described by Winnicott—is a process typical of the drives and of the life of the drives. At the very beginning, the sexual dimension and creativity go hand in hand: the sexual aspect lies at the very root of creativity, and creativity gives expression to the action of the sexual dimension when it comes to fruition in the service of the ego.

The theoretical problem arises from the fact that initially the hallucinatory process was described by Freud—in a manner similar to the model of dreams—as being linked to "object-less" narcissism and auto-eroticism, a process that is set up when the object is absent, precisely in an attempt to compensate for its absence. The hallucinatory process, however (and this is clear in Freud's last writings on the subject and appears to a considerable extent to be confirmed by recent research in the neurosciences), always occurs when there is an increase in drive-related tension; it is probably an "automatic" phenomenon, linked to the basic functioning of the human psyche, its very momentum.

When, thanks to hallucination, the process finds the object that it has created, there follows an illusion of self-satisfaction that is fundamental for the construction of narcissism. When the process does not find the object that it has created, this gives rise to auto-eroticism in so far as there has been a sufficient number of early experiences of creative illusion, and that these have left enough traces for them to be preserved "in memory" and activated in a sufficiently realistic way, so as to produce a kind of consolatory illusion. But, as Freud never stopped pointing out, auto-eroticism is ultimately always unsatisfying; it can never be more than a consolation.

The idea of hallucination being brought about by the absence of the object can still be found in many contemporary psychoanalytical papers: the work of the mind is seen as being based on absence or on a representation of the absent object. That conception is based on the contrast between perceiving and hallucinating, which, in turn, considers the process of perception to be relatively passive in nature and not, as all the research being done at present in the neurosciences never fails to demonstrate, a highly structured one. It implies that reality is a "given", not that it is gradually constructed as a psychical category and progressively enriched by experience. It conflates the moment when the process of symbol formation becomes manifest and the point at which it is created—it confuses, as it were, the second phase of the process with the process as a whole.

Hallucination is a perception-based representation of the object that is waited for, expected, desired, hoped for; it has to be able to fit into a present perception in order to "become real" and be fulfilled; that is, it has to find a sufficiently structurable perception in the individual's present time in order to be part of it. The *sumbolon* is this primary "putting together", this first reuniting of an internal process and an external "locality". If no encounter is possible, the result is a state of narcissistic disappointment and a feeling of distress. If that feeling persists, it will produce the kind of agony and a reaction of destructiveness which, for Winnicott, constitutes the fulcrum of pathological processes; it is only later, after there has been a sufficient number of experiences of fulfilment, that auto-eroticism will become a possibility.[1]

The second comment that I would like to make concerns the role and place of the object in setting up and maintaining the found–created process.

In many of his earlier writings, Winnicott focused above all on how the mother took care of her infant—mainly in terms of her holding, handling, and presenting the object—and on the way in which these various elements of maternal care contributed positively to the infant's mental development. In what he was saying at that time, it was already possible to sense that, over and beyond physical care in the strict sense of the term, Winnicott was attempting to define the mother's cathexis of her infant and the way in which she attunes to the needs of his/her ego. It is, of course, in those very early days of the baby's life, through the body and its sensoriality and sensorimotricity, that the earliest forms of communication are established; it is very much to Winnicott's credit that he was sensitive to that dimension, as we see in his various studies of the primary conditions required for a relationship to be set up. However, it was when he suggested that the mother's face played the part of a mirror that a watershed was reached in his theorisation of the overall meaning of primary communication.

Winnicott's hypothesis was that the function of the mother's face and of what it expresses in relation to the infant is that of reflecting back to the child his/her own internal states, or, at least, some message to do with these. When we read the chapter that Winnicott wrote about the function of the mother's face, it becomes obvious that, if the face as such plays indeed a very important part in this "mirror" role that he sees in the child's mother, it is above all her whole manner of "being present" that acts as a mirror for her infant. That is a variation on the idea of the found–created process (the infant has to see him/herself in the mother's face and in the way her body is physically present), but a variation that is one of the key elements of the process itself.

Classically, what is emphasised is the projective process: the infant finds what he/she created projectively. Winnicott, however, emphasises the complementary importance of the "feedback", the "return" processes through which the infant internalises the reflection that he/she perceives in the way in which the primary objects respond to his/her own movements and states of being. In pointing this out, Winnicott made a major contribution to the theory of narcissism through his description of the fundamental intersubjective vector that is present in that situation. Infants see themselves as they are seen; they "create" themselves as they are seen, experienced, and reflected by the mothering environment, and they identify with what is being reflected back to/of themselves. I think it appropriate at this point to relate this to what Marion Milner described in terms of the malleable (or pliable) medium. It is no doubt difficult to know exactly what each of them owes to the other; the ways in which they see the primary role of the mothering environment are very similar to each other.

Milner emphasises the fundamental part played, in the emergence of the process of symbol-formation, not only by illusion, as illustrated in the eponymous title of her most famous paper (1977), but also, for this to be properly set up, by an encounter with an object that is a sufficiently pliable medium; in other words, with an object that can let itself be transformed in accordance with the requirements of the infant's creative process. It is thanks to that good-enough malleability that the mothering environment can fulfil its role as "mirror"; by making itself malleable so as to respond to the infant's internal states and impulses, it can make adjustments to the reflection that gives substance to that narcissistic function.

I am now in a position to attempt to give a metapsychological description of the process of creativity—that is, to follow, step by step, the various phases and problems that arise in setting it up and allowing it to develop.

A metapsychological analysis of the process of creative activity

For Winnicott, this process originates in the hypothesis of the "theoretical first feed" and early traces of satisfaction. In the light of what we now know about the infant's innate skills, it could be said that he/she is born with some preconception (to use Bion's term) of the objects and encounters that are necessary for his/her development; therefore, the infant has from the outset a kind of expectation with regard to the primary environment. But that preconception is—to use a word that Winnicott himself very much appreciated—only "potential", and its hallucinatory activation—the way in which the infant begins to "present" to him/herself what is waited-for—must encounter an object sufficiently similar to the one that is expected for the primary found–created process to be set up. Conversely, if, indeed, the experience is sufficiently satisfying, the potential element will take on an initial shape that depends on what has been found. Here, we have to suppose that the preconception is, to some extent, malleable and that it can adapt itself to what the mother offers, if this is close enough to what her infant needs—in other words, if she is "good-enough". It is probable, too, that, although initially a significant level of adjustment is required of the maternal environment, with the repetition of such an experience and the infant's ongoing development, he/she becomes able to tolerate a less than perfect degree of adaptation and to do whatever is necessary for there to be a "good-enough" response to what is expected. There is, therefore, some leeway, some "play" in this process, even though this might be to a limited extent; a certain degree of psychical work is, thus, demanded of both participants.

One of the distinguishing features of this primary mode of relating is that it is "ruthless", as Winnicott put it. In other words, if it is to unfold properly, the infant should not have to take into account any specific characteristics of the state in which the mother finds herself. That particular aspect of the primary relationship can be understood in several ways. One would be to say that the baby is in an "object-less" state, that is, the presence of the external object is not acknowledged as such. The infant is, therefore, "ruthless" because of this non-acknowledgement of the object's existence. I am not sure that this is a correct interpretation of what Winnicott was saying, because it does not seem to correspond to the idea of ruthlessness. I would tend to say that the infant has to encounter a malleable-medium environment that adapts to his/her needs; at birth, the baby does have such a preconception—that is, that of an object able to put to one side (to sacrifice) its own wishes and states of being. To some extent, for the infant, that is one characteristic of the primary "breast", of the creativity that is reverberated by the primary breast. It is more an encounter with an object that wants to be made use of ruthlessly, one that wants to adapt to the infant's needs. This, no doubt, has some relationship to what Winnicott called the "pure female" element, which could be seen as a characteristic common to both the feminine and the maternal dimensions.

I spoke earlier of Marion Milner's idea of the "pliable medium", an object that can take on any form or shape since it has no particular one of its own. In my opinion, the logic underlying Winnicott's thinking has as its necessary complement the idea that the primary breast has to be a malleable/pliable medium.

Conversely, primary identification—the basis for the feeling of self-identity, and what Freud saw in the idea "I am the breast"—sets up within the infant a space for creativity built on the introjection of that characteristic of the early encounter with the object, with the object's "pure female" element, its pure female or "pure maternal" aspect. Primary potential creativity, female element, pliability and malleability of the responses—these combine and link together in the experience of being.

Formlessness and creativity

I would argue that the connection that I have just suggested between several of Winnicott's ideas is justified by what he said about the importance of the feeling of formlessness in the primary relationship with the mothering environment. The experience of the found–created breast does not account for creativity in its entirety; it is simply a starting point, one that is programmed more or less biologically if my hypothesis about the existence of an innate preconception of a breast that is adapted/adapting to the infant's needs is correct. True creativity implies that the infant can take possession of that primary experience so as to turn it into something that is appropriated, under his/her control, and not seen as a more or less automatic occurrence.

In 1920, Freud emphasised that the psyche must first of all make sure that it controls what it feels; to use a favourite metaphor of his, it has to "tame" what it experiences. He emphasised also the fact that the individual has to have a representation of that tamed experience in order for it to be truly appropriated. In France, André Green insisted on the fact that the moment at which an experience occurs is not the point at which it becomes meaningful.

Winnicott added to the metapsychology of the process of integrating a subjective experience through his fundamental idea, according to which the infant has to experiment with formlessness. These situations occur when babies have no internal constraints: they are neither hungry nor tired, there is no threat of an internal need arising, they are not under the pressure of external demands coming from the environment; they can just let themselves be and allow the traces of earlier experiences, the integration of which is so important, to come back inside themselves. Here, formlessness does not imply states in which any form or shape has been lost, situations that have lost all structure and are felt to be chaotic; it is a kind of receptiveness towards what is taking place or coming back into that state of internal relaxation. For such a situation to exist, the mothering environment must be both "containing" and "holding".

For Freud, the initial phase was one of "taming" the experience and the drive-related impulses that are part of it; that "tight grip" on the experience is, however, only a preliminary to the process of appropriation, a condition for its taking place. The infant then has to abandon any control over the experience and represent to him/herself what had earlier been lived through; in this way, the child can "give" it to him/herself and appropriate it more fully. In this second phase, the experience is brought back into play, and symbolisation can then emerge thanks to the reflexive processes that this implements. However, that phase is possible only if the infant has some space—receptiveness—for taking in that earlier experience (indeed, all earlier experiences), a space that is sufficiently formless for all of these experiences potentially to be taken in.

I can now link this to what I said earlier concerning the pure feminine element: this formless space is the result of the apperception of the capacity for pliable adjustment characteristic of the mothering environment, the outcome of the encounter between the infant's need to find a tailor-made environment that can adapt to his/her needs and impulses and one that is sufficiently pliable and malleable. Although, at the outset, the mothering environment must adapt itself almost perfectly to the baby's needs, it is also absolutely necessary for the infant to have some experience of an environment that is not instantly perfect, one that has some tension to it, one in which some effort towards adaptation and adjustment is necessary. The experience of the mothering environment actually endeavouring to adapt is just as important, if not more so, than the outcome itself—in any case, more important than any adaptation that is immediately and "magically" granted to the infant. This is necessary for the experience of potential transformation to be set up, with the idea that a suitable environment can gradually be created. This is a decisive moment in the establishment of hope. As Winnicott often said, once some degree of development has occurred, a "magical" environment is of little use to the infant. There is no contradiction between what Winnicott proposes here and Freud's very important idea of the work of the psyche; for Winnicott, however, that mental work is, above all, characterised by its "playing" aspect.

That work, in turn, also demands an adjusted/adjusting environment; there must once again be a degree of empathy in the mother with respect to the development of her infant's needs.

The capacity to be alone in the presence of the object

Another fundamental contribution that Winnicott made was his introduction of the idea that, between presence and absence, there lies an intermediate phase, one that is essential for the development of creativity.

As I pointed out earlier, the experience of formlessness is not one of disorganisation or of chaos. If formlessness is to be experienced from the very outset in a positive manner, this can happen only in the presence of the object, that is, with the help of the security guaranteed by the presence of the mothering environment. In Freud's famous description of the little boy playing with the reel, the child's grandfather was present and paying close attention to the boy's throwing the reel and pulling it back, but without intervening actively in the play itself. That play was "addressed" to him, but it took place with the little boy being "alone in his presence". This is a situation with which psychoanalysts are very familiar: during a session, the play of free associations takes place "in the presence of the analyst", that presence being a fundamental requirement for the play to occur, even without any direct intervention on the analyst's part.

When infants are playing alone in the presence of the object, they are reproducing in their play some detail or particularity of what they experience in their encounter with the object; their play is about playing with the object while the object itself is present. In this way, infants create the "mother" object within themselves. In their play, there is an internal representation of the object, which becomes the object in their play; from time to time, however, they have to turn towards the object that is actually present, as though to verify the impact produced on the object by playing with their internal representation of that object and the process of appropriation that this implies. In this way, they make sure that the object "survives" the appropriation that is present in their play; this potentially enables the internal representation of the object to be detached from its perception, as long as the object that is present allows this to take place. I shall explore *infra* some issues concerning the survival of the object with respect to the child's mental processes: this was the key question that, in *Playing and Reality*, Winnicott called "the use of an object"; I would, all the same, like to say a few words about what this "survival" implies in the context of being alone in the presence of the object.

First of all, following on from what I said in the preceding paragraph, the object must allow that experience to take place; in other words, it has to let the infant have some experience of formlessness without intervening or de-cathecting this. The object must also allow the play to be carried out while being present, once again without intervening or de-cathecting that playing. For example, the object—the child's mother, let us say—can read a magazine or, as in Winnicott's famous example, go on with her knitting; she can focus primarily on an activity linked to her own feminine dimension without becoming completely carried away by it or paying no attention whatsoever to her infant, and, at the same time, without becoming completely absorbed by what he/she is doing.

The survival of the object and the dialectics of creativity–destructiveness

The idea of the "survival" of the object is fundamental to the articulation between creativity and destructiveness in Winnicott's work. Every theory of creativity must take into consideration something to do with the role of destructiveness. In Winnicott's writings, that issue is a crucial one for the process of disillusionment, which itself lies at the heart of the acknowledgement of both dependence and love.

Once the object is found–created, the infant has an experience of a primary illusion that goes to the very heart of the beginnings of narcissism: the illusion that the object which is, in fact, "found" externally is the fruit of his/her own internal creation. That illusion is productive in so far as the illusion of creation contributes to the establishment of a nucleus of self-confidence that combines with the infant's trust in life and in the surrounding world, but it is based on an illusion that has gradually to be overcome without the capacity for illusion itself being destroyed in the process. Winnicott described one particular way in which this can come about: the name that I would give to it, by analogy with the experience of found–created, is that of "destroyed–found" or perhaps "destroyed–lost–found".

As I have pointed out, the perfect adaptation of the mothering environment, which is so typical of the earliest days of life, cannot last forever. Although continuing to be "good-enough", it has gradually to give way to a more approximative adjustment that necessarily and inevitably will, at times, be incomplete.

When this occurs, the infant experiences a kind of failure, a setback that weakens his/her capacity for creative illusion; the impression is that he/she has destroyed this. This, in turn, gives rise to an experience of despair mingled with helpless rage: an experience of destructiveness. The outcome of that experience depends on the mothering environment's response to the destructive anger that the infant expresses. This is where Winnicott's concept of the "survival of the object" (in the chapter on the use of the object) becomes most meaningful. The object must "survive" the manifestations of destructiveness—in other words, as Winnicott points out, it must not "retaliate" either actively or through some kind of emotional withdrawal. I would add something that seems to me to be implicit in Winnicott's thinking here (because he spoke only of negative characteristics): the object must show that it is still alive, that is, that it remains creative. To survive does not mean not being touched or affected by what the infant is communicating about his/her distress and helpless anger; it implies maintaining or re-establishing the relationship that existed previously.

If the object survives, the infant has the experience that what was thought to have been destroyed in fact has not been; the object, thus, lies beyond the infant's omnipotence, it can withstand that omnipotence: the object is another subject, whose way of being present, whose desires and whose internal impulses are not dependent on the infant even though they have something to do with him/her. Although the object can "mirror" the infant's internal states, it can also break free of that mirroring–mirrored relationship.

At this point, I would like to say something about the discovery of the object. All the work that is at present being done on the early phases of child development shows that the infant very quickly perceives that his/her mother and other people in his primary environment have their own separate existence—there is, in fact, no "pre-object phase", as was thought at one point to be the case. The issue is not one of "perception" but of "conception"; perceiving the object as separate is not at all the same thing as conceiving of it as "another subject", that is, as having its own wishes, experiences, and impulses. What is at stake in the experience of the survival of the object does not (indeed cannot, for this would be meaningless) have to do with the perception of the object, but with how the object is conceived. Experience enables the infant to discover that the object is external, external to him/her as a subject; it is, therefore (a term that I have devised in order to emphasise this point), another-subject. Since both of these elements are connected together and emerge through the same movement, it would perhaps be clearer were I to say that conceiving of the object as another-subject implies the conception of the subject also, that is, the conceiving of oneself-as-subject. Subject and other-subject no doubt both have their roots in the same movement; they are "the subjects of"—neuroscientists prefer the term "agents"—and arise from situations that are experienced.

Winnicott made a highly significant comment on this when he emphasised that, having gone through the experience of the object surviving his/her destructive anger, the infant becomes capable of a whole new set of subjective processes. The infant, says Winnicott, can distinguish between destroying the object in fantasy and its actual destruction in reality; this enables the infant to realise that he/she can be the subject of some internal momentum or other that is quite different from its external effect. In this way, conceptual categories can begin to be constructed, thereby making perceptions, sensoriality, and even drive-related activity meaningful.

Another major consequence that Winnicott noted was the emergence of love as such. His way of describing this movement, in *Playing and Reality*, is worth quoting in full:

> "Hullo object!" "I destroyed you." "I love you." "You have value for me because of your survival of my destruction of you." "While I am loving you I am all the time destroying you in (unconscious) fantasy." Here fantasy begins for the individual. (1971, p. 90)

As we can see, it is the individual's entire topographical structure that depends on being able, in a good-enough way, to have the experience that I call destroyed–lost–found (or found again).

That experience also has a significant impact on several aspects of creativity. First of all, primary creativity was "automatic" in the sense that it was not the work of any individual/subject acknowledged as such; it was experienced, but its basis lay in an illusion. Once the self-as-subject and another-subject have emerged, creativity becomes "purposeful"; it can be carried along by drive-related impulses that are "subjectivised", and, thereupon, matters relating to the introjection of the creative process can be explored.

Creativity and creation

Creativity is not creation; creativity is a potentiality, while creation implies the actual production of something. Creativity implies some aptitude for creation, an aptitude that is supported by a facilitating environment; creation implies the implementation of a process of creating that requires a structured ego, one that becomes structured through the mobilisation of the drive-related energy required by what is being undertaken.

That said, creation should not be thought of as being completely independent of the environment, which is and will remain a vital element for the individual throughout a significant part of the development of introjection and structuring of the drives. Between creativity and creation, Winnicott set up some intermediate forms that I shall mention in these final paragraphs. There are two domains in which creativity opens on to a kind of creation: that of dreams and that of play.

In so far as dreams give some shape, "materialised" by the hallucinatory process, to psychical processes, creativity and the subjective appropriation that it includes as a potentiality are, to some degree, actualised when dreaming takes place. As Freud never failed to point out, dreams are "work", a work of creation, one that calls upon the putting into practice of a series of processes that have to do with primary symbolisation. Dreams bring about a movement in which the raw psychical material described by Freud becomes a scenario and takes on a poetical and rhetorical value expressed through the dream (in the widest sense), involving a relatively organised construction that can be narrated to another subject and have some effect on him/her. Dreams act not only upon the dreamer, but also upon the person to whom they are addressed; that is why, in Winnicott's view, dreams lie on the side of reality.

Play also offers the creative potential a kind of realisation when it is played out, represented, or "materialised" in the *objeux*/objects it makes use of; this depends also on the individual including the idea of giving shape to a part of his/her raw psychical material, which requires some degree of symbolisation and integration.

There are, therefore, three scenarios involving creativity that emerge in Winnicott's work. The first emphasises creativity in its relationship with objects becoming other-subjects—this depends, to a considerable extent, on the responses of the objects involved, and no doubt influences the quality of the other two scenarios. The second is playing "alone in the presence of the object", which begins to break free of the impact of the object's response as long as the process of play is sufficiently adhered to by the object. The third is that of the dream stage, which, in its construction, is completely free of objects/other-subjects; its umbilicus, however, requires that it be taken up again in a relationship with another person.

Note

1. I am not referring here to the kinds of auto-sensuality that may be set up initially in order to compensate for the early absences of the object or for any lack of satisfaction.

References

Freud, S. (1914c). On narcissism: an introduction *S. E., 14*: 73–101. London: Hogarth.

Freud, S. (1920g). *Beyond the Pleasure Principle. S. E., 18*: 7–64. London: Hogarth.

Freud, S. (1921c). *Group Psychology and the Analysis of the Ego. S. E., 18*: 67–143. London: Hogarth.

Freud, S. (1937d). Constructions in analysis. *S. E., 23*: 257–269. London: Hogarth.

Milner, M. (1977). The role of illusion in symbol formation. *Revue Français de Psychanalyse, 5–6*: 844–874.

Winnicott, D. W. (1971). *Playing and Reality*. London: Tavistock.

CHAPTER SEVEN

Further reflections on Winnicott's last major theoretical achievement: from "Relating through identifications" to "The use of an object"*

Jan Abram

Elsewhere I have proposed that "the use of an object" constitutes Winnicott's final major theoretical achievement (Abram, 2008). Furthermore, following Winnicott, I have attempted to illustrate how this concept offers psychoanalysis a new psychoanalytic theory of aggression (Abram, 2012).

Here, I aim to present a further examination of Winnicott's concept "the use of an object" and to illuminate how it constitutes a distinct clinical concept that accounts for the fate of primary aggression.

The evolution of Winnicott's theoretical matrix

First of all, to appreciate the full measure of Winnicott's late concept, let me remind the reader of the chronological sequence of Winnicott's work in which I have identified three specific conceptual advances.

Phase one, 1935–1944: the environment–individual set-up

After 1944 it was no longer possible to see the individual without reference to the m/other. "There's no such thing as an infant" equates to there is no such thing as an individual. Each self is the outcome of the earliest and subsequent environment–individual set-up.

Phase two, 1945–1959: transitional phenomena

Winnicott made a claim for a "triple statement" about human nature in his paper on transitional objects (1953) concerning an area between inner reality and shared reality. It is "an area that is not completely subjective, nor completely objective", although it is, of course, a subjective phenomenon. The focus is on the "something" that is in between intrapsychic and interpsychic relating.

> It is an area which is not challenged, because no claim is made on its behalf except that it shall exist as a resting-place for the individual engaged in the perpetual task of keeping inner and outer reality separate yet inter-related. (Winnicott, 1953, p. 90)

Phase three, 1960–1971: the use of an object

This concept accounts for the "fate of the primitive impulse", that is, primary aggression. The problem with this issue, Winnicott said, was resolved when he wrote "The use of an object" (1969) in which he recognised that the destructive drive in the human infant required an object who would survive (see Abram, 2013a, p. 308). *Survival of the object* is the core concept in "the use of an object" and, thus, his final major theoretical advance.

A note on Winnicott's choice of titles

"The use of an object" was originally written in 1968 for a presentation given to the New York Psychoanalytic Society on 13 November 1968. Subsequently, it was published in 1969 in the *International Journal of Psychoanalysis*, with the same title. During the last two years of his life, Winnicott worked on two publications, *Playing and Reality* and *Therapeutic Consultations*. Masud Khan assisted him with compiling these books, which Winnicott would never see published as he died on 25 January 1971 and they were both published later that year. However, he was active in the selection of chapters for both books and he selected "The use of an object" to be Chapter Six in *Playing and*

Reality. Very little was changed for the 1971 publication, except the addition to the title ". . . and relating through identifications". I have often wondered why he added this phrase and I can only guess that it was because he wished to emphasise that the paper's aim was to illustrate how the human infant moved from object relating (which he designates as "relating through identifications") towards the *capacity* to use the object. In the paper, and across his work, it can be seen that he refers to primary identification as the earliest stages of object-relatedness, that is, the stage of development before the infant is imaginatively able to "put himself into the other's shoes". This latter capacity is referred to as "secondary identification", as he describes in Chapter Ten of *Playing and Reality*—"Interrelating apart from instinctual drive and in terms of cross-identifications". The capacity for "cross-identifications" is the outcome of a good-enough early environment. The subject who is able to use the object, according to Winnicott's thesis, has already accomplished the in between stage (a move from primary identification to cross-identification), and is, therefore, able to discern the other as separate and different (Me from Not-me), rather than a "bundle of projections".

The lead-up to Winnicott's conceptualising the use of an object

Let us now review the relevant formulations in Winnicott's work that led up to his proposals in the "use of an object".

Winnicott saw innate aggression as a "symptom of being alive" (Winnicott, 1989, p. 239). The newborn's kicks and movements are aimed at *discovering* the reality of the object. This "benign" aggression is mobilised by an instinctual force which makes the newborn's needs ruthless (Abram, 2007a, p. 21). This point will be elaborated later, linked with Winnicott's decision in his later work to use the word "destruction" instead of "aggression" as a way of qualifying the meaning of early aggression, that is, that it is object-related—"relating through identifications"—and, in order for a self to grow, the subject needs an object who will survive his primary aggression.

In the third and final phase of his work (1960–1971) (Abram, 2008, p. 1205), Winnicott examined the specifics of the psychic environment that facilitated the infant's sequential movement from "creatively apperceiving" to "objectively perceiving".

By the beginning of 1968, two years before he died, his formulations concerning the infant's journey from Me to Not-me took shape in "The use of an object".

Winnicott's original summary for the New York Society, 1968

It is well known that Winnicott first gave this paper to the New York Psychoanalytic Society and recently I have referred in more detail to the New York visit (see Abram, 2012). For this chapter, I will concentrate on Winnicott's main contribution and so, before going into more detail concerning the main argument in "The use of an object", let us first of all examine Winnicott's original "Summary" of his paper, which was posted in advance of the planned talk.

> Object relating can be described in terms of the experience of the subject. Description of object usage involves consideration of the nature of the object. I am offering for discussion the reasons why, in my opinion, a capacity to use an object is more sophisticated than a capacity to relate to objects; relating may be to a subjective object, but usage implies that the object is part of external reality.
>
> This sequence can be observed:
>
> 1. Subject relates to object.
> 2. Object is in process of being found instead of placed by the subject in the world.
> 3. Subject destroys object.
> 4. Object survives destruction.
> 5. Subject can use object.
>
> The object is always being destroyed. This destruction becomes the unconscious backcloth for love of a real object, that is, an object outside the area of the subject's omnipotent control. Study of this problem involves a statement of the positive value of destructiveness. The destructiveness plus the object's survival of the destruction places the object outside the area in which projective mental mechanisms operate, so that a world of shared reality is created which the subject can use and which can feed back into the subject. How this usage develops naturally out of play with the object is the theme of this talk.

It would help in my exposition if a reading of the following papers could be taken for granted:

1. (1966) The Location of Cultural Experience. *Int. J. Psa. 48*: 3, 368–72
2. (1962) Hogarth Press, London, 1965. Ego Integration in Child Development, (Chapter 4 in: *The Maturational Processes and the Facilitating Environment*) N.Y. I.U.P. – 1965, pp. 56–63
3. The Capacity to be Alone. *Int. J. Psa. 39*: 5, 416–20, 1958
4. Playing: Its Theoretical Status in the Clinical Situation. *Int. J. Psa. 49*, 1968 – still in press (Winnicott, 1968 in Abram, 2012, pp. 307–308)

The reader will note that both the 1966 and 1968 papers were chosen by Winnicott to be republished in *Playing and Reality.* Moreover, it is noteworthy that he advises that the recommended papers should be read in chronological order. This suggests his preference for an order of emphasis, that is, the location of early cultural experience, ego development, the capacity to be alone, and the theory of playing in the clinical setting.

Winnicott's formulations preceding 1968

Let us now focus on the salient concepts of each of the above papers in an attempt to track Winnicott's trajectory up to the point in 1968 when he prepares his paper, "The use of an object". It will become clear that each concept is intrinsically related to what I have suggested will be articulated as a theory of psychic survival.

1. In the " The location of cultural experience" (1967[1966]), Winnicott posits a "potential space" which, for the baby, is located *in between* the subjective object and the object objectively perceived. "From the beginning the baby has maximally intense experiences *in the potential space between the subjective object and the object objectively perceived,* between Me-extensions and the Not-me" (Winnicott, 1971, p. 100, original italics).
2. Earlier, in 1962, Winnicott had offered a departure from Freud by stating that the newborn's ego, distinct from the self, was provided by the mother in her state of primary maternal preoccupation—ego-relatedness. This is why he states, "There is no

id before ego". Therefore, at the very beginning "... instinctual life can be ignored because the infant is not yet an entity having experiences" (Winnicott, 1965b[1962], p. 56). A self has to be in place before the infant is able to "experience" emotions, otherwise s/he can only "react", which constitutes trauma.

3. Winnicott had introduced the term ego-relatedness in 1956 to describe the phase of absolute dependence when, in his terminology, the baby is merged with the mother and benefits from ego-coverage that emanates from the mother's primary maternal preoccupation. In his paper, "The capacity to be alone" (1958b), he had stated that this capacity was based on the introjection of an "ego-supportive environment"—a consequence of the early good-enough mother's attention and adaptation—that is, ego-coverage. In Klein's theory, this indicated the existence of a good internal object, while in Freud's theory, it indicated an ability to tolerate the "... feelings aroused by the primal scene". Here, Winnicott emphasises that the introjection of the good internal object and the resolution of the Oedipus complex could not occur without the "introjection of an ego-supportive environment" at the very beginning. The capacity to be alone is based on the paradox of being alone in the "presence of mother" (Winnicott, 1958b, p. 417).
4. The theory of playing was present in Winnicott's early paediatric work when, in the 1930s, he found that the "spatula game" could be used as a way of assessing the infant's emotional difficulties in first consultations (Winnicott, 1941). Later, the "squiggle game" became a natural successor to the earlier game for toddlers, as well as a helpful diagnostic tool for children and adolescents. In 1942, Winnicott had already observed that the "... child values finding that hate or aggressive urges can be expressed in a known environment, without the return of hate and violence from the environment to the child" (Winnicott, 1964c[1942], p. 43). Here, we find the very theme of the subject's attack and the object's tolerance to that attack would begin to crystallise in the papers of 1968. The critique of psychoanalytic technique is also raised (as it is in "The use of an object"), and Winnicott is unequivocal that "... interpretation outside the ripeness of the material is indoctrination ... a corollary is that resistance arises out of interpretation given outside the area of overlap of the patient's and analyst's playing together" (Winnicott, 1968, p. 597).

It should be clear now that the above four papers show how Winnicott's reformulations were moving towards a distinct "paradigm shift" in psychoanalysis (Loparic, 2012). This does not imply that instinct theory is irrelevant for Winnicott, but, rather, that from the infant's point of view, the instinctual/biological impulse might just as well be an external clap of thunder *before* the sense of self could develop, and a sense of self will only come about through a psychic environment capable of meeting the infant's biological and emotional needs (Winnicott, 1965d, p. 141).

Evidently, Winnicott thought that something was missing in psychoanalytic theory: "There is a phase prior to that which makes sense of the concept of fusion" (1989, p. 239). As already stated, Winnicott's original thesis on aggression in 1939 was that it was primary and simply "muscle erotism", and a "symptom of being alive", ". . . and had nothing to do with anger", let alone hate, sadism and envy. By this last decade of his work, he used the term "destructive", but both words—"aggression" and "destruction"—in Winnicott's language signify a benign force in the infant at the beginning (although the word "destruction", as we shall see, takes on a supplementary meaning in the use of an object).

In "Metapsychological and clinical aspects of regression within the psychoanalytic set-up" (1955a), Winnicott argued that Freud took for granted the early good-enough environment, and his work with neurotics, therefore, meant that he did not have the clinical data that analysts with borderline patients discover, although this is something that has recently been challenged (cf. Raphael-Leff, 2007). In "The use of an object in the context of Moses and Monotheism", Winnicott reiterates this point, stating his view that this is the reason that Freud did not theorise about the pre-fusion stage and the question of how the infant develops a capacity to think symbolically (Winnicott, 1989: 240–246). As already stated above, it is in this very late paper that Winnicott introduces a new thought when he suggests that the father has an important role at this pre-fusion stage of the subject's psychic life (Abram, 2007a, p. 38).

The father's imago, he suggests, starts off as a whole object in the infant's psyche as a presence in mother's mind, that is, the fact of the parental intercourse (Abram, 2007a, p. 39). I have suggested that this notion advances the concept of primary maternal preoccupation because Winnicott states that the *"father as a whole object at the beginning*" (my italics) constitutes an integrative force in the infant, a clear suggestion that the father (in mother's mind during her state of primary maternal preoccupation) is transmitted and internalised by the infant, which will lead to an ego capacity. Indeed, it seems clear that without the father in mother's mind, there is no such thing as survival of the object in Winnicott's theory (cf. Green, 2000).

Recently, following on from this final detail in Winnicott's work and in contrast to Green's proposal of the Other in the mother's mind, I have proposed the notion of the "paternal integrate" (Abram, 2013c). Let us now explore the area of illusion in Winnicott's work that is inextricably associated with transitional phenomena.

Illusion (of omnipotence)

Primary creativity, the theoretical first feed, and creating the object

Let us briefly discuss three of the key related concepts that Winnicott had already outlined before 1968: primary creativity, the theoretical first feed, and creating the object (Abram, 2007a, pp. 114, 209). This discussion is aimed at highlighting the core concept in "The use of an object" because it should elucidate an understanding of how and why it offers psychoanalysis a theory based on clinical experience, showing that there is no need for a speculative concept such as the death instinct. These concepts help us to understand how Winnicott conceptualised the stage pre-fusion.

As we saw above, for Winnicott, the Freudian theory of fusion of the instincts could only occur *after* the establishment of "unit status" or a "unit self" (Winnicott, 1955b, 1965c). This stage of emotional development cannot occur before the age of three or four months. And, as we have seen, the establishment of a self was contingent on the mother's survival of her infant's ruthless, destructive love. Winnicott emphasises that it is the biological need in the baby that has to be attended to by the emotionality of the m/other/psychic–environment; and it is this attending to the infant's biological need which, at the very early stage of life, is not separable from emotional need. It occurs through the mother's emotional response due to her deep identification with the infant's state of helplessness, and this constitutes what Winnicott describes as the "theoretical first feed".

> The theoretical first feed is represented in real life by the summation of the early experiences of many feeds. After the theoretical first feed, the baby begins to have material with which to create (Winnicott, 1988, p. 106).

Following Freud, Winnicott sees that the baby is born into the world equipped with a creative potential. This "inherited tendency", described as a predisposition to grow, is bound up with the sensations in the body and the baby's absolute dependence. The mother's ability to recognise her baby's predicament enables her to adapt to his needs, for example, offering her breast when he cries. Winnicott stresses that the mother's adaptation has to involve the mother's desire and enjoyment in order to provide what the baby needs through her deep "primary maternal preoccupation"—an intense and unconscious identification with her baby's predicament of absolute dependence (1958a). This very first contact between mother and infant is the beginning of a gradual building up of the baby's "illusion of omnipotence" which means that, from the baby's point of view, his need (hunger) creates the breast (food). Winnicott sees this as a crucial moment that constitutes the foundations for all further development. The mother's ability to adapt to her baby's needs facilitates in the baby/subject the "illusion of omnipotence". This experience is a necessary aspect of what he describes as "the theoretical first feed".

> At least until we know more I must assume that there is creative potential, and that at the theoretical first feed the baby has a personal contribution to make. If the mother adapts well enough the baby assumes the nipple and the milk are the results of a gesture that arose out of need, the result of an idea that rode in on a crest of a wave of instinctual tension. (Winnicott, 1988, p. 110)

The wave of instinctual tension is, for example, the sensation of hunger (or any other biological impulse). Hunger that is met through the mother's "adaptation to her baby's need" does not necessarily mean that she is able to provide the theoretical first feed. There are many more essential ingredients involved in the good-enough mother's ability to feed her baby (Abram, 2007a, p. 235). In Winnicott's final formulations of the mother–infant relationship, he focuses on the process of mother's adaptation to the infant's needs, and suggests that these ingredients culminate and constitute her "survival" of the newborn's ruthless need for her. As we have seen, in 1968 he explores how the good-enough external object survives the baby's primitive need. This is another aspect of what occurs at the theoretical first feed and is associated with the baby's excited states and the mother's capacity to identify and respond to her baby's communications. The "good-enough mother" *survives* due to her state of primary maternal preoccupation. The fact of the mother's survival facilitates the baby's ability to "create the object". In contrast, the mother who is not able to tolerate the baby's ordinary demands, but instead tends to feel attacked by the baby and even persecuted (as we saw in the mother of the 1939 paper on aggression), is the mother who does not survive for the subject (Winnicott, 1984).

Therefore, the "survival of the object" is central, a crucial fact in the early psychic life of the human being that either enables or disables the subject to move from object relating to object usage. Here is Winnicott's famous sequence:

> After subject relates to object comes subject destroys object (as it becomes external); and then may come "object survives destruction by the subject" . . . A new feature thus arrives in the theory of object relating. The subject says to the object: "I destroyed you," and the object is there to receive the communication. From now on the subject says: "Hullo object!" "I destroyed you." "I love you". "You have value for me because of your survival of my destruction of you". "While I am loving you I am all the time destroying you" . . . in unconscious fantasy. (Winnicott, 1969, p. 713)

A dissection of the sequence that leads from object relating to object usage

The reader will note that in his outline summary for the audience in New York (as shown above), Winnicott lists five stages to the sequence just quoted and features the words "relates", "destroys", and "use". Let us dissect the sequence and pay attention to the word emphasis.

1. Subject *relates* to object.

   This is the baby at the beginning of life who is unaware of the care he receives and is merged with the m/other during the phase of absolute dependence. The baby is ruthless during this stage—in a state of pre-ruth—and he cannot know about the demands he puts on the environment; indeed it is paramount that the baby is *not* made aware of what he is doing. The environment mother must protect him from this fact so that he can get on with the tasks involved in being out of the womb.

2. Object is in process of being found instead of placed by the subject in the world.

   The baby's needs are met and this leads to the object being experienced, although not yet consciously. The baby cannot yet be aware that the mother/object is a separate other. The process of finding out and moving towards more conscious awareness has to be given space and time. The baby is not yet ready to be aware because further crucial processes need to take place before he will be able to "place the object in the world".

3. Subject *destroys* object.

   The repeated and uninhibited ruthless demand for the environment's adaptation amounts to a continual destruction of the object. The ongoing destruction is not intentional, but, rather, a necessary process of "discovering" the externality of the object.

4. Object survives destruction.

   The mother's sustained capacity to tolerate the baby's endless demands because of her state of primary maternal preoccupation offers the infant a sense of continuity and reliability. Survival involves primary identification, mirroring or reflection, ego protection, processing, and, crucially, non-retaliation. The myriad aspects of the good-enough m/other's survival enables the baby to move from apperception to perception in the potential space between relating to subjective objects and perceiving objects objectively perceived. This phase of the baby's life takes him from absolute to relative dependence as he moves from total unawareness to a gradual awareness of the environment.

5. Subject can *use* object.

   The previous merger of the "environment mother" and "object mother" in the phase of absolute dependence gave the baby the impression that he had two different mothers. Due to the consistent survival of the object, this perspective has gradually changed and by now the baby is able to see that both mothers are actually one (Winnicott, 1963).

This sequence depicts the step-by-step process of the baby's aggression (biological urge/need) being survived (received and digested) by the external object, which simultaneously leads to the baby's internalisation, as Winnicott said, of the "ego supportive environment" (Winnicott, 1962, p. 63). The infant's primary aggression—that is, a benign instinctual impulse—forces the object to adapt (or not) to the baby's instinctual needs. At the very beginning the subject cannot differentiate between instinctual bodily need and the object's separateness. Good-enough adaptation to the needs of the newborn means there is also no differentiation for the infant between psyche and soma. This harmonious mix between psyche and soma, mother and infant, is incrementally internalised and culminates in the baby's intrapsychic "imaginative elaboration" about what is happening to and in his body.

Winnicott's principle thesis is that there is *no duality* in the biological/instinctual demand. In other words, he disagrees with Freud's theory of the duality of instincts because he states that, at the beginning, it is a movement concerning being alive and, therefore, it has no other intention except to *relate*, that is, to feel the extent of the boundary and to find the object for needs to be met.

The crucial moment in Winnicott's sequence of object relating to object use is that the object is there to *receive the communication*: that is, the object is able to *receive* the subject's loving destruction. It is this reception (which inevitably includes reflection) that I suggest constitutes the object's psychic survival. Because of the object's ability to receive, and, thus, survive, the subject will experience that his ruthless love has been survived by the object, because she—the object—continues to receive and reflect, respond and adapt. This is the essential experience of mutuality that will lead on to the establishment of an internalised "ego supportive environment" without which the subject is not able to distinguish between his/her projections and the integrity of the m/other.

The surviving and non surviving objects

Winnicott's late work, as I have described above, led to my attempt to extend his theory of psychic survival to formulate the notion of the surviving and non-surviving objects (Abram, 2005, 2007b). These two intrapsychic subjective objects result from the object's survival or non survival of the infant's primary aggression. My recent examination of Winnicott's very late concept of the 'integrate'—the third in mother's mind—has led to my proposal of the 'paternal integrate' (Abram, 2013b,c, 2014). This very late concept finally brings the crucial function of the early father into Winnicott's theoretical matrix without which there can be no true survival of the object.

References

Abram, J. (Ed.) (2000). *André Green at the Squiggle Foundation*. London: Karnac.

Abram, J. (2005). L'objet qui survit, D. Alcorn (Trans.). *Journal de la Psychanalyse de l'enfant, 36*: 139–174.

Abram, J. (2007a). *The Language of Winnicott: A Dictionary of Winnicott's Use of Words* (2nd edn). London: Karnac.

Abram, J. (2007b). L'objet qui ne survit pas. Quelques réflexions sur les racines de la terreur, D. Houzel (Trans.). *Journal de la psychanalyse de l'enfant, 39*: 247–270.

Abram, J. (2008). Donald Woods Winnicott: a brief introduction. *International Journal of Psychoanalysis, 89*: 1189–1217.

Abram, J. (2012). D.W.W.'s notes for the Vienna Congress 1971: a consideration of Winnicott's theory of aggression and an interpretation of the clinical implications. In: J. Abram (Ed.) (2013a), *Donald Winnicott Today* (pp. 202–230). Hove: Routledge.

Abram, J. (Ed.) (2013a). *Donald Winnicott Today*. Hove: Routledge.

Abram, J. (2013b). On Winnicott's area of formlessness: the pure female element and the capacity to feel real. *Bulletin of the E.P.F., 67*: 43–57.

Abram, J. (2013c). L'integré paternel. Atelier avec Haydée Faimberg CPLF 2013 (unpublished).

Abram, J. (2014). The paternal integrate and its role in the analyzing situation (forthcoming).

Green, A. (2000). On thirdness. In: J. Abram (Ed.), *André Green at the Squiggle Foundation* (pp. 39–68). London: Karnac.

Loparic, Z. (2013). From Freud to Winnicott: aspects of a paradigm change. In: J. Abram (Ed.), *Donald Winnicott Today* (pp. 113–156). Hove: Routledge.

Raphael-Leff, J. (2007). Freud's prehistoric matrix: owing 'Nature' a death. *International Journal of Psychoanalysis, 88*: 1345–1373.

Winnicott, D. W. (1941). The observation of infants in a set situation. *International Journal of Psychoanalysis, 22*: 229–249.

Winnicott, D. W. (1953). Transitional objects and transitional phenomena: a study of the first not-me possession *International Journal of Psychoanalysis, 34*: 89–97.

Winnicott, D. W. (1955a). Metapsychological and clinical aspects of regression within the psychoanalytical set-up. *International Journal of Psychoanalysis, 36*: 16–26.

Winnicott, D. W. (1955b). The depressive position in normal emotional development. *British Journal of Medical Psychology, 28*: 89–100.

Winnicott, D. W. (1958a). Primary maternal preoccupation. In: *Collected Papers: Through Paediatrics to Psychoanalysis* (pp. 300–305). London: Tavistock (2nd edition, with preface by M. M. R. Kahan, London: Hogarth and The Institute of Psychoanalysis, 1975).

Winnicott, D. W. (1958b). The capacity to be alone. *International Journal of Psychoanalysis, 39*: 416–420.

Winnicott, D. W. (1963). The development of the capacity for concern. *Bulletin of the Menninger Clinic, 27*: 167–176.

Winnicott, D. W. (1964c). Why children play. In: *The Child, the Family and the Outside World*. Harmondsworth: Penguin.

Winnicott, D. W. (1965a). *The Family and Individual Development*. London: Tavistock.

Winnicott, D. W. (1965b). Ego integration in child development. In: *The Family and Individual Development* (pp. 56–63). London: Tavistock.

Winnicott, D. W. (1965c). *The Maturational Processes and the Facilitating Environment: Studies in the Theory of Emotional Development*. London: Hogarth Press.

Winnicott, D. W. (1965d). Ego distortion in terms of true and false self. In: *The Maturational Processes and the Facilitating Environment: Studies in the Theory of Emotional Development* (pp. 140–152). London: Hogarth Press.

Winnicott, D. W. (1967). The location of cultural experience. *International Journal of Psychoanalysis, 48*: 368–372.

Winnicott, D. W. (1968). Playing: its theoretical status in the clinical situation. *International Journal of Psychoanalysis, 49*: 591–597.

Winnicott, D. W. (1969). The use of an object and relating through identifications. *International Journal of Psychoanalysis, 50*: 711–716.

Winnicott, D. W. (1971). *Playing and Reality*. London: Tavistock.

Winnicott, D. W. (1984). *Deprivation and Delinquency*, C. Winnicott, R. Shepherd, & M. Davis (Eds.). London: Tavistock.

Winnicott, D. W. (1988). *Human Nature*, C. Bollas, M. Davis, & R. Shepherd (Eds.). London: Free Association Books.

Winnicott, D. W. (1989). *Psycho-Analytic Explorations*, C. Winnicott, R. Shepherd, & M. Davis (Eds.). Cambridge, MA: Harvard University Press.

CHAPTER EIGHT

The use of an object: Winnicott and ternary thought*

Wilfrid Reid

The knowledge of knowledge

Winnicott provides new knowledges in psychoanalysis, first of all in introducing a new knowledge of knowledge. Implicitly, his work calls into question the rules of formal logic that allow us to give a status of truth to our theoretical propositions. Until Winnicott, analytic thought—like occidental science before the birth of quantum physics—remained faithful to the formal logic propounded by Aristotle. This logic is essentially based on the principle of non-contradiction.

According to this principle, confronted with two propositions, one of which is the logical negation of the other, if one is true then the other is necessarily false. This principle refuses the conjunction of proposition A and proposition non-A. Edgar Morin, philosopher and sociologist, has developed a new epistemology, the paradigm of complex thought, which invites us to give a moderate place in our thinking to the principle of non-contradiction. This paradigm of

* I wish to thank my colleagues, Prométhée Constantidines and Allanah Furlong, for their help with the English translation of my chapter.

complex thought describes the different aspects of this new knowledge of knowledge.

According to this paradigm, a new logic, a paradoxical logic, goes beyond the Aristotelian logic without totally invalidating traditional logic. The latter, foundation of the "old paradigm of the disjunction, reduction, simplification" (Morin, 2005), is still relevant in representing certain aspects of reality. But the paradigm of complex thought opens new horizons concerning our knowledge of reality and, specifically, our knowledge of unconscious psychic reality: Winnicott's work illustrates this perspective in a masterful way.

The three principles

Morin (2008) presents the paradigm of complex thought in his major work entitled *La Méthode*. This work, in six volumes, is encyclopaedic in character. For our purpose, I will describe only the basic elements of the new paradigm, which are the three principles of complex thought. The first principle is the dialogical principle. In paradoxical logic, two antagonistic concepts are not only opposed but, at the same time, nourish one another, are complementary. We find this paradoxical logic, for example, in the clinical paradox of the found–created. For Winnicott, to find and to create are simultaneously antagonistic and complementary. In the presence of the good-enough mother—a compelling incarnation of the dialogical principle—the infant will simultaneously experience finding and creating the breast; in fact, the experience of finding is a necessary condition for the experience of creating.

The second principle concerns organisational recursivity, a circularity existing between causes and effects. Effects become causes, just as causes become effects: "Individuals produce society which via the culture, produce individuals" (Morin, 2005). According to Winnicott (1988), each pole of the unity formed by this specific child with this specific mother contributes to the creation of this unity. The mother creates the child who creates the mother who creates the child in a virtual continuous movement, which can, however, be brought to a standstill depending on the evolution of the relationship.

The third principle of complex thought refers to the hologram. Each part of a hologram contains the quasi-totality of information about the represented object down to the smallest detail of its image. The hologrammic principle stipulates that if the part is in the whole, the whole is equally in the part. Biologically, each cell of the organism contains the totality of the genetic information of the organism. On the psychic level, for Winnicott (1988), "the theoretical first feed" gives birth, as much in its emergences as in its interferences, to the quasi-totality of the vicissitudes of the mother–child unity.

Ternary thought

Winnicott was never aware of the paradigm of complex thought. In fact, the first formulation of this paradigm appears in a work published in 1982 (Morin) entitled "Science avec conscience". Furthermore, according to Morin (1983), this paradigm does not exist by itself; it is its applications that shape the paradigm; it operates, totally unconsciously, in the spontaneous epistemology of scholars. Nevertheless, Winnicott had an intuition of this paradigm.

> The fact is that what we create is already there . . . So when I look at the clock, as I must do now, I create a clock, but I am careful not to see clocks except just where I already know there is one. Please do not turn down this *piece of absurd unlogic* – but look at it and use it. (Winnicott, 1986, p. 52, my italics)

Winnicott relies on this "absurd unlogic" to elaborate his work. The paradigm of complex thought substitutes ternary thought for traditional binary thought. Ternary thought is, indeed, the ferment of Winnicott's views on the unconscious. In this conceptual frame, all notional duality requires a triadic principal, including the connotation of an absent third notion. This absence is understood not as a non-existence, but, rather, as a hope, a potential presence. Binary thought involves a third excluded; in contrast, ternary thought reveals a third included. Following Winnicott's lead, André Green (2002a) explicitly introduces ternary thought into psychoanalysis by proposing the concept of "tiercéité", usually translated as "thirdness". This concept, without being formulated as such, impregnates all Winnicott's writings; it is especially illustrated in his conception of the loss of the primary object.

Winnicott (1971a) brings new insight into this foundational moment by distinguishing the interruption of maternal breast-feeding from the weaning of the infant, the latter an intrapsychic phenomena resulting from the disillusionment process. This interpsychic moment expresses itself in the mode of paradoxical logic: Winnicott mentions the child "who is just about becoming ready to be 'weaned', to be able to deal with loss without quite losing what is (in one sense only) lost" (1988, p. 35). When the baby is ready to assume it, the loss, thus, simultaneously exists and does not exist. This is the "effacement" of the object, according to Green (1993).

Winnicott's vision points to a specific metapsychological modality in the loss of an object. It is the hallmark of a successful illusion–disillusionment process; the mind becomes a palimpsest (Reid, 2012). In the "effacement" of the object, the object exists and does not exist. The mother is "there" in the mode of "not being there". Metapsychologically, this form of presence is called "absence". A good educator has to work at becoming useless. According to Lao-Tzu, vases are fabricated with clay but their usefulness depends on their internal emptiness. The mother will facilitate the status of the "absent mother" in the child's mind only if she herself can cathect the child in the mode of an "absent" object. A little known aspect of Winnicott's thought is the new perspective it offers on the father's role. He describes this role as a third part included in the mother–child duality when he evokes the father's presence in the mother's mind during the exercise of her maternal function (Abram, 1996).

The use of an object

This epistemological preamble sets up our intention to a reappraise the concept of the use of an object and to further draw out Winnicott's thought. This concept—located at a crossroad of the fundamental concepts of Freud's metapsychology—calls for a significant shift in our understanding of drive, psychic trauma and the analytic process. *The capacity to use the object refers to a specific modality of unconscious psychic activity.* This new *modus operandi* of the unconscious entails differentiation of the subjective and the objective objects. It marks the instauration of "the conception–perception gap" (Winnicott, 1971b).

For Winnicott, the use of an object is equivalent, in a certain way, to reality testing in Freud's thought. For Freud, as later Winnicott, was trying to understand how the change in the modality of cathexis of the object comes about in the transformation of the pleasure principle into the reality principle. Freud's description comprises two poles, that of the child's mind and that of external reality. The latter might be thought of as including the mother's mind in the designation of "extraneous help" (Freud, 1950a), but nowhere does he appear to take into account the specific character of the mother's unconscious psychic functioning. For Winnicott, on the other hand, the use of an object implies three poles: the child's mind, external reality, and the mother's mind as a distinctive pole. In his view, the mother works as a mediator between the child's mind and external reality in a more or less desirable manner, depending on her personal psychic characteristics. With Winnicott, the external help becomes a mother.

We can then see the close articulation between the theory of the parent–child relationship, the development of transitional processes, and the use of an object (Abram, 1996). Moreover, the use of an object refers essentially to the success of the found–created and the destroyed–found, which are the psychic processes equally responsible for the instauration of transitionality. Transitionality and the use of an object are two faces of the same *modus operandi* of the unconscious, transitionality designating the intrapsychic side while the use of an object addresses the interpsychic side.

At the end of the sequence of interpsychic events leading to the use of an object, Winnicott states firmly, "Here fantasy begins for the individual" (Winnicott, 1971c, p. 90). This notional duality of fact and fantasy thus acquires a triadic principle. In order for this duality to respect ternary thought, it must include a notion of absence (Green, 1990), a third space where all psychic content bears simultaneously the mark of fact and fantasy. This *modus operandi* of the unconscious unites an experience and a non-experience of the distinction between fact and fantasy. Such is the substance of "the illusion without which no contact is possible between the psyche and the environment" (Winnicott, 1978a, p. 223). Illusion, in different ways, constitutes the ferment of the mother–child relationship as much as the ferment of transitionality and the use of the object. Effectively, these three notions form a network in which each one can only be thought in continuity with the others.

The drive

In their positive vicissitudes, the unconscious process of the found–created and the destroyed–found form a passage from object-relating to use of an object. Such a perspective encourages a review of our conceptions of drive and of psychic trauma. For Freud, the sexual drive forms the basis of the unconscious mind. Yet, as we know, this model continues to be strongly questioned, all the more so in so far as its supporters have not always taken into account the new challenges met by this model in contemporary clinical experience.

Winnicott invites us to a new comprehension of drive, in fact, a new ontology of drive. In defending this hypothesis, we once more refer to the paradigm of complex thought. In Morin (2005):

> This "scienza nuova" assumes and renders explicit a new ontology which, not only accentuates relationship to the detriment of substance, but also emphasizes the emergences, the interferences as constituents parts of object. Not only is there a network formed by relationship, there are realities which are not essences, which are not formed of a sole substance, which are composite, produced by systemic interplaying but somehow endowed with a certain autonomy. (p. 67, translated for this edition)

It is as though Edgar Morin were describing the different dimensions of drive that are implicit in Winnicott's texts. Let us try to make explicit our propositions. First, the drive does not suddenly appear in the subject, but in the drive–object pairing formed by the mother–child unity. There is a relational inscription of drive. The emphasis is on "relationship to the detriment of substance". Second, "emergence" of drive represents a qualitative change in the unconscious mind. However, this emergence is not ineluctable. It can become the subject of various interferences depending upon the vicissitudes of the evolution of the drive–object pairing. In this regard, the psychoanalysts who repudiate the model of sexual drive would have a metapsychological understanding equivalent to a mirror undoubling of the processes of interference, impeding the emergence of this drive as a new quality of the mind.

Third, the drive does not express itself in the mode of an "essence", of a "being-there" at the beginning. Apart from the fact that it takes form in a relational frame, its initial content is always "composite".

Drive is "produced by the systemic interplaying" of the found–created and the destroyed–found. Fourth, the drive is "somehow endowed with a certain autonomy". From the drive–object pairing operating in the mother–child duality, it ultimately actualises itself as part of the individual mind of the child. In the process, there occurs a gradual subjectivisation of drive.

With Gauthier (2006), we consider the idea of "an ontogenesis of drive". Apart from the fact of its relational inscription, drive, in its psychic content, requires a process of transformation of the instinctual energy, a process that will be more or less facilitated according to the vagaries of the relational inscription. The emergence of drive as a new quality of mind is subsequent to a transformation that is, at one and the same time, processual and semantical/referential.

The relational inscription of drive

For Freud, the internal origin of excitation marks the instinctual character of excitation. According to this canonical definition, drive takes root directly in intrapsychic space, whereas for Winnicott (1971c), the drive originates in the mother–child unity. The vital or destructive quality of the drive does not take place, in an immanent way, in the instinctual movement; it is the response of the object that will determine the vital or destructive character of the primordial instinctual movement of the subject.

To illustrate, let us take a paradigmatic situation: a baby moves on his mother's lap. For one mother, he seems "full of life", there is no experience of, and then no actualisation of, destructivity. The baby will be spared the unconscious experience of his instinctual motion as a real destruction of the mother. This response of the object has permitted a successful operation of the destroyed–found, thereby opening the way to the use of an object.

In contrast, another mother could cry out, "Be careful, you will hurt mummy." As in the first scene, the instinctual motion begins "in the individual's omnipotence" (Winnicott, 1960). We are not referring here to omnipotence as a psychic content but as an organising principle of the psychic processes. In the second scene, omnipotence cannot be the object of internal processual transformation. The process of "individual's omnipotence" remains at a standstill without access to "the conception–perception gap" (Winnicott, 1971b). Thinking about destroying the mother and really destroying the mother has become equivalent in the mind. This response of the object introduces an "interference" which hinders the processual transformation of the individual omnipotence of the subject. The response of the object jeopardises differentiation between subjective and objective objects, and, consequently, the capacity to use an object.

The second mother, in psychotherapy, relates a recent event with her five-year-old child. She is tormented by the conviction of being "a bad mother". This subjective object ("the bad mother"), since it is not differentiated from the objective object, easily becomes reality. The mother sails in troubled waters in relationship with her son; at any moment, the spectre of the "bad mother" can appear suddenly in the reduced space of her intrapsychic metabolising capacity. When a clash happens with his mother, the child throws in her face, "Mummy, I don't like you." The child's words go straight to the mother's heart; she receives in a traumatic way a representation of herself at one and the same time spurned and unrecognised as a representation of herself. This representation of reality becomes reality. The mother can only respond with a slap; afterwards, she is crushed by the weight of her guilt. Is that not a bad mother's behaviour? She then rushes to her child begging for forgiveness. In spite of all her good intentions, this mother does not seem to possess a psychic organisation capable of surviving the "destructive" motions of her child. Such a psychic environment precludes a successful destroyed–found.

The principle of organisational recursivity alters our understanding of the process–content relation (Ody, 2005). According to Winnicott (1989a), "destructive aliveness" is the most primitive instinctual motion, a motion being simultaneously a psychic process and a psychic content. If the response of the object is good enough, the process produces the content that produces the process. The reciprocal playing of the process on the content and the content on the process modifies simultaneously the process and the content. The mind acquires an "aliveness" by virtue of being non-"destructive" enough to lay the foundation from which creativity can emerge to modify the processual character of destructivity; the latter ceases to be perceived as reality. Destructivity, henceforth, assumes a strictly virtual character wherein creativity exercises a counterweight, a very comforting rampart for the subject. This reciprocal playing of the process on the content and the content on the process transforms "the individual's omnipotence". The differentiation of subjective and objective objects induces a qualitative leap in the unconscious psychic functioning. I still remember an analysand experiencing this qualitative leap. He was astonished to discover "I thought 'that' and it was not 'that'!"

The psychic content of drive

If, at first, it concerns its relational inscription, the new ontology of the drive equally refers to its semantic content. The latter, as described earlier, will be "composite" at the beginning. How should we name this semantically "composite" content? Winnicott was uneasy with this matter and it was not, for sure, the reception of his conference at the New York Psychoanalytic Society in 1968 that would persuade him of the contrary. All through his work, he invites us to beware of possible misunderstandings, introducing many expressions. The primordial instinctual urge is, first, "almost synonymous with activity" (1978b, p. 204), then "we mean spontaneity" (1978b, p. 217). Elsewhere, it becomes "simply a symptom of being alive" (1989a, p. 239) or "such things as eagerness" (1989a, p. 240).

This heterogeneous content derives from a paradoxical logic appealing simultaneously to two antagonistic and complementary notions. This primordial instinctual motion, this "destructive aliveness" (Winnicott, 1989a), corresponds to a processual indifferentiation which would initiate two distinct processual vicissitudes depending on the degree of facilitation or interference of the mother–child relational frame. Winnicott (1989a, p. 239) mentions the metaphor of fire. "I quote from Pliny who (in playing tribute to fire) writes: 'Who can say whether in essence fire is constructive or destructive?'" Depending on its context, the first instinctual motion will induce a "constructive" or "destructive" process, a process bearer of psychic life or death. Better still, in a positive avatar of this instinctual motion, will abruptly appear a differentiation between a process bearer of life and a process bearer of death with a priority to aliveness over destructivity; at first an instinctual dualism known as creativity–destructivity will emerge in a theoretical time preceding the dualism auto-conservation–sexuality.

In the beginning, "the individual's omnipotence" of the child pole of the mother–child unity produces an immoderate intensity of tension "composed" of a mixture of spontaneity, sensoriality, and motricity. The "good-enough" response of the object facilitates the sharing of immoderate tension in such a way as to permit its "good-enough" modulation. Access to a living mind arises in the emergence of the instinctual dualism creativity–destructivity. Dealing positively with the intense tension, in the relation with the other as well as with oneself, the mind can unconsciously adopt its experience as properly libidinal; the pleasure principle becomes the organising principle of the mind. There is, therefore, a complementarity between Freud's instinctual model and Winnicott's; the emergence of the dualism creativity–destructivity can now be seen as a preliminary condition to activation of the dualism auto-conservation–sexuality under the auspices of the pleasure principle. Freud's instinctual model auto-conservation–sexuality describes a model in which drive has been subjectivated. In the "afterwardness" of Winnicott's thought, Freud's instinctual model would be a tributary of an ego visited by destructivity.

The death drive

Winnicott was explicit in disagreeing with Freud about the death drive. This open disagreement had the unfortunate consequence of leading to an underestimation of Winnicott's paradoxical contribution to the notion of a death drive. Each theorist, in his own way, tried to conceptualise what prevents the establishment of the pleasure principle. Freud formulates the hypothesis of a primary destructivity, appearing directly, in the form of an auto-destruction of the subject; Winnicott, on the other hand, postulates the existence of a "destructive aliveness", arising in the drive–object pairing formed by the mother–child unity. Winnicott (1988) proposes the existence of an instinctual unity where the drive is potentially destructive. Destructivity does not occur directly. It is secondary to the failure of transformation of the primordial instinctual process. At the beginning, this process is understood as indeterminate with respect to the positive or negative quality of its semantic content: "Who could say whether in essence fire is constructive or destructive?" The mother–child relational frame "precipitates" out of this indeterminate primordial drive a positive or negative variation.

With a good-enough response of the object, we observe a transformation of the instinctual process. The response "constructs" the found–created and the destroyed–found in such a way as to promote differentiation between conception (representation) and perception (external stimulus) and consequent capacity to use the object. The emergence of the creativity–destructivity drive dualism allows the mind to be mobilised by a process bearing psychic life. In the absence of a good enough response of the object, fire becomes destructive; the destructive potentiality of the drive ceases to be virtual; it becomes active in the form of "annihilating destructivity" [annihilating = *néantisante* in French] (Green, 2002b), which often leads the subject to an evacuation of his own psychic activity. The drive process that mobilises the mind is the bearer of psychic death. Would the concept of creativity be Winnicott's responses to the metapsychological concerns behind Freud's proposition of the concept of death drive? Winnicott (1986, p. 39) means by creativity "a doing by impulsion" which partakes of a being in opposition to "a doing by reaction" where "the word "being" has no relevance".

The creativity–destructivity drive dualism defines the subject as existing, as living. This first dualism appears as a necessary condition for the effectiveness of the auto-conservation/sexuality Freudian dualism. Creativity—"a basic place to operate from"—represents a mobilising process for the mind, a process exercising a pressure, a primordial characteristic of the drive. It is a bearer of psychic life. It produces a doing by im/pulsion; we modify the writing of the term "impulsion" to emphasise the subjective effectiveness of the drive, henceforth in phase with its canonical definition as "internal". The emergence of the creativity–destructivity dualism renders operative the auto-conservation–sexuality dualism. In the opposite case, the non-emergence of creativity has negative consequences for the subject: "The activities that indicate that the person is alive are simply reactions to stimulus . . . Withdraw the stimuli and the individual has no life" (Winnicott, 1986, p. 39). The mind is governed by an "annihilating destructivity" which crushes psychic activity, a destruction of any activity that would be generated by the subject. The function of the mind is reduced to a simple reading of perception: "The essential is the 'centration' on the object as origin and cause of all the internal movements of the subject" (Green, 2012, my translation).

"La dame au docteur" is a good illustration of the psychic emptiness, of the unconscious auto-annihilation of the self. With her analyst's silence, the ground gives way under her feet. "La dame au docteur" is thus named because, during a long period of psychotherapy, a question was often floated by her during sessions: "What do you think, Doctor?" Only the doctor, it seemed, was able to think as soon as a question arose and the questions occurred non-stop. Annihilating destructivity was central to her unconscious processes; it took multiple expressions. In her forties and still living with her mother "la dame au docteur" had never known any real sentimental engagement.

The unconscious annihilation manifests itself in a quasi-pure form in an exchange with her analyst. This exchange happened while she was vituperating against her mother, who was pressuring her into accompanying her on a visit to some relatives.

The analyst: "The question: 'Do I want to accompany my mother?' This is a question that does not exist."

The patient: "Yes, yes, I asked my mother: 'Why, Mum, don't you ask me if I want to go with you?'"

The analyst: "'Why, Mum, don't you ask me if I want to go with you?' The question: 'Do I want to accompany my mother?' This is a question that does not exist."

The patient: "So it is very serious . . ."

Of course, this recognition does not immediately modify the patient's annihilating dynamic. Nevertheless, and progressively, the patient established a new relation with herself, a relation that did not necessarily migrate through the relation with the other. She developed the capacity of being alone in presence of the other, another formulation of Winnicott's ternary thought. With time, she got in touch, painfully, with the feeling of awakening from a "deep sleep" of over forty years. She eventually experienced being "alone facing the drive in the presence of the other" (Roussillon, 2008). She then felt her first sexual feelings, on an ego-syntonic mode. A non-equivocal sign of an opening to the libidinal experience, she will be drawn to a poetical expression of her erotic feelings. We are far from the nightmares of the beginning of her psychotherapy, where men "throw projectiles at my thighs".

The psychic trauma

With his new formulation of the nagging theoretical problem of human destructiveness, Winnicott introduces a new understanding of psychic trauma as impeding the passage from object relating to the use of an object. The notion of psychic trauma never ceased to haunt the psychoanalytic movement. More than 100 years after the abandonment of neurotica, the theme of the 2005 International Congress of the IPA, psychic trauma, was introduced in the following manner: "Is it preferable to see trauma as a purely intrapsychic manifestation, perhaps an inevitable part of the development or else a response to the external events?" (IPA, Newsletter 2005).

Can we avoid passing from Charybdis to Scylla, from the external to the internal, or from the internal to the external? Freud, in the turning point of 1897, discovered a spatio–temporal logic proper to the unconscious; it has a hallucinatory quality; unconscious processes "equate reality of thought with external actuality, and wishes with their fulfilment – with the event – just as happens automatically under the dominance of the ancient pleasure principle" (Freud, 1911b, p. 225). Laplanche (1976) identifies the presence of the hallucinatory in this crucial turning point; however, he brings out an apory unelaborated by Freud.

> And if the element of reality in external perception is not the result of learning, hallucinations are to the very same extent not available to being corrected by any training or experiential or testing process. The hallucination *is or is not*, and when it is, it is absolutely useless to imagine a procedure allowing one to demonstrate to the hallucinator that he is wrong. (p. 61, original italics)

"Hallucination is or is not". The author clearly shows how any paradigm of either/or cannot very well take into account the hallucinatory register. Winnicott's genius casts light on a triadic principle at work: the notional duality of hallucinatory satisfaction *vs.* real satisfaction now includes reference to a third and "absent" notion: a satisfaction simultaneously hallucinatory and real in the found–created.

In this way, Winnicott will revive the role of the hallucinatory and give it a central role in his metapsychology. Save for a few exceptions ("We need to be able to think hallucinatorily" (Winnicott, 1989b,

p. 157)), he will not use the term "hallucinatory". In his language, it will be designated as "the individual's omnipotence". The psychic processes of found–created and destroyed–found which guide the way to the use of an object represents successive transformations of the hallucinatory. Psychic trauma is now located in the obstacles to these transformations:

> In psycho-analysis as we know it there is no trauma that is outside the individual's omnipotence . . . changes came in an analysis when the factors enter the psycho-analytic material in the patient's own way, and *within the patient's omnipotence.* (Winnicott, 1960, p. 585, original italics)

Illusion, in its different transformations, all through development, remains the ferment of psychic life. If transitionality, the most advanced form of illusion, performs an anti-traumatic function for the mind (Kluzer-Usuelli, 1992), then the failure of its establishment condemns to a traumatic functioning.

Winnicott proposes a conception of psychic trauma with multiple levels. In addition to the traumatic event, he underlines the traumatic character of the environment that does not produce a good-enough response when needed. This response, if good enough, avers actualisation of the "destructive potentiality of the drive". In this manner, Winnicott draws attention to the existence of a traumatic potentiality inherent in the human mind. Consequently, we can factor out three different levels of trauma: the trauma-as-event, the trauma-as-environment, and the "structural trauma" as-a-traumatic-potentiality-proper-to-the mind (Reid, 2010). We rightly take stock of the traumatic potentiality of the child's mind when we recognise the need for the environment to prop up "for the child the divine prerogatives of creating the world which surrounds him" (Ribas, 2000, p. 52, translated for this edition). Winnicott's contribution illustrates the pertinence of abandoning a certain external–internal dichotomy in order to think about reciprocal interactions among the various levels of the psychic trauma in a perspective of organisational recursivity or circularity.

The analytic process

Patients without the capacity to use the object require a new conception of analytic process and, consequently, a modification of the analytic method. The use of an object results in thought processes subjectively experienced as distinct from perceptual processes. The accepted or refused interpretation is generally received as an interpretation that is a "thought" on the part of the analyst. In these persons, the mind is accessible to meta-communication. When the capacity to use an object has not been reached, subjective and objective objects remain undifferentiated. The disavowed subjectivity of the subject is deposited in the object in such a way to produce an "incriminating objectivation out of the mind" (Green, 2012) [in French: "*objectivation accusatrice hors-psyche*"].

> Returning to psycho-analysis, I have said that the analyst is prepared to wait till the patient becomes able to present the environmental factors in terms that allow of their interpretation as projection. . . . In the course of time, the patient becomes able to make use of the psycho-analytic interpretations of the original traumata as projections. (Winnicott, 1960, p. 585)

How can we work with patients for whom traumatic factors in the environment have been considerable; how can they eventually become accessible to interpretation? Perhaps Botella's notion of negative trauma shows a way:

> Trauma comes from negativity. Something should have happened for a healthy evolution; it is the absence of a primordial psychic fact which is traumatic, a negative trauma, in the sense that it is neither thought nor perceived and does not leave any trace on an usual mode of memory. (2005, p. 22, translated for this edition)

Winnicott's work has alerted us to the traumatic potential inherent in a primitive/immature mind confronted with immoderate intense tension. "Something has not happened" to avert the triggering destructivity of drive, destructivity which, at the beginning, is only virtual, "potentially destructive".

The analytic work must be situated either before or beyond interpretative work, aiming at restoring the psychic processes of found–created and destroyed–found and, thereby, facilitating a processual transformation in "the individual's omnipotence". The stake of the survival of the object has to be given another round:

> In psychoanalytic practice the positive changes that come about in this area can be profound. They do not depend on interpretative work. They depend on the analyst's survival of the attacks, which involves and includes the idea of the absence of a quality change to retaliation. (Winnicott, 1971c, p. 91)

The incapacity of using an object calls for a modification of analytic technique. Interpretation is no more in the forefront and the elaboration of countertransference becomes crucial for "survival" (often by both parties) of the analysand's "destructive aliveness". Moreover, a great deal of patience is required when the bond is experienced in a state of subject/object indifferentiation.

In conclusion, the concept of the use of an object commands a reformulation of Freudian metapsychological concepts, not to invalidate them, but to permit them to be more in phase with the challenges of contemporary psychoanalysis. The concept of the use of an object reveals itself as having great heuristic value in the conduct of analytic cures. Both theoretically and therapeutically, the use of an object represents a major conceptual breakthrough in post-Freudian psychoanalysis.

References

Abram, J. (1996). *The Language of Winnicott: A Dictionary of Winnicott's Use of Words*. London: Karnac.

Botella, C. (2005). Enjeux pour une psychanalyse de demain. In: F. Richard & F. Urribarri (Eds.), *Autour de l'œuvre d'André Green, enjeux pour une psychanalyse contemporaine* (pp. 11–31). Paris: PUF.

Freud, S. (1911b). Formulation on the two principles of mental functioning. *S. E., 12*: . London: Hogarth.

Freud, S. (1950a). *Project for a Scientific Psychology*. *S. E., 1*: . London: Hogarth.

Gauthier, M. (2006). Troisième topique et psychanalyse d'enfant, *Revue française de psychanalyse, LXX*(5): 1483–1489.

Green, A. (1990). L'analyste, la symbolisation et l'absence dans le cadre analytique. In: *La folie privée, psychanalyse des cas limites* (pp. 63–102). Paris: Éditions Gallimard.

Green, A. (1993). *Le travail du négatif*. Paris: Les Éditions de Minuit.

Green, A. (2002a). De la tiercéité. In: *La pensée clinique* (pp. 259–308). Paris: Éditions Jacob.

Green, A. (2002b). *Idées directrices pour une psychanalyse contemporaine*. Paris: PUF.

Green, A. (2012). *La clinique psychanalytique contemporaine*. Paris: Ithaque.

IPA (2005). Newsletter.

Kluzer Usuelli, A. (1992). The significance of illusion in the work of Freud and Winnicott: a controversial issue. *International Review of Psycho-Analysis, 19*: 179–187.

Laplanche, J. (1976). *Life and Death in Psychoanalysis*, J. Mehlman (Trans.). Baltimore, MD: Johns Hopkins University Press.

Morin, E. (1982). *Science avec conscience*. Paris: Fayard [reprinted Paris, Seuil, 1990].

Morin, E. (1983). Peut-on concevoir une science de l'autonomie? In: P. Dumouchel & J.-P. Dupuy (Eds.), *L'auto-organisation, De la physique au politique* (pp. 326–333). Paris: Seuil.

Morin, E. (2005). *Introduction à la pensée complexe*. Paris: Éditions du Seuil.

Morin, E. (2008). Réédition de l'ensemble de *La Méthode* (2 volumes). Paris: Seuil.

Ody, M. (2005). Notes théoriques et cliniques sur la tiercéité. *Revue française de psychanalyse, 69*(3): 861–868.

Reid, W. (2010). Les avatars du trauma structurel ou les voies psychiques de l'accomplissement du désir, *Revue française de psychanalyse, LXXIV*(1): 51–69.

Reid, W. (2012). Le palimpseste de la psyché ou l'effacement de l'objet comme paradigme de la tiercéité, *Revue française de psychanalyse, LXXVI*(5): 1595–1601.

Ribas, D. (2000). *Donald Woods Winnicott: psychanalystes d'aujourd'hui*. Paris: PUF.

Roussillon, R. (2008). *Le transitionnel, le sexuel et la réflexivité*. Paris: Dunod.

Winnicott, D. W. (1960). The theory of parent–infant relationship. *International Journal of Psychoanalysis, 41*: 585–595.

Winnicott, D. W. (1971a). Transitional objects and transitional phenomena: a study of the first not-me possession. In: *Playing and Reality* (pp. 1–25). London: Tavistock Publications.

Winnicott, D. W. (1971b). Tailpiece. In: *Playing and Reality* (p. 151). London, Tavistock Publications.

Winnicott, D. W. (1971c). The use of an object and relating through identification. In: *Playing and Reality* (pp. 86–94). London: Tavistock Publications.

Winnicott, D. W. (1978a). Psychoses and child care. In: *Through Paediatrics to Psycho-analysis* (pp. 219–228). London: The Hogarth Press and the Institute of Psycho-analysis.

Winnicott, D. W. (1978b). Aggression in relation to emotional development. In: *Through Paediatrics to Psycho-analysis* (pp. 204–218). London: The Hogarth Press and the Institute of Psycho-analysis.

Winnicott, D. W. (1986). Living creatively. In: C. Winnicott, R. Shepherd, & M. Davis (Eds.), *Home Is Where We Start From: Essays by a Psychoanalyst* (pp. 39–54). New York, London: W. W. Norton & Company.

Winnicott, D. W. (1988). *Human Nature*. C. Winnicott, M. Davis, & R. Shepherd (Eds.), London: Free Association Books.

Winnicott, D. W. (1989b). New light on children's thinking. In: C. Winnicott, R. Shepherd, & M. Davis (Eds.), *Psycho-Analytic Explorations* (pp. 152–157). Cambridge, MA: Harvard University Press.

Winnicott, D. W. (1989a). Comments on my paper "The use of an object". In: C. Winnicott, R. Shepherd, & M. Davis (Eds.), *Psycho-analytic Explorations* (pp. 238–240). Cambridge, MA: Harvard University Press.

CHAPTER NINE

Thoughts on "Cultural experience and its location"

Laurie Wilson

At the start of his brief seminal essay, "The location of cultural experience", Winnicott observed that Freud "did not have a place in his topography of the mind for the experience of things cultural" (1971, p. 95).

Noting that he had previously hypothesised transitional space as the location of play, Winnicott tackled the issue of culture itself in this essay. He equated it with "what life itself is about". "You may cure your patient and not know what it is that makes him or her go on living. It is of first importance for us to acknowledge openly that the absence of psychoneurotic illness may be health, but it is not life" (1971, p. 100).

As a psychoanalyst, I have often seen patients who have lost their way or who have never experienced a sense that life is worth living. But I have learnt that this is rarely a problem for the artists I have worked with. After much reflection, I have concluded that this is the case because artists are almost invariably involved with projects that are produced in the transitional mental space that Winnicott so ably described in "The location of cultural experience". The products that artists create and invite others to share suggest they have found a pleasure and/or heightened awareness of what life is really about.

The patients with the greatest difficulty in thinking that life is worthwhile are usually stuck in work and relationships that allow for little, if any, playfulness—a stuckness that is often characterised by a fear of uncertainty. Since uncertainty is an inevitable part of play, it is an essential aspect of art and all kinds of creativity. By its nature, it must refer to something that has not existed before; thus, novelty frequently leads to unexpected experience.

The initial concerns Winnicott expressed in his essay involved the place and nature of cultural experience. He described these as ongoing non-climactic phenomena that occur in a "place" that is both a separation and not a separation. Rather, they are a form of union. Those occurring in the play area have infinite variability in contrast to "the relative stereotypy of phenomena that relate either to personal bodily functioning or to environmental actuality" (1971, p. 98)—by which he meant the external world of phenomena. In everyday terms, Winnicott notes that "it is non-instinctual satisfactions that make a baby begin to be, to feel that life is real, to find life worth living" (1971, p. 97).

Which brings us to the theme of safety. Both creativity and cultural experience are dependent on a feeling of safety—not just psychological safety but actual physical safety. For example, if a battle or a fire were raging nearby, the instinctive reaction of most individuals—including most creative individuals—would be directly related to protecting the self from danger. With the exception of combat photographers or filmmakers, most artists, poets, and composers would not be concerned with producing work in the midst of such actual danger.

"Cultural experiences", Winnicott wrote, "provide the continuity in the human race that transcends personal experience" (1971, p. 100). I think this has to do with the need for transmission between one person and another—whether that other is alive and present, imagined, or yet to be born—of something that is both personal and transcendent. Something that, according to Winnicott, is located in the potential space between the individual and the environment and must inevitably partake of both.

Winnicott argues that such potential space is best established in the earliest periods of life between the mother figure and the baby. Once internalised, it can be sustained, if not overly stressed.

Noy (1972, p. 246) describes how the artist child learns from the perceptual preferences of the mother. Thus, a mother who sings many lullabies to her infant will probably promote musicality. Children learn how to connect to the mother figure through shared perceptual pathways. Although genetic giftedness plays a crucial role, it is easy to see how many individuals from many generations of the Bach family could carry on a consistent tradition of excellence in music making. So many members of that remarkable family were talented and experienced musicians that Bach family gatherings invariably turned into music fests.

Phillip Setzer, one of the two violinists of the Emerson Quartet, explained once to a group of interested psychoanalysts how differently the same Beethoven quartet can sound depending on which of the two violinists played the first and second parts. When the group rehearsed the piece with him (Setzer, 2008) playing first violin, it would have one relatively consistent, particular sound. But if Eugene Drucker were scheduled to be the first violinist, the group would have to rehearse all over again, because the music and the performance would have a different sound.

Setzer described other variations within a tradition that exemplified to me precisely what Winnicott was describing as a variablility within a cultural tradition based on the ability to play and be sensitive to nuance and uncertainty. For example, Setzer related a story about Mstislav Rostropovich playing Shostakovich's cello concerto, which the composer had written expressly for him. For the first performance, Shostakovich had made markings in the score and rehearsed the famous cellist until he was playing it exactly the way the composer wanted it. Years later, after Rostropovitch had performed the piece about two hundred times, Shostakovich was in the audience and was shocked, almost horrified, at the way the piece seemed to have been transformed. As Rostropovich's experience of the concerto deepened over time, he kept finding new ways to interpret the music, though each time he played the notes exactly as Shostakovich had written them.

One other story that tells a similar tale comes from a poet I know, Jim Glaser. When he first writes a poem, it partakes of his thoughts, feelings, and recent experience. Rereading it a short time later, he has no trouble connecting the words of the poem with his recent experience. If, however, he puts the poem aside and turns to it months or even years later, the memory of his original thoughts and feelings exists, but new emotional material affixes itself to the poem. Indeed, it often appears in a very different light with new associations, associations that are new enough to move him to retitle it and, thus, alert the reader to new way of experiencing the very same words (Glaser, 2012).

Listening to and watching the performance of a great string quartet such as the Emerson reveals several other Winnicottian ideas about cultural experience. Each musician in the group has a distinct role to play. All perform at the highest level of artistry, precise in their playing of the notes and fully alive to the emotional depth and breadth of the composition. At the same time, they can immerse themselves in the emotional depth of their particular part while almost simultaneously keeping contact with one another.

At the beginning of each movement, their attentive regard is obvious. They have to start off together, but, once under way, particularly if they are playing a richly, even fiendishly, complex work such as a late Beethoven quartet, they continue to communicate over and through the transitional space among them. Sometimes, a musician can catch a quickly shared eye movement; most often it is through their playing one voice of a fugue, following the next and rippling on to the last voice until they return to the same notes and rhythms. The concentrated consonance of four musicians sounding like a single instrument can be seen as the height of civilisation and cultural experience.

Even the sophisticated, highly cultured audiences that usually attend a performance by the Emerson Quartet appear to take part in the play between and among the four musicians. Listening silently with rapt attention, careful not to interrupt the players' concentration by coughing or clapping in between movements, such audiences seem to become one with the performers, sharing the heightened experience that has been forged out of the score.

Setzer related to the group of analysts that the Emerson Quartet had experiences that were similar to the story of Shostakovich and Rostropovich with the cello concerto, noting that, over time, they would come to perform the same piece of music in very different ways. They found that, with repeated experience of a familiar score, new depth and emotional resonance seemed to appear in the music, demanding a revised way of performing it.

Any opera lover will have had the following experience: one performance of hearing Verdi's masterwork *Traviata*—with soprano A playing Violetta—will convey a world of different emotional and musical meanings and responses from hearing it performed by soprano B.

This variation in the margin of the way a piece of music can sound is a central example of cultural power and endurance. If the composer has produced a rich enough composition, there is room for a wide range of interpretations—from the most heated emotional and full-bodied example of Artur Rubinstein's performances of Chopin to the precise, cooler, and, for many people, equally beautiful playing of Maurizio Pollini. Even more obvious is the difference in the way Andras Schiff and Glenn Gould play Bach. Both perform the music with exquisite precision and deep emotional resonance, but sound entirely different.

Two other instances of variability pointing to cultural experience that can endure over time is Mozart *vs.* Anton Salieri (so poignantly presented in the film *Amadeus*) or, less famously, Mozart *vs.* Johann Stamitz. In Mozart's music, there is always an element of surprise—that is, uncertainty, whereas, in the more pedestrian compositions of Stamitz or Salieri, we hear the same sounds, the same intervals, the same melodic cadences repeated over and over again. We are almost never surprised. While it is true that a routine performance of an otherwise splendid composition by Mozart or Beethoven can leave an audience unmoved or uninspired, this is, in my experience, somewhat rare.

Winnicott argues that cultural experience begins with creative living and is first manifested in play. Although he does not exactly say it, he implies that the play must be vital and that any cultural experience that does not partake of, and convey, a sense of vitality will not endure. It will certainly not add anything to civilisation.

For example, when we look at a portrait by Rembrandt, we are entranced not just by his exceptional skill with form, line, and colour, but also by the ways he brings the sitter to life. I believe that the unique quality of Rembrandt's portraits reflects his ability to portray not just one feeling on the face and in the gestures of his sitter, but, rather, the play of several feelings simultaneously. The same can be said of the portraits by Francisco Goya, or Rogier van der Weyden. If any of these masters is compared to their contemporaries, who may approach their skill in capturing the physical likeness of the sitter but lack the gift of conveying his or her aliveness, we can immediately detect the difference without always being able to explain it. We, and countless other viewers, will not be drawn back to look again and again at a technically excellent portrait that fails to capture the vitality and spirit of the sitter.

Leonardo's *Mona Lisa* is surely a case in point. Uncertainty is embedded in her expression. Is she smiling seductively, contentedly, mysteriously? Her evocative face has fascinated millions and has rarely been matched by any other artist. Her look is more overtly complex and mysterious than the ambiguous—I would go so far as to call it ambivalent—demeanour we see in Rembrandt's portraits. That very ambiguity is—by its double or triple nature—uncertain. By its complex and vital nature, it partakes precisely of the kind of play Winnicott has noted at the heart of cultural experience.

The excitement engendered by uncertainty is that of not knowing what truly lies behind the sitter's expression. It is an ongoing excitement that never seems fully resolved. It requires a viewer to be drawn into the engagement, the pre-conscious questioning that occurs in the presence of great art. Why am I so fascinated? What makes me want to look at this object? Why do I find it so beautiful, awe inspiring, or compelling?

When a work of art engages the attention of many viewers or listeners over time, we might ask: Does it partake of "image magic", the term coined by Ernst Kris to describe an artist's conscious or unconscious goal of bringing a work of art to life. Balzac's fictional painter, Frenhofer, and the ancient world's legendary sculptor, Pygmalion, were exemplars of imaginary artists who could turn oil paint and canvas or marble into living beings. The ancient Egyptian word for "sculptor" was "he who brings to life"—a fitting name for an artist in a culture with pronounced views on the enduring nature of life after death.

I hypothesise that most artists, poets, and composers seek to create something similar, something that is vital. They might call it by different names, such as wanting the painting or novel to be effective, or "to work", but their common goal is to produce something that attracts and holds attention. It might not be an object of beauty, but it must be compelling—and that is not likely to be the case if there is no internal psychological freedom to play and explore novelty. To achieve a cultural experience in the Winnicottian sense, safety is best combined with a sense of fullness—of having something worth communicating and sharing. Winnicott writes about transcendence, and it is not surprising that many artists intend that their creations will become transcendent art objects that will endure over time and space.

In his essay on the location of cultural experience, Winnicott (1971, p. 100) writes that "The potential space happens only in relation to a feeling of confidence on the part of the baby ... confidence related to the dependability of the mother-figure or environmental elements". It might seem like something of a leap, but I believe that what Winnicott describes as "the dependability" of the mother or the safety of the environment in the potential space between mother figure and baby is just as crucial as uncertainty for cultural life to exist and to thrive.

When a civilisation is in a state of upheaval or grave uncertainty about its future, cultural experience tends to be one of the first casualties. As has often been noted, in the face of traumatic conditions, such as war or natural disasters, reality functioning might increase and neurotic interference with the perception of reality often diminishes. It is not safe to be very neurotic under such stress. Equally true is that it is not safe to be playfully imaginative when survival itself might require that one pay constant heed to the dangers of external reality. Thus, the creation of cultural products, which require large amounts of time and attention and a high level of ego functioning, are often foregone during periods of external danger.

I believe that time is a factor of great importance for creativity and culture. While some individuals can thrive or only be productive in the face of a deadline, most artists I have met and worked with in my clinical practice do their best work when they sense they have enough time to experiment and, if necessary, to redo a piece as many times as they need to make it "right". Beethoven was the quintessential reviser, and his scores are covered with the many changes he made until a sonata, concerto, opera, mass, or symphony sounded the way he wanted it to sound. Mozart was famous for having the entire composition ready at one go, needing only to write down the notes to achieve perfection.

Even when an environment can supply a sense of security and consistency, there may still be a missing element necessary for what Winnicott means by culture.

When Winnicott (1971, p. 101) addresses the problem of deprivation, he notes that "A deprived child is notoriously restless and unable to play, leading to an impoverishment of capacity to experience in cultural field". Years ago, as an art teacher and therapist working with boys and girls from impoverished neighbourhoods, I often saw how meagre were most of their art works. It was not just an issue of intelligence or even of talent; rather, it seemed to be a difficulty in being able to sustain attention while producing something as "useless" as a cultural product. Who needs a painting when hunger or fear dominates life?

Children from more comfortable environments—and here I do not mean financial or socioeconomic comfort, but psychologically safe environments that offer the consistency of loving care and a reliable and expectable surround—could and did produce much more complex and "interesting" art objects. For example, a drawing of a school playground by such a child would include at least several types of play equipment (such as balls, bats, basketball hoops, skipping ropes) and at least two children with enough physical detail to discern their age and gender.

A sense of safety and reliability—when the mother's love is displayed or made manifest—gives the baby a feeling of trust or confidence in the environment. In other words, I can make art or music because I believe someone will want to see or hear what I make. Especially when that someone else will not be envious. Creative individuals have the best chance of thriving if the people in their immediate environment do not intrude on their earliest efforts and provide support.

Two examples come to mind from twentieth-century art, where extraordinarily gifted sons were not imposed upon by their artist parents, whose status and accomplishments could have been used to persecutorily invade the private worlds of their children. Both Pablo Picasso and Alberto Giacometti had fathers who were successful painters. In Picasso's case, his father handed over his palette and brushes to his son once he saw how superior were the boy's gifts. Giacometti's father, Giovanni, was one of Switzerland's renowned post-Impressionist painters. He quickly recognised Alberto's exceptional skill and was proud, rather than envious, of his ability (Wilson, 2003, pp. 57–58).

The generosity of these two artist parents made exploration safe for their fearless progeny. And it is probably true that one element of the friendship between Picasso and Giacometti was related to their similar experiences of having artist fathers who protected them from envious attack and supported their talent as they went on to world fame.

As a clinician, I have worked with talented patients who have not always been so fortunate—in one case a painter whose father could not have been more different from those of Picasso and Giacometti. The artist father of my patient threatened, or actually attempted, to kill his son when he showed signs of achieving artistic success. For the young male painter, the father's psychological persecution impeded the development of his career for decades. While he had no trouble producing a large opus of exceptional work, he faltered any time there was a possibility of selling his art and enhancing his career. He could be highly successful and uninhibited in his day job, because it was in a realm that did not threaten the father.

Taking a leap away from the cogent clinical examples of individuals who had to develop compliant false selves in order to survive childhoods marked by adults' intrusions into safe internal space, I argue that some cultures—or some aspects of many cultures—are so rigidly organised and allow for so little individual responses to life questions that play and cultural experience are largely snuffed out. If there is only one way to worship, only one way to celebrate life's milestones, only one way to be an adult male or female, the stereotypes imposed on the individuals in that particular culture prevent them from having a playful and creative response to their spiritual, maturational, and sexual–social needs. This is not to say that enduring traditions, whether religious, familial, cultural, or otherwise, cannot generate extraordinary creative cultural achievements.

Christian church architecture is an example. Evolving over time, cathedrals went from their origins as Roman basilicas (banks)—with a single central aisle leading to a rounded or square enclosed and unadorned end—to elaborate Gothic structures with pointed arches, flying buttresses, elaborately carved capitals and friezes. In specific geographic areas, or when guided by individual sculptors, stonemasons, or architects, such buildings were often stylistically unique while being simultaneously part of a larger tradition of church architecture. Consider, for instance, the cathedrals at Bamberg and Chartres and the abbeys of Cluny and Moissac.

When artistic tradition stiffens with stereotyped ways of producing art, civilisation is stifled. Nineteenth-century academic painting often placed high barriers against novel artistic solutions. The French

Impressionist painters are a well-known case in point. Young, fresh painters, such as Monet and Renoir, whose playful experimentation led to a critically important breakthrough in the history of art, were faced with an Academy that awarded prizes and exhibition spaces only to those artists who conformed to the "rules". To dare to do something different from tradition—"the way it is"; "what my parents taught me"—is terrifying because the child or adult artist might end up isolated and not allowed back into safe, feasible space. "Interplay between originality and acceptance of tradition is one more example of interplay between separateness and union", as Winnicott observed.

The fundamental point of Winnicott's essay is that cultural experience occurs in a place in between two different objects or phenomena. "This potential space depends on experience that leads to trust. It can be looked upon as sacred to the individual and it is here that the individual experiences creative living" (1971, p. 103).

I believe that this fundamental point can be seen and comprehended if we think about how necessary it is for creative individuals or groups to have a welcoming audience. With visual artists, that may mean a gallery dealer who supports the work and the artist, or an art critic who writes positively about the work, or even a small network of people who understand and admire the work. The twentieth-century American artist, Louise Nevelson, was sustained for decades by the dedicated support of her family and several dealers who, even if they could not provide funds or sell her work, gave her the courage to continue. In some instances, they wrote eloquently about her sculpture, in others, they made sure that it was well exhibited and brought to public attention.

While Nevelson, like many artists, sometimes claimed to have achieved success entirely on her own, a careful study of her actual trajectory—from talented beginner to world fame—is marked by significant help from others (Wilson, forthcoming). Such significant help is often unmentioned and forgotten, much in the way an infant is not likely to recall the mother's ministrations from his or her earliest years. Yet, what has happened in that potential space can last forever.

References

Glaser, J. (2012). Interview with author. Sleepy Hollow, New York, August 15.

Noy, P. (1972). About art and artistic talent. *International Journal of* Psychoanalysis, *53*: 243–249.

Setzer, P. (2008). Music and imagination: finding consensus in the Emerson String Quartet. April 15, 2008, Philoctetes Center, New York City.

Wilson, L. (2003). *Alberto Giacometti: Myth Magic, and the Man*. New Haven, CT: Yale University Press.

Wilson, L. (Forthcoming). *Louise Nevelson: All for Art*. New York and London: Thames and Hudson.

Winnicott, D. W. (1971). The location of cultural experience. In: *Playing and Reality* (pp. 95–103). London: Tavistock.

CHAPTER TEN

The mirror role of mother and family in child development: a reflection

Angela Joyce

The provenance of this chapter, derived from a paper given to a conference in London in 1967 under the title, "The predicament of the family: a psychoanalytical symposium", is rooted much earlier in Winnicott's writings, as he explored the milieu in which a child comes to experience him/herself as existing in the world in a real way. Winnicott, the psychoanalytic and paediatric clinician concerned with "doing something and doing it usefully" (Winnicott, 1986, p. 102), was also a theoretician of health and his concerns could be said to be an extended contemplation around living, being, feeling real; he is renowned for his attention to the subtleties of those factors that interfere with the inherent tendency towards development and health. The metaphor of the mirror applied to both development and the clinical process underlines his focus on processes *between* child and the environment (mother in the first instance) rather than simply within the baby: *between* analyst and analysand. However, this late paper in his canon can be said to break new ground in moving that focus from the initial mouth–breast relationship (with its links to drive theory in psychoanalysis) to the significance of the gaze and, thus, the complexity of the link between baby and mother, in the constitution of the self at the beginning of life.

An observation: a three-day-old baby, Corey, third boy in the family, is restless in his cot, though not crying. His mother, Anne, picks him up, saying ,"I think you might be hungry; I think it's time for a feed" and settles herself to feed him. She is rather brusque in her movements, and indicates to the person with her that she anticipates some pain when her baby latches on to her breast. She talks about the struggle he has to get latched on, his small mouth perhaps not big enough for her ample nipple. The observer responds sympathetically that it always takes time to get used to it (meaning for both: the grip of the baby's mouth on the nipple). When the mother offers the baby her breast, he hesitates and she tells him to yawn, to open his mouth wide, but as he struggles he gets another idea, catching sight of her face, and is immediately captivated, his eyes brightening and widening as he gazes at his mother's face. With almost imperceptible irritation, Anne says to him that he does not want it (the feed). The other person intervenes, saying that he seemed more interested in her face, and, after a moment`s hesitation, Anne follows his lead and responds, brightening and widening her gaze at him, imitating his eyebrows as they raise; for what seems like a long half a minute mother and infant are held in mutual rapture. Baby Corey breaks the gaze connection and takes the nipple into his mouth, sucking vigorously. His mother makes a sound of pain and the expression on her face shows a mixture of acceptance and fortitude.

This vignette is replete with the complexity of the good-enough environment at the beginning of a baby's life. This mother and baby are not alone; there is a third, a neighbour who is interested in what happens between mothers and babies. There are intimations of irritation in the baby's restlessness and the mother's tone, but also a sense that they are trying to get together, if only . . . And they manage it as the mother is able to respond contingently to her baby's searching gaze, once she has been supported to see the baby and what he wants. "What does the baby see when he or she looks at the mother's face?" Winnicott rhetorically asks, replying, within the metaphor of the mirror, that "he sees himself or herself". Mother's face mirrors what the baby is presenting and "what she looks like is related to what she sees there".

Corey seems immediately captivated by his mother's face, but it is he who, through his gaze, demands that she looks at his. He is setting the agenda, creating, one might say, his "environment mother" as she shows her recognition of him in her imitation of his raised eyebrows, widened and bright eyes now in response to what she almost missed in her anxiety to get to the feed. Their mutuality feeds him, readies him for the milk feed he turns to with gusto and appetite. His "legitimate experience of omnipotence" (Winnicott, 1971, p. 131) has not been violated. In Anne's responsiveness to her baby, she gives him the possibility of a rich elaboration of his nascent self, mediated through the mutual connection of their gazes. We might suggest that his seeing himself reflected in his mother's eyes gives form to that experience: that moment of his searching for connection through his eyes which is met by his mother's responsiveness registers his nascent self bathed in that recognition. This is the establishment of the sense of existing, of feeling real in the world for the sighted baby in a form that is visual to add to those other sensory modalities that Winnicott describes as fundamental for the baby: the mother's care-ful holding and handling of his/her body. We now know, through developmental research conducted since Winnicott's death, that the neonate has the capacity for cross-modal perception, so that his/her sensory experiences are transposed in the brain (Meltzoff, 1981). This lends itself to the integration of psyche–soma in the context of the relationships the baby has with others.

It is interesting that Winnicott does not privilege sound in his account of infancy, as this is the sensory modality that is first available to the baby: healthy babies can hear from the third trimester of pregnancy. Sound, the voice and its utterances are also the primary medium for communication in psychoanalysis. We might argue that the baby's different sensory modalities and how they are tended by the mothering person give form to these earliest intimations of the self. The quality of the mother's look in her gaze at her baby, the tone of her voice as she speaks to him/her, the tenderness or otherwise of her touch in holding and handling, all evoke experiences in the baby which are registered as modes or idioms of the self (Bollas, 1989; Wright, 2009). For Winnicott, this is the expression of primary creativity, facilitated by the mother's adaptations to the particularity of this baby, so that the baby who can afford to look and see because the mother is there to see him/her can look creatively, make what he will of what is there to be seen. This feeds the baby's psyche, his capacity for imaginative elaboration of his bodily, sensory phenomena. This matches the mother's imaginative elaboration of her baby: she sees what is there to be seen, but "seeing" is an active process and she actively participates in the creation of her baby in this way; not distorting through projective processes, but elaborating in her psyche her experience of her baby for him to see and of which he can make what he will. In the analytic setting, we might also say that the analyst's responses to the analysand's communications (gleaned through the analyst turning "his own unconscious like a receptive organ towards the transmitting unconscious of the patient" (Freud, 1912e, p. 115)) give form to those communications and, thus, enable the analysand to more fully inhabit his/her own idiom.

This is health, the "normal" aspects, as Winnicott describes it, of individual emotional development. Mother is the baby's first mirror, but even in this short observation it is hard not to see that mothers were never intended to do the hard job of mothering alone! This mother, Anne, still recovering from the birth of her baby (he is three days old here) and encountering again the realities of what having a baby does to her body, anticipates the very real physical pain she suffers as she encourages her baby to take her milk. She is stalwart, but in need of support; one can also infer the depth of mixed emotion Winnicott had so helpfully enunciated in "Hate in the countertransference" (1982a). There, among the eighteen reasons why mothers hate their babies, Winnicott lists

> the baby is a danger to her body in pregnancy and at birth; he hurts her nipples even by sucking which is at first a chewing activity; he is ruthless, treats her as scum, an unpaid servant, a slave; at first he does not know at all what she does or what she sacrifices for him. Especially he cannot allow for her hate. (p. 201)

This picture of mother is one of disturbance; she is inevitably disturbed in her body and in her psyche and mind in giving herself over to the gestation, birth, and nurturing of her baby. Her "normal illness" of primary maternal preoccupation reflects this disturbance as she is plundered by her baby, and, in one of Winnicott's BBC talks, "What irks?", motherhood is robustly recognised as being, at times, boring and irksome: "the care of small children can be irksome no matter how much they are loved and wanted" (2002, p. 140). In that talk, what Winnicott chooses to explore about "what irks" is far from the usual content of parents' conscious complaints. He goes deeply and simply into the fact that to be available to her children, mother has to be a "free house" (p.145) for a time; that nothing of her is sacred as her privacy is invaded (originally in her pregnancy, when the baby is literally inside her body); that she cannot defend herself successfully from this without at the same time depriving her child of some essential element—the feeling that she is accessible. It is only a limited but absolutely necessary time: "she had her secrets once and she will have them again. And she will count herself lucky that for a while she was infinitely bothered by the infinite claims of her own children" (2002, p. 145).

> They lose everything. What they gain is that in the course of time, they can recover, because their children gradually give over this perpetual staking of claims and are glad that mothers are individuals in their own right, as indeed they themselves quickly become. (Winicott, 2002, p. 148)

And who would be a mother?—"who indeed but the actual mother of children" (2002, p.146). For the mother, then, the task becomes one of recovery of herself in concord with her baby's pace, as the maturational process proceeds.

"Good-enough mothering" allows for wide variation; to be good enough is not to be perfect and, paradoxically, perfection is not good enough. To be human is to be fallible, and this is an ingredient of the care provided by the ordinary devoted mother. *Good enough, but not perfect*. The experiential build-up for the baby is precarious because it is human and fallible. The human environment *needed* is imperfect and free from mechanical reliability, and tolerant of the imperfection that enriches the connection between mother and baby. The imperfection is paradoxical, as the baby needs predictability that is, at the same time, fallible. It is an individual mother adapting to her baby`s individual needs, full of trial and error and learning from the experience of being with this person now at this point in time, accumulating history so that a sense of time evolves with past and present and the promise of the future. It means that the mother has to be able to give herself over to the experience, to be disturbed by it. For some mothers, this is very frightening, and they can never give themselves over completely. Perhaps we are in an age now where our post-industrial society has little tolerance for this natural pace and providing mothers with the support for this profound adaptation to their newborn.

In Winnicott's view, the good-enough mother depended upon her own experiences of having been well mothered herself. In her childhood fantasies playing with dolls, he saw the girl as preparing herself imaginatively for the time she would become a mother. There is now a rich literature on the intergenerational transmission of good-enough and unhelpful or traumatising experiences of being parented. It is connected with the development of new psychotherapeutic modalities that address the psychopathology that can emerge in the parent–infant relationship as it is lived, with the purpose of intervening to disrupt that transmission and halt the repetitions down the generations. In that context, I have treated many mother–infant pairs[1] where factors from the parental history threaten to rupture the baby's developing self. In one such family, the issue of mirroring or its failure down the generations was critical.

Clinical case of a baby and her mother

This clinical case is of a baby and her mother seen together in psychoanalytic parent–infant psychotherapy. It demonstrates the intergenerational impact of the failure of mirroring in the mother–infant relationship, and how this transmission can be interrupted through a therapeutic intervention which takes account of these processes.

Baby Emma had been conceived through donor insemination because the mother's partner (who was of a different race) had become infertile through infection since the birth of their older child. As a consequence of their unresolved conflict over this decision, these parents had made a choice of donor that meant this baby bore no resemblance to her mother's partner. In this choice of donor, Emma became the "wrong baby" in the minds of her parents for a variety of reasons, though consciously because she did not fit in to the image they had of the child they wanted in their family, or of themselves as parents to such a baby. The father refused to come to the treatment, but Emma and her mother were seen together weekly over a period of a year from when Emma was twelve weeks old.

In the first session, the mother, Felicity, told me their story while baby Emma (aged twelve weeks) lay on the baby mat between her mother and me. Felicity emphasised her drive since childhood to have children and she had sought to extend what she saw as the perfection of the family she had created thus far by having a second child. The birth of "wrong baby" Emma had faced her with the terrible sense that this perfection had been ruined. Emma was quintessentially English, with fair skin, light brown hair, and blue eyes, just like her mother. Felicity had been a girl who had created babies in her play, families who, I learnt, would compensate for her empty, lonely childhood with a chronically depressed mother and elderly father. In that first meeting, there was very little engagement between this mother and the baby; in fact, Felicity was so full of her tormented preoccupations about the baby's origins, her revulsion at Emma's appearance, in Emma's unmistakable "otherness" because she did not look like her partner, that there seemed no space for baby Emma as Emma in the room. Felicity's paradoxical feelings about Emma's appearance saturated her discourse: she was disgusted by Emma's pale skin, prone to angry red outbursts of eczema, as she was with her own pallor, and yet it was the baby's "otherness" that she linked this to; "other" in that she was fathered by another, unknown to her, who did not give Emma the pretence of being born of the father of her son; other genetic material that was alien to the family.

Felicity's fantasy family of babies about whom she had ruminated since her early childhood was ruined by this "wrong baby". And I was faced with a baby so vigilant of this frightening, only fleetingly available mother that she could barely risk a glance at me as this new person she might get to know. Emma's gaze was fixed on her mother's face and, from time to time, Felicity would smile at her. Felicity's face seemed to crack at these moments, but soon other expressions of pain, rage, sorrow, etc. would cloud her face and I would see these feelings mirrored in Emma. Baby Emma became the mirror to her mother's disturbance, and, in being seemingly locked in her vigilance, her own states received little, if any, confirmation. In the early sessions, she did not look at me or respond much to my talking to her, and when she did eventually, she gazed at me in a solemn way which was rather lifeless.

Felicity's story emerged of a child and adult who had used ruminatory thinking to escape from a lonely and empty childhood where she never felt seen by her chronically depressed mother. Predominantly, Felicity seemed to have replaced her old and familiar ruminations about herself and her life with those of Emma as the "wrong" baby. There was a great risk that the therapy sessions could become another place where Felicity's ruminations dominated and Emma was cast adrift. In these ruminations, Emma frequently fell out of her mother's mind, which was full of another baby, or a life with which she, Emma, as a real live baby, could not compete. There seemed little possibility at first that Felicity could mourn the loss of her imagined baby so that she could make space for the reality of Emma now as her real baby, and, thus, provide for Emma an experience of being seen and therefore able to begin to psychically exist with a sense of realness.

Technically, then, I was faced with a familiar dilemma in parent–infant psychotherapy: how to manage the competing needs of the patients in the room without over-identifying with either one or the other. Felicity's discourse was both compelling and, in some way, repellent. In my countertransference, I found that her identification of Emma as the "wrong" baby actually propelled me away from her in my sympathies and towards her baby. I was drawn towards this vulnerable baby Emma, who, nevertheless, was also not very attractive: she was big and had red, inflamed skin; she did not invite me in to attend to her. Something of her predicament as this "wrong" baby was already in the way she was in the room. It did not seem in those early sessions that Emma could find a way into her mother's heart in such a way that she might eventually be more "right" than "wrong"; in her reluctance to look at me, it seemed I could not, initially, provide a bridge so that she could be and feel seen by me, to hold her over, so to speak, until her mother could see her.

Within approximately six to seven sessions, however, I began to see a change: the perinatal period is one of great possibility. As Felicity had spoken, I had included Emma many times, talking to her about her mother's feelings and how painful it was for both of them that the decisions that day of her conception had led to this sense that she was somehow the wrong baby. Emma, in her baby way, gradually became interested in my speaking to her and she began to look at me. She began babbling and we often had little "conversations", taking turns, when I would talk to her about her predicament with her mummy and in her family. I would match her affect with my tone of voice, hold her gaze, and wait for her to return to me when she turned away. This began a process of recognition and Emma could be helped to feel recognised as having her own experience of this situation.

Felicity, at first, was anxious and disconcerted by my behaviour in this way. She was worried about these difficult and painful feelings being so out in the open in Emma's presence. However, very quickly she became interested in my interest in how Emma experienced her life with her mother. This representation of the baby by the therapist as an emergent, experiencing person in her own right, this "mirroring", is a powerful communication to a parent (as well as to the baby), especially when the baby in some way is depersonalised or not seen as a full human being. This was the case for Emma and Felicity. In being the "wrong" baby, Emma was at great risk of not having the experiences through which she could feel real and alive, qualities that Winnicott recognised as fundamental to living well.

Felicity began to tell me about her early life, which was strangely echoed in Emma. She had hated how she looked from an early age, never used a mirror, and hated herself and her "disgusting" habits; she fidgeted and scratched, especially her head. She told me that if she had her head shaved, it would be there for all to see: the scabs from a lifetime of picking herself. She also had a fantasy that she was invisible and could not be seen by other people. Emma was also developing the same "habits" as she scratched at her raw skin, red from eczema. When I made these links, Felicity was shocked and she became more attentive to her treatment of her baby in these repetitive ways. Her sympathy for her baby was galvanised as I talked about her sense of disgust at Emma's pink English body that did not belong to her husband and Felicity's self-disgust as a baby and young child whose mother seemingly had retreated into chronic depression, unable and unwilling to provide an affirming, life-giving mirror in her gaze upon her daughter. She described her mother as looking like the person in Munch's painting of *The Scream*, a truly terrifying image of a mother for a baby or young child to see. The repetition through generations of these ways of being can be as powerful as the intrapsychic repetitions observed in psychoanalytic practice with individuals (Fraiberg et al., 1975). The loosening of the repetitions leaves space for the baby to come into her own, and, indeed, Emma began to show something of her own personality as a feisty, engaging little girl.

It was not so straightforward for Felicity to relinquish her representations of Emma as the "wrong" baby even if she was challenged in these different ways. Felicity remained eloquent in her description of Emma as a wrong child, an alien, a weirdo, all these images filling her mind so that she could rarely see Emma in her own right. The ordinary psychosomatic unity of mother and baby in pregnancy and the post natal period which supports the "normal illness" of "primary maternal preoccupation" (Winnicott, 1982b) was deeply flawed by the meanings of the artificial insemination by donor to Felicity which were elaborated on many different levels. She had been impregnated with an "alien", which was so linked to her sense of herself as a "weirdo", and now was preoccupied with this. Her obsessional thinking was a pre-existing defensive structure which gave her some sense of existence in the context of her depressed and frightening mother, and now was the vehicle for these ruminations as she became the mother of her own daughter. We might link this material to Winnicott's comments in the "Mirror" paper about Francis Bacon's art, most particularly his representation of the human face in contortions and distorted.

The metaphor of the mirror was a very powerful one for Felicity as it was so linked in her consciousness with her dread of seeing herself in the mirror. The idea that she was Emma's first mirror was shocking to her, but also eventually helped her look for a part of herself, linked to the lost baby of her imagination, that could be there to see Emma for herself. This began the process of mourning and renunciation of the imagined baby which was not just the baby who would slip seamlessly into the family identity, but had its origins in her as a little girl playing with dolls, expressive of her wishes to be the "seen" baby of her absent mother. She had no memories of being attended to by her mother; no nice comments about looking pretty that help a little girl feel pride in herself. She conveyed her sense of her mother's self-absorption and narcissistic resentment that her children needed anything that took her away from herself, and became aware for the first time of how she was repeating this with both her children. She had adored her mother and longed for her; she said that one can only be loved unconditionally by one's children but for now she could not see how deep were her own narcissistic needs from Emma and how this reversed the usual relationship between a mother and baby. Her baby's need for this unconditional love from her was only fleetingly available.

I took up the sense of humiliation she felt in her desperation to reach her mother. She found the link I made with her humiliation now in having a baby who did not fit in to her wished-for ideal family, and this fact being so visible for all to see, very moving. To talk about this with the baby present meant that the impact of these ubiquitous elements of her mother's mind could be addressed in the immediacy of the session. I recognised Emma's intense interest in her mother's emotional expressions as Felicity recalled these matters and, through my including Emma in our discourse, I was able to support Felicity in her growing recognition of Emma's position and to have more sympathy with her. Felicity's need to be loved and claimed by Emma reflected her relationship with her own mother, now re-presented in her relationship with her baby. For Emma to be allowed to be herself with her own baby needs, freed from the transference repetition of a toxic mother–daughter relationship from the previous generation, was essential.

Despite these very painful feelings, the work with mother and baby fostered an increasing possibility for emotional connection and recognition by Felicity of Emma's separate identity and emerging personality. Emma was becoming less vigilant and there was increasingly direct interaction when Felicity was more present for her baby. She began to talk about feeling a bit better and then the beginnings of loving feelings towards Emma. I had the sense of "two Emmas" in Felicity's mind, a "wrong" one and a "right" one. Emma was, in response, becoming more of an engaging baby; she smiled, more often held her mother's gaze intently; there was less of a sense of her gaze being anxiously vigilant; instead there was pleasure and interest. Indeed, Emma could now begin to look and see, as Winnicott described, looking creatively: her own personality began to emerge, interested in her surroundings, determined and persistent in her acquisition of her developmental milestones. She related to both her mother and me in a playful, direct way and was also able to convey the variety of feelings she had with some expectation that they would be responded to. Although her eczema remained, it functioned as a barometer to her emotional states and it was increasingly less raw. Although I was concerned about a defensive precocity in her, she seemed to be developing the basis of a robust self that could sustain her in difficulty.

The mirror in psychoanalytic treatment

Freud used the metaphor of the analyst as mirror in his 1912 paper "Recommendations to physicians practising psycho-analysis" (Freud,

1912e, p. 118). In the context of a discussion about the risk of suggestion within an analytic treatment, and, indeed, one about the place of the person of the analyst in that treatment, Freud says "The doctor should be opaque to his patients and, like a mirror should show them nothing but what is shown to him" (p. 118). The tone of this sentence is one of stern warning, implying that Freud was worried that analysts might be too personal with their analysands, endangering the neutrality of the analytic setting within which the free associations could reveal the patient's unconscious complexes. To be "opaque", however, suggests a hard, ungiving surface which reveals nothing. The mirror can only show what is shown to it. Freud's mirror seems curiously static, and this tone seems to reflect his concern with the possibility of the intrusion of things too personal from the analyst that could ruin the psychoanalytic setting. Freud saw little, if any, therapeutic use in the countertransference; rather the contrary. However, Roy Schafer, in his discussion of Freud's technical papers (Schafer, 1983), interprets Freud's use of the mirror metaphor as "not legitimising stiff formality, impassivity and remoteness" (p. 24). He, Schafer, regards the analyst as mirror as an active, transformational process and says that the choice of this metaphor was not well chosen.

In Winnicott's use, the "mirror" becomes something alive and affirming; it is potentially a transformational object (Bollas, 1985). We have seen, in the mother–infant relationship, that it is through the mother's capacity to see, to recognise her baby as him or herself, not projecting something so that what she sees is a distorted baby self, that is so essential to the baby's establishment of a sense of aliveness and realness. Mother, here, is an active, imagining person, elaborating in her psyche the baby that she holds and cares for, but in the baby's terms. In this way, she gives form in her psyche to what she sees and baby, in turn, feels seen and recognised, gradually elaborating and giving form and representation to his/her psychosomatic experience of being cared for in this way by mother. Winnicott also saw the practice of psychoanalysis as analogous to this description of the early mother–infant relationship. He says "Psychotherapy is not making clever and apt interpretations; by and large it is a long term giving back what the patient brings. It is a complex derivative of the face that is there to be seen" (1971, p. 137). To be seen and, in analysis, to be seen by one's analyst as one really is, can be complex and difficult. Nevertheless, Winnicott avers that the patient is ultimately grateful, as it is through being seen that one comes to feel alive and real. The analyst, like the mother, has to do this "well enough" (1971, p. 138).

Bollas, an analyst who has written very much within the Winnicottian tradition, has been concerned with the coming into being of one's personal idiom. This is an elaboration of Winnicott's concept of the True Self, which implicitly requires the mirroring function of the mother to permit it to flourish. In *Cracking Up* (Bollas, 1995), Bollas discusses what he calls "the ego's desire to express the intelligent process of living" (p. 42). He regards this as "the eros of form" (p. 43), the drive to find expression for internal urges, to give them representation and then communicate them, form "populating the inner world with excitement and objects of desire" (p. 43). This form, or representation, in the inner world emerges out of the intimacy of the earliest connections between baby and mother. It is an aesthetic that is distinctive, idiosyncratic, and unique to the person that that baby becomes. In the analytic setting, then, the analyst as mirror becomes the agent through which the analysand gives form to his/her inner urges; form which, perhaps in many of the patients seen in present day practice who have never felt seen, has never been given substance in the inner world as a consequence of the absence of maternal mirroring in infancy, and then never communicated to the external world recognised.

The television eyes dream

A young woman came to analysis very unsure whether she wanted to see me; she found me cold and "too neutral"; she had wanted something more. But she stayed, very unsure that she wanted me as her analyst. In my countertransference, I had an awareness of being with someone who was telling me she did not really want to be with me. In the third year of her analysis, during which time this dynamic had been worked on from time to time, and after she had broken up with another boyfriend whom she felt did not really want to be with her, she brought a dream image. In the dream she was with a previous boyfriend (with whom she had had a similar relationship of not feeling wanted) and she was looking at his face, particularly his eyes. She was aware that she was not looking into his eyes, but looking *at* them; in fact, in the place of his eyes there were two television screens and it was these she was looking at. In her associations to the dream image, she emphasised the "looking at" and not "into", and conveyed a sense of the unresponsiveness of the television screen eyes that had no depth. There was no way that she could make a connection with the non-image on the screen.

It seemed that this image could be dreamed, remembered, and reported, and then worked upon, out of the analytic work around the dynamic of seeking and being with someone she did not want and who did not want her, or was not available to be with her. This was being repeated in her external life, particularly in her seeking a partner, and it came as the intensity of these feelings was abating somewhat in the transference–countertransference situation in her analysis, although, at the same time, the risk and uncertainty of the emotional connection between us was tangible. The antecedents in the patient's life from which this phenomenon arose included an early history of having been born unplanned long after her older siblings, which coincided with her maternal grandmother's death. Her mother had been depressed when she was a baby and then her father, to whom she was closer, left the home when she was around seven years of age and it was some years before she saw him again. The dynamic she brought into the analysis and then was expressed in the dream image was of a relationship with an object whose preoccupations (the television screen eyes) rendered them opaque and unavailable. The lack of cathexis of her by her object (the mother's depression, compounded by the later loss of the father) now illustrated by the television eyes, suggests an early failure of the mirroring that Winnicott writes about. It suggests that this patient, as a baby, was most probably left with the sense of not being able to connect, see *into* the eyes, which would have helped her to feel recognised and also wanted. The analytic "neutrality" which she had experienced as coldness was the first manifestation of this experience in the transference and communicated to me so powerfully in my countertransference.

Some months after this dream, the analysis began to feel very precarious; the patient frequently was silent. This was not long after the summer break and I had reminded her that I would be away for several days the following month. She arrived for her early morning Tuesday session looking dishevelled and ill and was silent for much of the session after telling me that she was not going to work, and had not the day before, as she could not face it. On the Wednesday, she told me that she was thinking of ending her analysis as it and everything was useless. After a while of working with her sense of hopelessness and her conviction that her analyst and analysis were useless to her, I put to her that this covered over her fear that both had become too important to her and that my reminding her again of my coming absence had filled her with despair; she could not risk her thoughts with an analyst who left her feeling so despairing. Shortly afterwards, she followed this simple link with a revelation that she had had several thoughts this week that she could not face telling me; she was too embarrassed, but now she felt somewhat easier and then told me of an image (not a dream) she had had of cockroaches pouring out of her body, implying that she was referring to her sexual body. She said this made her feel disgusted with herself. In working with this material, I noted the sense of embarrassment, a feeling associated with shame, in turn with being seen by another, her analyst, whom she now feared looked at her with disgust. There was also the link with her sense of her mother, whom she had recently been talking about feeling disgusted by, and so this image suggested her identification with her disgusting and disgusted maternal internal object. In the transference, it seemed that I was now the disgusting object who saw her disgusting self, expressed in her anxiety about how I would respond to her speaking of the image of the cockroaches pouring out of her.

The genital sexuality in this material is significant, but it is imbued with meaning from an earlier developmental stage, which I suggest can be understood in terms of the mirror function of the mother. One might also say that the sense of shame comes from being seen by the other and "found wanting", which is how I first thought of writing about this piece. The baby who is wanting, and found wanting, that is, disappointing to the maternal object, is greatly at risk of not feeling seen as in the mirror metaphor, but seen through the prism of the mother's eyes that cannot see the wanting baby. Instead, in this material, the baby's wanting is seemingly disgusting and this could be said to give form to that particular representation of the self and maternal object in this patient's inner world.

When she returned for her Thursday session, she was in a very different state of mind, now in touch with some hope. At one point, I commented on how unwell she had looked on Tuesday and she was astonished that I had seen her, recognised her as being in that state, seemingly not expecting that I would notice; I would say, not having an internalised sense of a mirroring maternal object who could notice her and recognise her state without in some essential way distorting it.

Conclusion

The imaginative elaboration by the other and what it contains of the capacity to imagine ourselves is the continuity signalled by Winnicott (and in a different register by Lacan, whose "mirror stage" Winnicott references in this paper in a way to distinguish himself from). It necessarily involves, as the establishing condition, the issue of development of the self and its place in a world that precedes the baby. If, in his article on the mirror stage and its contribution to the constitution of the ego, Lacan emphasises the role of the (misrecognised) image in the development of the subject, Winnicott links the capacity to imagine oneself to the (m)other's capacity to provide an incipient awareness of the idea of a self that derives from the environmental functions of that other/mother. In the first example, newly born baby Corey's encounter with his mother becomes bathed in her responsiveness to his wanting, seeking gaze. On the other hand, baby Emma is initially only seen as the wrong, weird, alien baby and is at high risk of her nascent self being imbued with these reflections of her mother's representations of her own self. The example of the dream of the television eyes implies that this young woman's early experiences had interfered with her capacity to feel alive and real beyond the surface; she looked at the surface of the television eyes but could not look into them. The dream suggests that she is seeking, perhaps because of the work of her analysis, a deeper connection, the wish to look into and see, be seen, and to feel wanted.

Winnicott's proposal of the significance of the mother's capacity to mirror her baby's states through her gaze (but implicitly also her multi-sensorial care) locates the establishment of the self firmly in the matrix of their dyadic relationship. In his canon, this is a paradoxical phenomenon, as it is an essential feature of the baby's illusion of omnipotence, where, in his experience of his primary creativity, the baby also feels this recognition comes from within himself. The mother's recognition in her gaze of what the baby shows her confirms the baby's creativity, the creation of his self, paradoxically absolutely dependent at this point on mother's capacity to sustain that creativity in her baby. Over time, she will be able to relinquish this position, as Winnicott put it in "What irks?": "And it's when your children exist in their own right that you can afford to do so too. You can afford to be yourself, with your secrets, which brings you back (although with a difference) to where you were before you were invaded by your children" (Winnicott, 2002, p. 148).

Note

1. The Anna Freud Centre in London pioneered an adaptation of psychoanalysis to treat babies with their parents when there was risk of the baby's development being derailed consequent to difficulties in the attachment relationships (Baradon et al., 2005).

References

Baradon, T., Broughton, C., Gibbs, I., James, J., Joyce, A., & Woodhead, J. (Eds.) (2005). *The Practice of Psychoanalytic Parent–Infant Psychotherapy: Claiming the Baby*. London: Routledge.

Bollas, C. (1985). *The Shadow of the Object*. London: Free Association Books.

Bollas, C. (1989). *Forces of Destiny*. London: Free Association Books.

Bollas, C. (1995). *Cracking Up*. London: Routledge.

Fraiberg, S., Adelson, E., & Shapiro, V. (1975). Ghosts in the nursery: a psychoanalytic approach to the problems of impaired infant–mother relationships. *Journal of the American Academy of Child Psychiatry, 14*: 387–421.

Freud, S. (1912e). Recommendations [to physicians practising psycho-analysis] on analytic technique. *S. E., 12*: 109–120. London: Hogarth.

Meltzoff, A. N. (1981). Imitation, intermodal coordination and representation in early infancy. In: G. Butterworth (Ed.), *Infancy and Epistemology* (pp. 85–114). London: Harvester Press.

Schafer, R. (1983). The atmosphere of safety. In: *The Analytic Attitude* (pp. 14–33). London: Karnac.

Winnicott, D. W. (1971). The mirror-role of mother and family in child development. In: *Playing and Reality* (pp. 130–138). London: Tavistock.

Winnicott, D. W. (1982a). Hate in the countertransference. In: *Through Paediatrics to Psychoanalysis* (pp. 194–203). London: Hogarth Press.

Winnicott, D. W. (1982b). Primary maternal preoccupation. In: *Through Paediatrics to Psychoanalysis* (pp. 300–305). London: Hogarth Press.

Winnicott, D. W. (1986). Varieties of psychotherapy. In: *Home Is Where We Start From* (pp. 101–111). London: Penguin.

Winnicott, D. W. (2002). What irks? In: *Winnicott on the Child* (pp. 139–154). Cambridge, MA: Perseus.

Wright, K. (2009). *Mirroring and Attunement*. London: Routledge.

CHAPTER ELEVEN

Ruptures and reconnections: play as a thread for sewing up?*

Massimo Vigna-Taglianti

In this chapter, I will attempt to tackle the subject of *ruptures*, taking as my starting point a number of differing perspectives that are, in fact, deeply interwoven.

We know that the warp and weft of life is continually inscribed with personal and interpersonal lacerations and restitchings, and that the forms of psychic suffering in many ways resemble fractures subsequently darned with more or less unsuccessful attempts at disharmonious self-soldering. Psychoanalysis, too, which deals with these ruptures and attempts to provide patients with more stable and harmonious recompositions than those they have individually adopted up to that moment, has not been, and is not, devoid of "splits": suffice to recall the theoretical rifts that have occurred in the history of psychoanalytic thought (within Freudian thought itself, between Freud and Jung, between Freud and Ferenczi, between Melanie Klein and Anna Freud, to cite only a few).

* This paper is a revised version of the presentation read at the 27th EPF Annual Conference in Turin, Italy, 10–13 April 2014, on "Ruptures".

So, I will analyse the issue of *rifts* and *restitchings*, taking into consideration three different levels in which these phenomena can be expounded. The first is the historical level and concerns the ruptures and discontinuities that have occurred during the evolution of psychoanalytic thought. The second—belonging to the internal world—regards those "tears" in the interpersonal fabric of the subject's early relationships with his own primary objects, which translate into "cracks" in the psychic container, with a resulting deficit of the capacity to symbolise. The third pertains to what happens in the analyst's room, since such ruptures, which originated in the intersubjective dimension and became intrapsychic via an introjective path, are reproposed and come to life in the here and now of the analytic relationship thanks to transferral repetition. This repetition, in my opinion, does not only take place in the wake of a deadly compulsion to repeat but, instead, in the attempt to find a symbolic solution to a traumatically interrupted task: what cannot be remembered is, in fact, brought into play in the transference through the *agieren* (Freud, 1905e, 1912b, 1914g).

I have spoken of rifts, but also of restitchings.

With regard to this, I shall propose and discuss the hypothesis that playing, in psychoanalysis, represents a sort of sewing thread, both theoretical and clinical, capable of carrying out a fundamental function in the reparative recomposition of the above-mentioned levels of rupture. Its conceptual formulation has, in fact, represented in the history of psychoanalysis a crucial theoretical turning point that has served to sew up a dramatic rift in psychoanalytic thought. At the same time, playing emerges as an intrinsic component of the therapeutic process and an indispensable tool (on a par with dreams and free associations) available to the analyst for tackling and recomposing the complex forms of rupture of the thinking faculties that originated in a there and then and come to life again in the here and now of the analyst's room.

As an ideal terrain for discussing these aspects, I have chosen what, in its turn, might appear paradoxically to be a *territory of rupture*, that is, child psychoanalysis. I believe this is a field in which all the levels I have mentioned previously emblematically converge: both the events linked to the rifts that occurred in the history of psychoanalytic thought and those—inevitably interwoven among themselves—regarding the early failures of the container–contained relationship and their reactivation in the therapeutic relationship.

So, child analysis may be a territory of possible rupture, but it is also a terrain for research and fertile recomposition. While some authors believe, in fact, that child psychoanalysis is a modified form of adult analysis, others maintain that there is absolute continuity between the essential therapeutic processes involved in the treatment of children, adolescents, and adults, except, obviously, for the specific traits relative to changes in ways of expression and communication (Frankel, 1998; Vigna-Taglianti, 2014).

Child psychoanalysis: two "godmothers" and a "tailor"

Sigmund Freud's work was so extensive and his thinking has subsequently met with so many reworkings that it accounts for the various roots of the two main doctrinal trends that have dominated the sphere of child psychoanalysis: on the one hand, inspired by the work of Anna Freud; on the other, linked to the theories of Melanie Klein.

Anna Freud centred her attention on the processes of normal and pathological development: focusing on the relative immaturity of the child's ego, she believed that a period spent building a positive relationship with the young patient was of fundamental importance, thus becoming the upholder of a pedagogical model aimed at developing the resources of the ego which in their turn would allow a gradual introduction of potentially anxiety-inducing interpretations of unconscious material. Contrary to what occurred during adult analysis, these interpretations could not be focused on the transference since she hypothesised that children, still too dependent on primary objects, would be unable to establish a transference relationship with the analyst (A. Freud, 1936, 1971a,b,c).

The theoretical standpoint of the other leading voice, Melanie Klein, was profoundly different. She believed that a transference neurosis could easily develop in children and that in them, as in adults, the transferral situation occurred to the extent in which a method was used with them that corresponded to the one used in adult analysis: that is, far from any pedagogical view and capable of analysing in depth the negative impulses directed at the analyst (Klein, 1932).

Moreover, Klein maintained that the transference corresponded more to unconscious fantasy than to a constellation of impulses and defences transferred from the relationships with parental imagos to the analyst. She did not conceive of the transference only in terms of references directed at the analyst, present in the patient's material. Her ideas were far more extensive and needed a technique by which the unconscious components of the transference itself were inferred from the global nature of the material. In fact, according to Klein, the patient was inevitably led to deal with the conflicts and anxieties that he relived with the analyst, making use of the same systems used in his far distant past (Klein, 1952).[1]

The treatment of historical and conceptual events that were necessary for sewing up what was emerging as the umpteenth "rift", capable of causing splits at the institutional level as well as in psychoanalytic thinking, lies outside the aims of this chapter. Suffice to recall here all the human and theoretical effort made by the analysts of that generation, in a London bombarded by the Nazis, that culminated in the famous and hotly debated "Controversial Discussions" and the subsequent "gentlemen's agreement", which allowed the British Psychoanalytical Society and the analytic community to come to a compromise, subsequently demonstrated over time to be highly "enlightened" (Rayner, 1991).

I will, therefore, limit myself to considering one of the theoretical aspects that developed from that and to pointing out the fundamental contribution of the work of "sewing up" carried out by Donald Winnicott in order to overcome this conflict and to further the evolution of psychoanalysis. Thinking independently, he made an extraordinarily creative and original effort to bridge the classical elements of Freudian psychoanalysis and the innovative ideas proposed by Kleinian thinking.

A key element of Winnicott's work was to bring together the intrapsychic dimension and the interpersonal one through the formulation of concepts of transitional space and objects. Transitional objects are created by the child in his internal reality; he then finds these objects again in external reality (Winnicott, 1971b). The pivotal cornerstone of transitional space is *play*, an activity during which the subject provides his own contribution in terms of psychic reality but, at the same time, has to deal with the other, who *really* exists in the external world.

Winnicott postulated that transitional space lies at the basis of playing: through playing we can use aspects of the internal world and make sure that they come into, and make up a part of, the external world, sharing them with others. Yet, at the same time, when playing, we use objects of the external world in a symbolic way in an attempt to represent and to understand something relevant to our psychic reality.[2]

In *Playing and Reality*, Winnicott defined psychoanalysis as a highly specialised form of playing in the service of communication with oneself and others (Winnicott, 1971a): in fact he affirmed that psychotherapy takes place in the overlap of two areas of playing, that of the patient and that of the therapist. So psychotherapy, for Winnicott, has to do with two people playing together and the corollary of this is that where playing is not possible, then the work done by the therapist is directed towards bringing the patient from a state of not being able to play into a state of being able to play (Winnicott, 1971a).

This view of analysis as an experience that is manifested in an intermediate space between two areas of play restores dignity and value to all the dimensions of the analytic situation, psychic reality, objective reality, and intersubjective reality, happily integrating the perspectives of Melanie Klein and Anna Freud. Thanks precisely to this specific activity of "oscillation"—inherent in playing—among such elements of psychic life, it is possible to arrive at recognising, integrating, and symbolising unrecognised and dissociated aspects of experience (Bromberg, 1994; Fonagy, 1995; Freedman, 1985).

The analytic setting: an ideal playing field for the rebirth of thinking

Increasingly frequently, in clinical practice, we have to deal with traumatic events characterised by the fact that *something that should have happened did not happen* and the subject is left lacking that work of affective significance necessary to subjectivisation (Balint, 1963; Botella & Botella, 2004) and to feeling that he and his own feelings are "real" (in the sense of Winnicott's realness). These situations are based on rigid and repetitive past relational sequences characterised by such a deficit in mirroring or reverie that the individual's subjectivity is wounded and his autonomous psychic existence is damaged. These sequences take shape in the mind as experiences that, by virtue of the damage inflicted on the representative faculty, belong to the sphere of the not named and the not symbolised.

The therapeutic encounter with patients who are seriously harmed at this level has inevitably led psychoanalytic research to focus its attention on the importance of the construction and/or reconstruction of the mind's symbolic capacity. Concerning this point, numerous authors, even from differing psychoanalytic traditions, concur that today the analyst's principal task is to restore the thought functions necessary for becoming capable of dealing with previously unbearable and unrepresentable psychic suffering: a necessarily preliminary work to that on splitting or repression (Borgogno, 2007; Ferro, 2009, 2011; Ogden, 2009).

This view of the analytic process has its roots in the Bionian concept of containment. By 1958, Bion had already intuited that if the patient was denied the opportunity for a normal use of projective identification, this provoked serious problems: with such a denial, the analyst, in fact, destroyed an extremely important bond (Bion, 1958). In introducing the concepts of containment and negative capability, Bion added functions to the analyst's tools that were not interpretative but participative, making the analytic situation more interpersonal (Bion, 1962a, 1965, 1970).

Regarding this point, Grotstein (2004, 2007) recently described Bion as one of the founders of intersubjectivity and emphasised the clinical meaningfulness of Bion's concept of becoming, which denotes the analyst's capacity to work in such a way that his own unconscious resonates with that of the patient's, getting "into the skin" of the analysand while remaining, at the same time, in his own. In other words, for Grotstein, the analyst must temporarily become the analysand.

In these situations "interpreting" becomes a crucial element in the analysis, not so much in the traditional sense of giving interpretations, but, rather, in the sense of personifying—for long periods and also unknowingly—specific characters and roles from the patient's history and internal world. This aspect (explored by Klein in "Personification in the play of children" of 1929) is something which, with Franco Borgogno, I have focused on in various works, emphasising how essential it is for the analyst to "lend" his emotional and symbolic functions, "experimenting emotions in search of an author" for however long is necessary, so that the patient will eventually be able to find them within himself (Borgogno, 2013; Borgogno & Vigna-Taglianti, 2009, 2013; Jacobs, 1986, 1991; Ogden, 1994a; Vigna-Taglianti, 2004).[3]

In fact, the characters that patients unconsciously come to play and interpret through the acting out that is intrinsic to repetition are those aspects of themselves that—as Frankel wrote in 1998—they are unable to accept as theirs and to show to the world with ease: those parts of the self that do not seem able to meet the other in a satisfactory manner. Playing offers an approach to this problematic part of one's personality: you can be something and then immediately afterwards repudiate it; playing allows one to come into contact with unrecognised and delegitimised aspects of the self by controlling the ways and times. In this sense, analysis would seem to have been conceived deliberately for playing: the analyst offers himself as a transitional object and can be used as the other character necessary for unknowingly representing the individual drama that is acted out in the transference (Frankel, 1998; Khan, 1974).

From this standpoint, it becomes essential to view the setting, in line with Winnicott, not as an inert space, but as an empathic environment capable of restoring to the analysand his experiences "understood", in such a way that they can be further worked through mentally by the patient himself with the help of the analyst.

Such a setting takes the form of a "three-dimensional", transitional, playful space; a potential space for growth in which all the various components—narrative and symbolic, but also pre-symbolic and acted—of the transference relationship can develop and so allow the individual who has never managed to become himself to construct the meanings of his own subjective experience. Precisely in this potential space, the serious game that is analysis takes place: it is an intermediate space shared by the analyst and the patient in which creative transformations are produced (Bollas, 1987, 1993; Winnicott, 1971a).

An analysis conceived in this way cannot be carried out by an ideally "neutral" analyst, or, better, neutrality has to be thought of as an uninterrupted activity between identification and dis-identification: in order to preserve it the analyst will always have to resort to his capacity for being identified with the patient, yet also quite distinct.

The transformative potential of analysis lies in the dialectic participation of the analyst in a role now of "old" object, now of "new" object (Greenberg, 1986, 1996; Mitchell, 1993): for the analysis to be truly mutative, the therapist must, in fact, be capable of activating the patient's pre-existing fears and hopes. However, at the same time, something new and unexpected must happen within the relationship that can lead to a gradual remodelling of his internal object representations through a well-calibrated balance between interpretation and containment as therapeutic factors, in dialectic tension with each other.

Breaking the ice: from the Arctic to the tramp's touch

The case of child analysis that I will now illustrate represents a condition of total emotive–affective iciness, a *sideration* of the ego, and sheds light on two aspects that are quite important in my opinion: (1) the psychopathology can, after all, be conceived as being determined by different degrees of impossibility in transforming one's emotions into a thought rich in affects; (2) the analyst's task is primarily to restore and provide the patient with the tools for thinking through the obligatory passage of acting, playing and talking.

For Winnicott (1960, 1965), the crucial failure in the primary relationship occurs when a "not-good-enough" mother fails to adequately disillusion her child, not helping him in the growing process that allows him to perceive shared reality as real. This happens in particular in situations in which the subjective-object-mother is unable to survive the infant's vigorous muscular aggressions and hate; this hate can then become a terribly catastrophic sentiment generating anxiety and destructiveness that is difficult to manage psychically, in particular if she retaliates. This destructiveness will inevitably trigger defence mechanisms, so that it can be acted in various forms or, on the contrary, be massively inhibited (Winnicott, 1971c,d).

From a Bionian standpoint, a failure in maternal reverie and a deficient alpha function seriously condition the progress of the interpsychic container–contained relationship, not allowing the small child to come into contact with his raw emotions and damaging the construction of the psychic space that is necessary for being able to transform them and, thus, provide a meaning that can be shared. Bion (1962b) maintains that this potential infantile catastrophe connected to the relationship with a mind that is not only incapable of welcoming projections and digesting them, but, even more, restores them further "contaminated" by its own suffering, provokes the installation in the individual's internal world of a projective-identification-rejecting-object, with which he identifies. An obstructing object, as Grotstein

(2007) has more recently defined it: an object, I would add, with marked characteristics of emotive impenetrability and impermeability, the result of a loss of real affective intimacy with the parents, and especially with the mother.

Tommy's experience seems to be emblematic in this sense; his story begins when he was four with the onset of autistic traits that coincided with such a serious destructuring of language and such a marked regression in motor and cognitive acquisitions that he was admitted to hospital with suspected neuro-degenerative disease.

Interviews with his parents described the story of an apparently carefree child, although, in fact, very isolated and too calm, who spent many hours alone in his room intent on leafing through children's books portraying prehistoric animals, all of whose names he knew by heart, a fact proudly exhibited by his parents as proof of his precociousness and intelligence.

However, some things had happened in the months preceding the consultation that had totally upset that quiet—although disquieting—routine. First of all, the birth of a baby brother, to whom Tommy appeared virtually indifferent, except for the fact that he had increased his behaviour of withdrawal, progressively isolating himself in his books or in repeated screenings of the same cartoons. Shortly after that, Tommy underwent an unexpected hospital admission in a provincial paediatric hospital, while on a short holiday, where mothers were not allowed to stay overnight. His parents identified this separation as the trigger: a devastating break between a before, in which everything seemed to be going well, and an after in which Tommy began to regress. In fact, as the assessment progressed, distinctive traits of the parental couple emerged: the mother had great difficulty in tolerating and managing her children's aggressiveness and psychic pain, while the father had a rigid and obsessive way of controlling every aspect of external and internal reality.

A diagnosis of pervasive developmental disorder was made and the child began psychotherapy, which lasted for three years, in the National Health Service. Quite rapidly, Tommy regained adequate language use and the autistic traits improved to such an extent that he was able to begin primary school and to establish relationships—with a certain amount of difficulty—with his schoolmates.

When Tommy was ten, his parents came to me: they had noticed that he was again tending to isolate himself and the National Health child psychiatrist had advanced a hypothesis of Asperger's. In fact, the child was once more shutting himself up for hours in his room where he drew up long lists of dinosaurs and other animals, or ran about alone for hours waving his hands around. At school, although he was diligent and obedient, he gave the impression of being "late": he was always "up in the clouds"; he learnt adhesively and was often teased by his schoolmates, who gave him the nickname "alien" because of his bizarre ways (Figure 11.1).

When we began treatment with Tommy (at that time extremely withdrawn), he asked me from the first sessions to concretely and invariably "interpret" the role of a "blockhead" student who had to carry out, from dictation, a very difficult task: to draw up, in an obsessive way, interminable lists of wild animals belonging to various natural habitats. In those moments he was completely identified with a tyrannical teacher—a sadistic and icy adult—who despised and devalued every childish emotion and need.

This game, in fact by no means playful at the beginning, gave a first shape to the profound emotional freezing of his mind: this frozen state underwent a gradual "thaw" only after a huge amount of dramatisation work that gave heart and voice to the terror of a child scared of getting in touch both with his own affective desertification and with his own raw emotions, in their wild state (Figures 11.2 and 11.3).

Tommy's business card
Controlling raw emotions and primitive anxieties

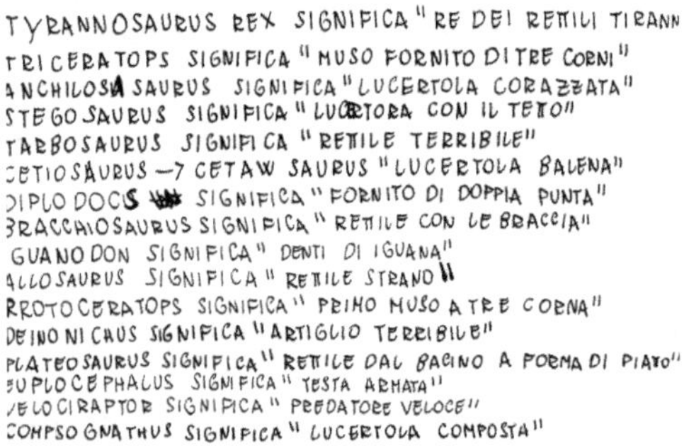

Tommy's writing

DINOSAURS –>DEINOS SAUROS
"TERRIBLE LIZARDS"
Tyrannosaurusrex means "king of the tyrant rep les"
Triceratops means "three-horn face"
Anchilosaurus means "fused lizard"
Stegosaurus means "roof lizard"
Tarbosaurus means "alarming rep le"
Cetiosaurus – cetus saurus – means "whale lizard"
Diplodocus means "double beam"
Brachiosaurus means "arm lizard"
Iguanodon means "iguana tooth"
Allosaurus means "strange lizard"
Protoceratops means "first horn face"
Deinonychus means "terrible claw"
Plateosaurus means "flat-pelvis lizard"
Euoplocephalus means "well-armed head"
Velociraptor means "speedy thief"
Compsognathus means "elegant lizard"

Figure 11.1. Tommy used to make these kinds of lists at home or in the assessment sessions, and also later in therapy.

Habitats
The Arctic

Tommy's writing

Marching across the "Big Chill"
Antarctica

Tommy's writing

The Tundra

Tommy's writing

Figure 11.2. The different habitats, in some way highly symbolic of progressive transformations in his primitive internal world and in the relationship. We started from the Arctic and, in our journey, we crossed the "Great North" and the "Big Chill".

Trials of Thaw
The swamps

Tommy's writing

Thaw starts . . .

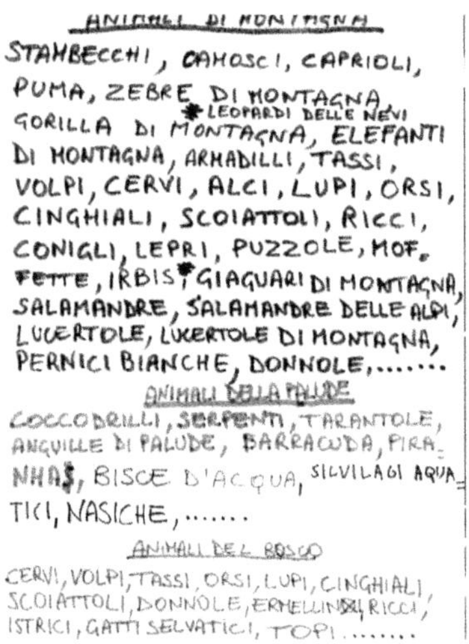
ANIMALI DI MONTAGNA

STAMBECCHI, CAMOSCI, CAPRIOLI, PUMA, ZEBRE DI MONTAGNA, *LEOPARDI DELLE NEVI GORILLA DI MONTAGNA, ELEFANTI DI MONTAGNA, ARMADILLI, TASSI, VOLPI, CERVI, ALCI, LUPI, ORSI, CINGHIALI, SCOIATTOLI, RICCI, CONIGLI, LEPRI, PUZZOLE, MOFFETTE, IRBIS* GIAGUARI DI MONTAGNA, SALAMANDRE, SALAMANDRE DELLE ALPI, LUCERTOLE, LUCERTOLE DI MONTAGNA, PERNICI BIANCHE, DONNOLE, ...

ANIMALI DELLA PALUDE

COCCODRILLI, SERPENTI, TARANTOLE, ANGUILLE DI PALUDE, BARRACUDA, PIRANHA$, BISCE D'ACQUA, SILVILAGI AQUATICI, NASICHE, ...

ANIMALI DEL BOSCO

CERVI, VOLPI, TASSI, ORSI, LUPI, CINGHIALI, SCOIATTOLI, DONNOLE, ERMELLINI, RICCI, ISTRICI, GATTI SELVATICI, TOPI ....

Mountain animals

Ibex, chamois, roe deer, puma, mountain zebras, mountain gorillas, snow leopards, mountain elephants, armadillos, badgers, foxes, deer, elk, wolves, bears, wild boar, squirrels, hedgehogs, rabbits, hares, polecats, skunks, mountain jaguars, salamanders, alpine salamanders, lizards, mountain horned dragons, rock ptarmigan, weasels . . .

Marsh animals

Crocodiles, snakes, tarantulas, swamp eels, barracuda, piranhas, water snakes, swamp rabbits, proboscis monkeys . . .

Forest animals

Deer, foxes, badgers, bears, wolves, wild boar, squirrels, weasels, stoats, hedgehogs, crested porcupines, wild cats, mice

Analyst's writing

Thaw goes on . . .
The pond

Tommy's writing

Thaw goes on . . .

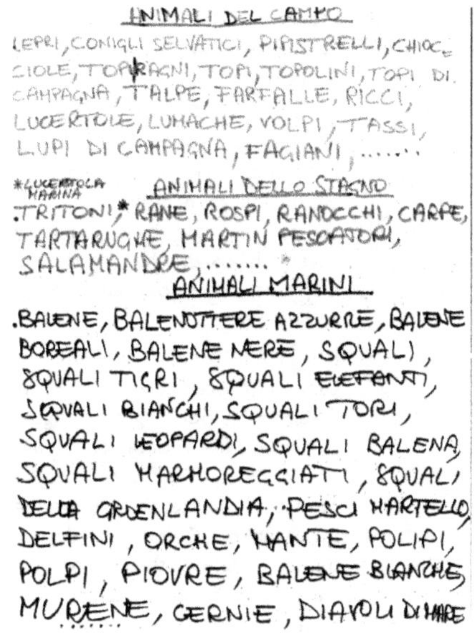

Meadow animals

Hares, wild rabbits, bats, snails, mice, rats, voles, field mice, moles, butterflies, hedgehogs, lizards, foxes, badgers, grey wolves, pheasants . . .

Pond animals

Marine iguana, frogs, toads, green frogs, carp, turtles, kingfishers, salamanders . . .

Sea animals

Whales, blue whales, Sei whales, black whales, sharks, tiger sharks, elephant sharks, great white sharks, bull sharks, leopard sharks, whale sharks, spotted wobbegong sharks, Greenland sharks, great hammerhead sharks, dolphins, killer whales, manta rays, octopus, giant squid, white whales, moray eels, dusky grouper, giant devil rays . . .

Analyst's writing

Figure 11.3. Through the Antarctic, the Tundra, the Taiga, we arrived at the Swamp, maybe the first signal of Thaw, and finally we arrived at the Pond, at the Meadow, at the Sea; there is no more ice, but water and earth, and I want to remember that life comes from the Ocean.

I immediately understood that I had a small but dogged scientist in front of me—a "Linnaeus of the psyche"—who made me detachedly catalogue a psychic reality that he could not come into contact with. To help him construct a thinking apparatus capable one day of representing such impulses and emotions (the animals in the lists), I myself had to personify and interpret a small child who was able to feel the terror in front of each of these bizarre animals (Figure 11.4).

Regarding this point, I believe it to be important that, for a long time during these interactive sequences, I experienced myself progressively invaded by feelings that ranged from tiredness to boredom, right to despair and to an almost physical sensation of "deadly" iciness. By means of working through my emotional response I under-

The Linnaeus of the Psyche
Frozen emotions

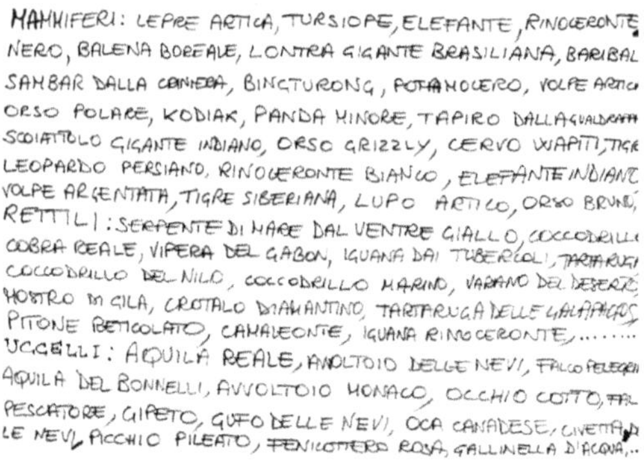

MAMMALS: Arctic hare, bottlenose dolphin, elephant, black rhinoceros, Sei whale, giant otter, American black bear, sambar deer, binturong, bush pig, Arctic wolf, polar bear, Kodiak brown bear, red panda, Malayan tapir, Indian giant squirrel, grizzly bear, elk, tiger, Persian leopard, white rhino, Indian elephant, silver fox, Siberian tiger, brown bear . . .

REPTILES: yellow-bellied sea snake, crocodile, king cobra, Gaboon viper, green iguana, tortoise, Nile crocodile, saltwater crocodile, desert monitor, Gila monster, eastern diamondback rattlesnake, Galapagos tortoise, python reticulatus, chameleon, rhinoceros iguana . . .

BIRDS: golden eagle, bearded vulture, peregrine falcon, Bonelli's eagle, cinerous vulture, Sardinian warbler, osprey, snowy owl, Canadian goose, pileated woodpecker, greater flamingo, moorhen . . .

Analyst's writing

Figure 11.4. Here is an example of Linnaeus's work: a list of animals produced by the interplay between Tommy and me during one session.

stood that in those moments, in a primitive transference–countertransference game, I became the depository of powerful deadly aspects. This happened both when Tommy freed himself of not very vital parts of his self, by projecting them into me, and when—identified with a glacial obsessive object that was unable to manage emotions and vitality—he dissociated into me a child dimension that up until then had been completely frozen and split.

To survive such treatment while playing along, in the attempt to give an emotional significance to his playing that could be shared, represented not only a preliminary work for laying the basis for future symbolisation, but also an essential process in the therapy, since, through role-reversal, Tommy concretely probed from close up the capacity of my mind to survive an experience with "agonising" characteristics. It was indispensable for me to activate a constant dynamic process of identification and dis-identification: a sort of empathic immersion and emersion that allowed us to reach that emotional closeness that is at the same time care and knowledge (Bolognini, 2004).

Through various years of analysis, all this led us to metaphorically journey through all the "Rooms of a Museum of Emotional Sciences": from the natural habitats (the Arctic, the Antarctic, the taiga, the steppes, the marshlands) we passed on to collections of bizarre animals (Figures 11.5, 11.6, and 11.7):

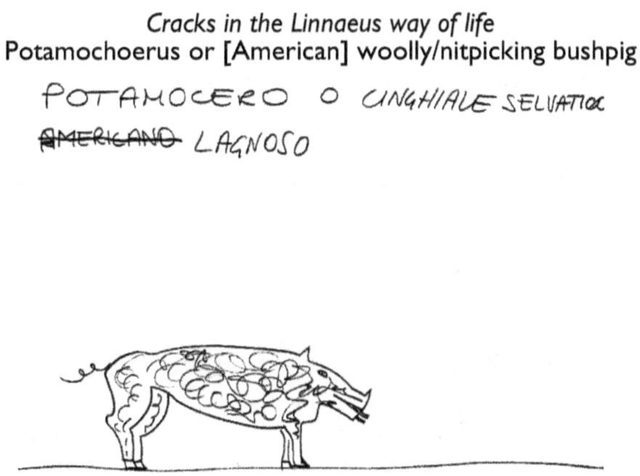

Figure 11.5. Analyst's drawing: in Italian LANOSO (woolly) sounds like LAGNOSO, which means NITPICKING.

Figure 11.6. Analyst's drawing following Tommy's advice.

Meeting human aspects
Woolly mammoth or woolly elephant with sabre tusks

Figure 11.7. Analyst's drawing: homo sapiens appears . . .

and then to the most frightening monsters (Figures 8 and 9),

Werewolf and exectioner

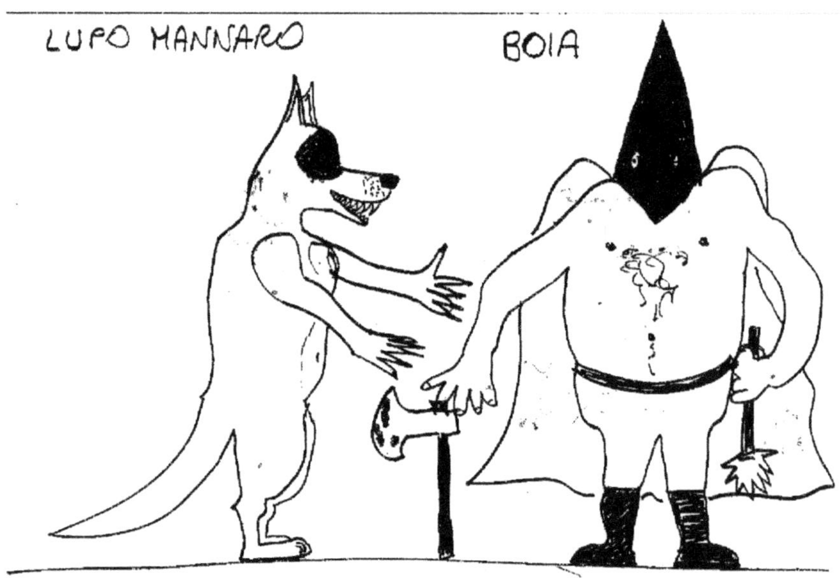

Figure 11.8. On Tommy's instructions, the analyst draws monsters.

Zombie and skeleton

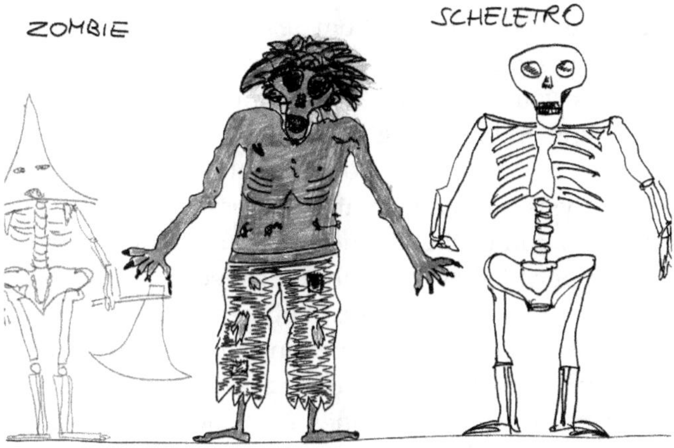

Figure 11.9. The analyst draws monsters following Tommy's request to draw "terribly frightening ones".

to end finally at *Horrorland* (Figure 11.10), a vivid representation of his nightmares, up until then not describable.

HORRORLAND PARK

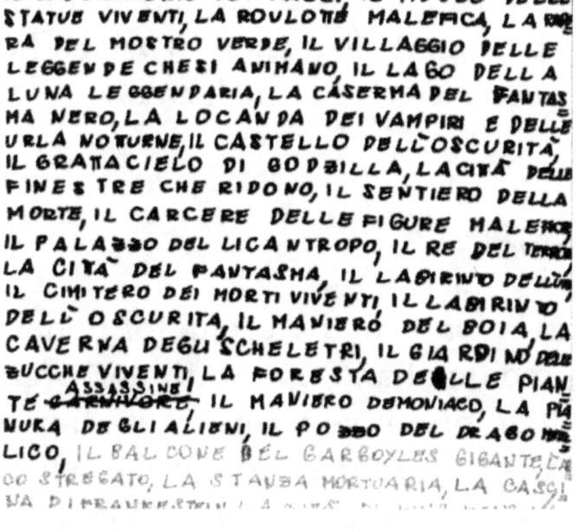

HORRORLAND PARK

Terror Tunnel, Bar of Horrors, Ghost Tower, House of Blood, The Mummies' Somersault, Vampire Grotto, Forest of Shadows, Room (Flat) of Evil, Black Man's Pazrking Space, Zombie Park, Forest of the Full Moon, Mysterious Game, "Who has seen him/her" Camping Ground, House of Fear, Lab of Mad People, Museum of Living Statues, Evil Caravan, The Clearing of Green Monster, the Village of the Awakening Legends, The Lake of the Legendary Moon, Barracks of the Black Ghost, Inn of Vampires and of Night Howls, Castle of Obscurity, Godzilla's Skyscraper, Town of Laughing Windows, Path of Death, Prison of Evil Figures, Palace of the Werewolf, King of Terror, City of Ghosts, Maze of Howl, Graveyard of Living Dead, Maze of Obscurity, Hangman"s Mansion, Skeleton Cavern, Garden of Living Pumpkins, Forest of Killer Plants, Devil's Mansion, Plain of Aliens, Well of the Metallic Gragon, Balcony of the Giant Gargoyles, The Enchanted Arch, The Mortuary, Frankenstein's Farm, King Kong's City

Figure 11.10. Tommy's writing.

In practical terms, the possibility for sharing such anxieties, "putting them down in black and white", but also dramatising them through role-reversal, made them less violent and finally representable: in doing this, Tommy could really learn to nominate and master them, as well as to "play" them himself, becoming increasingly capable of feeling and showing his emotions.

I feel it is important to point out that after about three years from the start of analysis (undertaken at three sessions a week) and abetted by the intensification of the instinctual component linked to puberty, something happened that can only be called a catastrophic change. Tommy began to show strongly phobic–obsessive symptoms that concerned, above all, a fear of becoming ill via contagion. This reacquired fragility terrified him, preventing him from going to the swimming pool or from going on outings with the Scouts, something that he had done up until then without blinking an eye. In the sessions, this anxiety manifested itself through repeated communications, made in an almost robotic-like way, of the type: "I saw a tramp today while I was coming to you. I'm afraid he might have touched me . . . did he touch me, do you think?"

Through the very patient but highly rewarding work of legitimising the fact that being touched can be very frightening, we passed from the concreteness of the tramp's touch towards awareness of a world inside where we feel touched by a meeting with the other, a meeting that can arouse unknown, violent, and threatening emotions: real content-killers for the mind. So, through playing, we arrived at verbalising the deep anxieties that emerged. Tommy could then begin to relinquish the sterilising control over his feelings and open up to dependence, reaching moments of profound regression in which he fell fast asleep during the session, exhausted like a small child.

Conclusions

This clinical material seems to me to be particularly useful for underlining how playing represents, on the one hand, the warp and weft based on intersubjective actions where primitive forms of the transference–countertransference dynamics take shape and, on the other, an indispensable tool for really reaching the patient in his core of deepest and unthinkable suffering (Ogden, 1994b).

For this objective, it is fundamental that the subject perceives that he is free to move in a setting capable of actively adapting itself to his needs: a close relative of maternal holding in its significance of a sustaining–containing environment. A psychic milieu with these characteristics allows the analyst a non-intrusive contact with all the levels of the patient's mind, through participating in his play and through using interpretative comments offered from an intermediate position between the analysand's reality and the analyst's reality (Altman et al., 2002). The analytic process can then, through regression, assume the characteristics of a *real* new opportunity to heal the patient's psychic suffering.

In this chapter, I have developed the idea that playing represents a creative integration of aspects of psychoanalytic theory that were previously conflictual and split: a *thread* capable of sewing up the theoretical rifts in psychoanalytic thought and of "mending" the psychic lacerations that afflict our patients, both adults and children. In fact, playing not only represents the main way for getting to the child's primitive fantasies and internal world (just as free associations and dreams do in adult analysis), it is also the cardinal pivot of that intermediate space where the psychic transformations, necessary to make thinkable those aspects of the experience that were previously unrepresentable, can occur safely—without scotomising the fragile conditions of the ego in favour of interpreting the unconscious fantasy and primitive drives and, at the same time, without overestimating the importance of external reality. From my point of view, therefore, playing means weaving ideo-emotive threads that are, of themselves, capable of repairing the weft or of spinning the warp of the subject's representative capabilities: a specific form, equivalent to dreams, of the waking dream thought theorised by Bion.

Through illustrating a clinical case, I have attempted to show how old relational fractures are reactivated in the complex identifying interplay of the analytic couple and what functions the analyst has to bring into play to successfully provide the patient with containing, communicative, and interpretative tools that can set in motion the representability of these "tears" that were unthinkable until that moment.

I have also advanced the hypothesis that playing allows the affects in the analytic setting to be unleashed through dramatisation, which is illusion *par excellence*, thus setting in motion the transformations

(Klauber, 1980, 1987; McDougall, 1986, 1989). To facilitate the spontaneous emergence of dramatisation in the patient, the analyst must proceed by allowing himself the same profound freedom of being intuitive and spontaneous: affective truth, which uses the inherent incisiveness of metaphor and of play, is, in my opinion, a decisive factor in the psychoanalytic cure.

To enliven and make more shareable this theoretical–technical perspective based on the idea that there is not so much an unconscious to unveil but, rather, a capability for thought to develop (Ferro, 2005; Ogden, 2005), I chose what is, in my view, a paradigmatic terrain for shedding light on the complexity regarding ruptures in the psychic container and the analytic work necessary for attempting to find a remedy: the terrain of child psychoanalysis. What is more, I believe that the analyst has to deal every day with a cracked, broken, split and lacerated "child", also in the analysis of adults. Indeed, I believe that there are split and unthinkable aspects concerning this infantile dimension of the mind that in the most various ways and forms—from the most deadly and silent to the most insane and screamed—urgently exert pressure on the transference–countertransference dynamic asking to be recognised, signified, and thought, at times for the first time, in the hope of finally finding a path for bein—not without pain—integrated into the internal world and authentically and creatively brought into "play" in interpersonal relationships.

Notes

1. Other metapsychological cornerstones were also the object of confrontation: (1) the nature of the unconscious fantasy; (2) the role of destructiveness as the main pathogenic element at the expense of child sexuality; (3) the dating of various developmental events, such the onset of the Oedipus complex and the organisation of the superego, which Klein brought forward to the first months of life (Klein, 1928). All this led to intensifying a profound theoretical conflict that assumed dramatic tones and, at times, ideological connotations.
2. Taking their cue from Winnicott, Fonagy and Target (1996) pointed out that playing is, by its very nature, a "pretending to", since whoever plays adopts new roles, imagining himself to be attentively observed by another person. "Pretending" means being able to straddle between two

states of the self at the same time. We can, therefore, define playing as a bridge between the perceptive and the imaginary: in pretending, we equate and, at the same time, differentiate the internal world from the external one (Ogden, 1986; Vygotsky, 1976).

3. Theodore Jacobs was the first to use the term "enactment" in his 1986 work entitled "On countertransference enactments". In the attempt to go beyond the pejorative and judgemental significance by then inherent in the term "acting out" (Boesky, 1982), he introduced this concept to describe behaviour, both verbal and non-verbal, implemented by the patient, or unconsciously by the analyst, or even by both analytic partners, that emerges directly from the transference–countertransference matrix and that is capable of channelling within it a conflicting relational dynamic that, up until then, had escaped being consciously grasped. Indeed, for Jacobs, enactment is also always a re-enactment: in it, a typical way of managing the intra- and interpsychic conflicts that had already been precociously used by the patient during his life is reproposed. In other words, Jacobs conceives enactment as a window that opens not only on the current state of the transference–countertransference relationship, but also on aspects of the patient's history. In a wider context, connected to a greater degree to a bi-personal psychology and to a more interactive idea of analysis, the concept of enactment is used today to indicate an analytically important event that involves the patient and the analyst reciprocally and contemporaneously through reciprocal induction and unconscious collusion. However, there is currently no unanimous opinion among the various psychoanalytical schools about this phenomenon. For those European analysts who are more tied into the Kleinian tradition or the Independent one (Rosenfeld, B., Joseph, J., Steiner, Little, Coltart, Bollas, Symington), it remains an event that signals a transference–countertransference collusion deriving from the analyst's lack of control: if this collusion is subsequently grasped and worked through, it can sometimes be transformed into developmental growth for the analytic pair. However, even in American psychoanalysis—where the concept was, in fact, coined—the positions are not unanimous and there are singular controversies that animate a fertile debate regarding enactment and adjacent technical aspects, such as, for example, self-disclosure (Chused, Ellman, Renik, & Rothstein, 1999). On the one hand, there are analysts more inclined to tradition (such as Chused, 1991; Gill, 1979; Jacobs himself, 2002, 2007; Poland, 1988; Schwaber, 1992) who, while appreciating the value of the countertransference, of the enactment and of the intersubjective perspective in analysis, emphasise the prevalent use

of such tools as vehicles for exploring in depth the mind of the patient. At the extreme opposite, there are other authors, such as McLaughlin (1987, 1991; McLaughlin & Johan, 1992) and Renik (1991, 1993), who, instead, conceive psychoanalysis as a constant series of unconscious enactments, big or small, that in any case involve both patient and analyst: these are inevitable and ubiquitous events linked to the intrinsic interactive flow of the analytic relationship, whose working through would allow the analysis and, therefore, comprehension of the analytical facts and of the patient, to progress. As a result, Bass (2003) has proposed differentiating these ways of conceiving enactment by using an upper case "E" to describe the exceptional ones and a lower case "e" for all the others.

References

Altman, N., Briggs, R., Frankel J., Gensler D., & Pantone, P. (2002). *Relational Child Psychotherapy*. New York: Other Press.

Balint, E. (1963). On being empty of oneself. *International Journal of Psychoanalysis, 44*: 470–480.

Bass, A. (2003). "E" enactments in psychoanalysis: another medium, another message. *Psychoanalytic Dialogues, 13*: 657–675.

Bion, W. R. (1958). On arrogance. *International Journal of Psychoanalysis, 39*: 144–146.

Bion, W. R. (1962a). *Learning from Experience.* London: Heinemann.

Bion, W. R. (1962b). The psycho-analytic study of thinking. *International Journal of Psychoanalysis, 43*: 306–310.

Bion, W. R. (1965). *Transformations: Change from Learning to Growth.* London: Tavistock.

Bion, W. R. (1970). *Attention and Interpretation: A Scientific Approach to Insight in Psycho-Analysis and Groups*. London: Tavistock.

Boesky, D. (1982). Acting out: a reconsideration of the concept. *International Journal of Psychoanalysis, 63*: 39–55.

Bollas, C. (1987). *The Shadow of the Object: Psychoanalysis of the Unthought Known*. London: Free Association Books.

Bollas, C. (1993). *Being a Character: Psychoanalysis and Self Experience.* London: Routledge.

Bolognini, S. (2004). *Psychoanalytic Empathy*. London: Free Association Books.

Borgogno, F. (2007). *Psychoanalysis as a Journey*. London: Open Gate Press.

Borgogno, F. (2013). *The Girl Who Committed Hara-Kiri and other Clinical and Historical Essays.* London: Karnac.

Borgogno, F., & Vigna-Taglianti, M., (2009). Il rovesciamento dei ruoli: un "riflesso" dell'eredità del passato piuttosto trascurato. *Riv. Psicoanal., 54(3)*: 591–603. Role-reversal: a somewhat neglected mirror of heritages of the past. *Italian Psychoanalytic Annual, 3*: 93–102, 2009.

Borgogno, F., & Vigna-Taglianti, M. (2013). Role-reversal and the dissociation of the self: An exploration of a somewhat neglected transference–countertransference process. In: R. Oelsner (Ed.), *Transference and Countertransference Today* (pp. 219–313). London: Routledge.

Botella, C., & Botella, S. (2004). *The Work of Psychic Figurability: Mental States without Representation*. London: Routledge.

Bromberg, P. M. (1994). "Speak! That I may see you": Some reflections on dissociation, reality, and psychoanalytic listening. *Psychoanalytic Dialogues, 6*: 55–71.

Chused, J. F. (1991). The evocative power of enactments. *Journal of the American Psychoanalytic Association, 39*: 615–639.

Chused, J. F., Ellman, S. J., Renik, O., & Rothstein, A. (1999). Four aspects of the enactment concepts: definitions, therapeutic effects, danger, history. *Journal of Clinical Psychoanalysis, 8*: 9–61.

Ferro, A. (2005). *Seeds of Illness; Seeds of Recovery: The Genesis of Suffering and the Role of Psychoanalysis*, London: Routledge.

Ferro, A. (2009). Transformations in dreaming and characters in the psychoanalytic field. *International Journal of Psychoanalysis, 90*: 209–230.

Ferro, A. (2011). *Avoiding Emotions, Living Emotions*. London: Routledge.

Fonagy, P. (1995). Playing with reality: the development of psychic reality and its malfunctions in borderline personalities. *International Journal of Psychoanalysis, 76*: 39–44.

Fonagy, P., & Target, M. (1996). Playing with reality: I. Theory of mind and the normal development of psychic reality. *International Journal of Psychoanalysis, 77*: 217–233.

Frankel, J. (1998). The play's the thing. How the essential processes of therapy are seen most clearly in child therapy. *Psychoanalytic Dialogues, 8*(1): 149–182.

Freedman, N. (1985). The concept of transformation in psychoanalysis. *Psychoanalytic Psychology, 2*: 317–339.

Freud, A. (1936). *The Ego and the Mechanism of Defence*. London: Hogarth Press.

Freud, A. (1971a). Four lectures on child analysis: introduction to the technique of child analysis. In: *The Writings of Anna Freud* (Vol. 1) (pp.

3–62). New York: International Universities Press.

Freud, A. (1971b). Normality and pathology in childhood: assessment of developments. In: *The Writings of Anna Freud* (Vol. 6) (pp. 3–273). New York: International Universities Press.

Freud, A. (1971c). Child analysis as a subspeciality of psychoanalysis. In: *The Writings of Anna Freud* (Vol. 7) (pp. 204–222). New York: International Universities Press.

Freud, S. (1905e). *Fragment of an Analysis of a Case of Hysteria. S. E., 7*: 7–122. London: Hogarth.

Freud, S. (1912b). The dynamics of transference. *S. E., 12*: 97–108. London: Hogarth.

Freud, S. (1914g). Remembering, repeating and working-through. *S. E., 12*: 145–156. London: Hogarth.

Gill, M. M. (1979). The analysis of the transference. *Journal of the American Psychoanalytic Association, 27S*: 263–288.

Greenberg, J. R. (1986). Theoretical models and the analyst's neutrality. *Contemporary Psychoanalysis, 22*: 87–106.

Greenberg, J. R. (1996). Psychoanalytic words and psychoanalytic acts: a brief history. *Contemporary Psychoanalysis, 32*: 195–213.

Grotstein, J. S. (2004). The seventh servant: the implications of a truth drive in Bion's theory of 'O'. *International Journal of Psychoanalysis, 85*: 1081–1101.

Grotstein, J. S. (2007). *A Beam of Intense Darkness. Wilfred Bion's Legacy to Psychoanalysis.* London: Karnac.

Jacobs, T. (1986). On countertransference enactments. *Journal of the American Psychoanalytic Association, 34*: 289–307.

Jacobs, T. (1991). *The Use of the Self.* Madison, CT: International Universities Press,

Jacobs, T. (2002). Secondary revision. On rethinking the analytic process and analytic technique. *Psychoanalytic Inquiry, 22*: 3–28.

Jacobs, T. (2007). Listening, dreaming, sharing: on the use of the analyst's inner experiences. In: S. Akhtar (Ed.), *Listening to Others. Developmental and Clinical Aspects of Empathy and Attunement* (pp. 93–112). New York: Jason Aronson.

Khan, M. (1974). *The Privacy of the Self.* London: Hogarth Press.

Klauber, J. (1980). Formulating interpretations in clinical psycho-analysis. *International Journal of Psychoanalysis, 61*: 195–202.

Klauber, J. (1987). *Illusion and Spontaneity in Psycho-Analysis.* London: Free Association Books.

Klein, M. (1928). Early stages of the Oedipus conflict. *International Journal of Psychoanalysis, 9*: 167–180.

Klein, M. (1929). Personification in the play of children. *International Journal of Psychoanalysis, 10*: 193–204.

Klein, M. (1932). *The Psycho-Analysis of Children.* London: Hogarth Press.

Klein, M. (1952). The origins of transference. *International Journal of Psychoanalysis, 33*: 433–438.

McDougall, J. (1986). *Theaters of the Mind: A Psychoanalytic Approach to Psychosomatic Illness.* London: Free Association Books.

McDougall, J. (1989). *Theaters of the Body: Illusion and Truth on the Psychoanalytic Stage.* London: Free Association Books.

McLaughlin, J. T. (1987). The play of transference: some reflections on enactment. *Journal of the American Psychoanalytic Association, 35*: 557–582.

McLaughlin, J. T. (1991). Clinical and theoretical aspects of enactment. *Journal of the American Psychoanalytic Association, 39*: 595–614.

McLaughlin, J. T., & Johan, M. (1992). Enactments in psychoanalysis. *Journal of the American Psychoanalytic Association, 40*: 827–841.

Mitchell, S. A. (1993). *Hope and Dread in Psychoanalysis.* New York: Basic Books.

Ogden, T. H. (1986). *The Matrix of the Mind: Object Relations and the Psychoanalytic Dialogue.* New York: Jason Aronson [reprinted London: Karnac, 1992].

Ogden, T. H. (1994a). The concept of interpretive action. *Psychoanalytic Quarterly, 63*: 219–245.

Ogden, T. H. (1994b). The analytic third: working with intersubjective clinical facts. *International Journal of Psychoanalysis, 75*: 3–20.

Ogden, T. H. (2005). *This Art of Psychoanalysis. Dreaming Undreamt Dreams and Interrupted Cries.* London: Routledge.

Ogden, T. H. (2009). *Rediscovering Psychoanalysis. Thinking and Dreaming, Learning and Forgetting*. London: Routledge.

Poland, W. S. (1988). Insight and the analytic dyad. *Psychoanalytic Quarterly, 57*: 341–369.

Rayner, E. (1991). *The Independent Mind in British Psychoanalysis.* London: Free Association Books.

Renik, O. (1991). Countertransference enactment and the psychoanalytic process. Paper presented to IPTAR, NY Academy of Medicine.

Renik, O. (1993). Analytic interaction. Conceptualizing technique in light of the analyst's irreducible subjectivity. *Psychoanalytic Quarterly, 62*: 553–571.

Schwaber, E. A. (1992). Countertransference: the analyst's retreat from the patient's vantage point. *International Journal of Psychoanalysis, 73*: 349–361.

Vigna-Taglianti, M. (2004). Transfert regressivo e transfert persecutorio:

trasformazioni del Sé e funzioni analitiche [Regressive transference and persecutory transference: Transformations of self and analytic functions]. In: F. Borgogno (Ed.), *Ferenczi oggi* [Ferenczi Today]. Turin: Bollati Boringhieri.

Vigna-Taglianti, M. (2014). Toy stories. The child psychoanalyst at play between relation and interpretation. *Italian Psychoanalytic Annual, 8*: 155–173.

Vygotsky, L. S. (1976). Play and its role in the mental development of the child. In: J. S. Bruner, A. Jolly, & K. Sylva (Eds.), *Play: Its Role in Development and Evolution* (pp. 537–554). New York: Basic Books.

Winnicott, D. W. (1960). The theory of the parent–infant relationship. *International Journal of Psychoanalysis, 41*: 585–595.

Winnicott, D. W. (1965). *The Maturational Processes and the Facilitating Environment: Studies in the Theory of Emotional Development*. London: Hogarth Press [reprinted London: Karnac, 1990].

Winnicott, D. W. (1971a). *Playing and Reality*. London: Tavistock.

Winnicott, D. W. (1971b). Transitional objects and transitional phenomena. In: *Playing and Reality* (pp. 1–25). London: Tavistock.

Winnicott, D. W. (1971c). Mirror-role of mother and family in child development. In: *Playing and Reality* (pp. 11–118). London: Tavistock.

Winnicott, D. W. (1971d). The use of an object and relating through identification. In: *Playing and Reality* (pp. 86–94). London: Tavistock.

CHAPTER TWELVE

Mirroring, mirrors, and proto-oedipal constellations

Maria Rhode

In his paper, "The mirror role of mother and family in child development", Winnicott described his main aim in doing psychoanalytic work as "giving the patient back what the patient brings" (1971, p. 117). This, he wrote,

> is a complex derivative of the [mother's] face that reflects what is there to be seen. I like to think of my work this way, and to think that if I do this well enough the patient will find his or her own self, and will be able to exist and to feel real. Feeling real is more than existing; it is finding a way to exist as oneself, and to relate to objects as oneself, and to have a self into which to retreat for relaxation. (p. 117)

For all the patients whom Winnicott described in this paper, "feeling real" was a central preoccupation. For some of them, so was being able to feel that they existed at all. Winnicott suggested that, in favourable circumstances, the baby might feel "When I look, I am seen, so I exist" (p. 114). This would depend on the mother's capacity to reflect in her facial expression what she feels about the baby, rather than her own preoccupations or defences.[1] "In other words, the mother is looking at the baby *and what she looks like is related to what she sees there*"

(p. 112, original italics). On this most primal level, then, we are what we see, and what we see depends on the other's capacity to see us.

These formulations are of profound importance in relation to patients whose sense of identity is fragile or who suffer significantly from existential anxieties. They overlap, to some degree, with other concepts, such as Bion's maternal reverie (Bion, 1962) and Meltzer's aesthetic reciprocity (Meltzer, 1987; Meltzer & Harris Williams, 1988), but the differences are significant. Winnicott's mirroring reflects "what is there to be seen", while Bion's reverie is more to do with the mother's role in allowing the baby to integrate feelings that were previously intolerable, so that his mind can grow. Meltzer's concept of aesthetic reciprocity (Meltzer, 1987; Meltzer & Harris Williams, 1988) concerns the passionate response of mother and baby to what they experience as beautiful in each other. Like Winnicott, Meltzer emphasises that this is not a matter of formal, physical beauty, but of the emotion that is expressed in recognising such beauty as might be present. Thus, Meltzer notes that far more "beautiful mothers" are mentioned in analysis than objectively exist in the population, while Winnicott points out how different is "the man who falls in love with beauty . . . from the man who loves a girl and feels she is beautiful and can see what is beautiful about her" (p. 113). Meltzer does imply that the absence of an aesthetic response from the mother can make human contact hard for the baby to sustain, but he does not focus so much on the primal sense of existing that is Winnicott's main concern.[2] (It was Searles' concern as well when he wrote (1984, p. 47) that the analyst's facial expression allowed borderline or psychotic patients to find their way to object relatedness: "each participant's facial expressions 'belong' as much to the other as to oneself; that is, the expressions of each person are in the realm of transitional phenomena for both of them".)

Winnicott emphasised that "the actual mirror has significance mainly in its figurative sense" (p. 118). Thus, "when the average girl studies her face in the mirror she is reassuring herself that the mother-image is there and that the mother can see her and that the mother is *en rapport* with her" (p. 113). In normal development, that is, mirroring by the mother underlies the child's relationship with the physical mirror, and where there have been problems with the mother's mirroring function, these will be reflected in the child's use of actual mirrors later in life. For example, he describes a woman who had many strengths, but was completely unable to face the world until she had "put on her face" and in this way got "the mirror to notice and approve. The woman had to be her own mother" (p. 114). I have myself treated a woman patient who had recovered from adolescent anorexia and self-harming, but who retained a degree of body dysmorphic disorder[3] so that all mirrors outside her own flat seemed to reflect her as ugly and disgusting. It was only the mirror in her own bedroom that showed her an image she could find tolerable: a vivid illustration of her profound lack of faith in the reception she could expect from a separate other. The eyes of the other she related to seemed to resemble those described by Steiner (2011) as engendering shame and humiliation rather than those of Winnicott's mirroring mother.

Winnicott acknowledged the influence of Lacan's (1949) paper on the *stade du miroir* (Lacan, 1977). However, he emphasised that his own primary concern was with the mother's live mirroring face rather than with the physical mirror: with the affirmation of the baby's existence rather than with a reflected image of the baby's body that the baby identifies with but that is alien to his felt experience or True Self. Children do, of course, produce material that brings Lacan's formulations immediately to mind. For example, a latency-aged boy with a diagnosis of Asperger's syndrome and many borderline features methodically touched all the parts of his face, as though he were making sure that they were where they were meant to be. When I suggested that this was what he was doing, he answered, "You wake up in the night, and bits of you are gone, you can't see them. Then you go to the mirror and you see they're all there, but the mirror tricks you." The contrast is striking between this child's experience of bodily fragmentation and the mirror image of an intact body that feels alien and alienating. However, in the case of this boy at least, this Lacanian contrast occurred within the context of transgenerational problems that had greatly complicated his parents' efforts to see him as himself; his mother, who had been profoundly depressed when he was born, had named him after her own brother, who had died in childhood. I would understand his experience of a "Lacanian" mirror image as following on from a problematic experience of "Winnicottian" maternal mirroring. Indeed, one of the arresting aspects of Winnicott's formulations is the possibility they provide of theorising transgenerational transmission of trauma: what Fraiberg and her co-workers (1975) called "ghosts in the nursery".

Physical mirrors

In this chapter, I will focus on the use of physical mirrors by children on the autistic spectrum, whose sense of identity is often so rudimentary and fragile and whose bodily existential anxieties and experience of physical fragmentation can be so extreme (e.g., Haag et al., 2005; Tustin, 1972, 1986). Their characteristic difficulty in making eye contact is well known; so is their terrified need to be in control of other people, so that one might not expect them to be able readily to benefit by the mirroring function provided by a separate other. However, they can generally make use of physical mirrors that are under their control in order to work on issues to do with their continuing existence and with problems concerning their relation to others. Children with autism tend to focus on people's surface characteristics (Meltzer, 1994; Tustin, 1981, p. 12), so that the shiny surface of a mirror or television screen links readily with the shining surface of the human eye. Since witnessing the creative use that a boy with autism made of a tiny mirror that happened to be part of the dresser in the dolls' house, I have made a point of providing a framed mirror that is large enough to reflect much of the room, but small and light enough for the child to manoeuvre.[4] The usefulness of providing a physical mirror is not confined to work with children on the autistic spectrum: Sinason (1999) has remarked on it with learning-disabled patients, another group for whom issues surrounding the sense of self are centrally important.

One of the key points to emerge from Winnicott's paper is that looking in the mirror can be object-related, rather than narcissistic. This area was also explored by a number of analysts working in the USA within a different theoretical framework, and who based their formulations largely on the material of psychotic patients. For example, Elkisch (1957) linked her patients' fascination with their mirror image to reports by Roheim (1919) and Rank (1989) concerning beliefs and taboos relating to mirrors in the fields of literature, mythology, and anthropology. The commonly held fear that seeing one's reflection meant the loss of one's soul (or death) was, Elkisch suggested, the obverse of the psychotic patient's belief that finding his mirror reflection might be a means of finding or re-finding his lost identity. She linked this to the play of Freud's grandson in front of a wall mirror: he crouched down so that his reflection disappeared, only to find it again when he stood up. His accompanying commentary, "Baby gone" and "Baby there [da]", exactly paralleled his commentary in the "Fort-Da" game in which he threw away and retrieved the cotton-reel (Freud, 1920g). This similarity, in itself, implies a link between losing and refinding one's mirror reflection (and with it one's sense of existing) and losing and refinding the mother whom the cotton-reel symbolised (Rhode, 2010). Such a link accords with Winnicott's formulations on the mother's mirror role and illustrates the kind of object-related concerns that may be expressed by preoccupation with one's reflection. Similarly, Lichtenstein (1964), who took up many of Elkisch's suggestions in his paper "The role of narcissism in the emergence and maintenance of a primary identity", pointed out the difference between being in love with oneself—as in narcissism—and being "in love" with one's mirror reflection in the eminently serious way that Elkisch described in her patients (1964, p. 51). As he put it, "the primary identity is always based on a mirroring experience" (1964, p. 54).

An extensive experimental literature exists on the capacity of both normally developing children and children with autism to recognise themselves in the mirror. Engaging with this literature in detail is beyond the scope of this chapter, but it is interesting to note that normally developing children under laboratory conditions sometimes identify their own shadow or mirror reflection as a member of their immediate family (Fontaine, 1992; Zazzo, 1995). As Athanassiou (2006) has pointed out in her absorbing psychoanalytically based discussion of these studies, recognising oneself in the mirror presupposes the ability to distinguish between virtual space and actual space, which, in turn, implies the acquisition of representational capacities.

Many children with autism have not acquired representational capacities, and those who have done so often show considerable fluctuations in their ability to access them. As Segal (1957) argued, representational or symbolic capacities depend on the child's working through of the depressive position with regard to an other whose separateness is acknowledged. This is inherently problematic for children with autism, who tend to experience bodily separateness as having a part of their body torn away (see, for example, Tustin, 1972). It also immediately raises issues to do with the early triadic relationships that are implicit in the notion of separateness.

In the clinical examples that follow, I consider a number of ways in which children with autism relate to the physical mirror. These vary in respect of the child's representational capacities; they also vary in respect of the child's implicit conception of a primitive parental couple. I hope to illustrate how, in the context of a therapeutic setting, a physical mirror can serve as a bridge between the child and the therapist, as well as helping to elucidate the child's anxieties and budding phantasy life. I shall suggest that a triadic structure is not invariably experienced as a potential interference with the mother's or therapist's mirroring function: it is also essential to the establishment of safe contact, provided that the child does not feel overpowered by the presence of a third element.

Who is the child in the mirror?

A mirror reflection cannot provide reassurance that one continues to exist until one can recognise it as one's own. This is a capacity that babies acquire in the course of development: most animals never do so, and respond to their mirror image as though it were another living creature, which they attempt to locate by looking behind the mirror. Similarly, very young (or disturbed) children will look behind the television to find the people whom they see on the screen: they cannot yet make the distinction between real and virtual space.

This makes it understandable that some children with autism do not respond to their mirror image by feeling reassured. Instead, they might react with fear to their own reflection, as though it were a real and threatening other person, or else the uncanny double described in Elkisch's quotations from Roheim and Rank. In any event, it is as though the child's existence in the real world were endangered by its own image in virtual space. Once virtual space is seen to be a representation of real space, the mirror reflection can be recognised as belonging to the child and can serve as a source of reassurance that underpins the sense of an enduring self. It can also provide a means of exploring how far this sense is strengthened or undermined by the existence of others.

Early triadic structures

Anthony, a latency-aged boy with severe autism, gazed for long periods at his own reflection. He did not allow me to catch his eye in the mirror, as though he and his reflection were to constitute a couple that excluded everyone else. I seemed to be in the role of a rival who competed with him for space; in his case, space in the mirror's reflecting surface, much as Britton (2003) described in "Narcissistic problems in sharing space". Previously, Anthony had upended a cow so that it balanced on the mirror on its muzzle and had described the cow and its reflection as "Mummy and Daddy", as though they were narcissistic parents who were mirror images of each other and left no room for him. Sometimes, he enacted the role of a pop star, holding a pretend microphone as though it were a mirror that reflected his expression of blasé superiority as he basked in the adoration of his fans. During these performances, I was completely ignored. I took this as a communication of how he experienced a mutually adoring parental couple that had eyes only for each other. Perhaps being part of such a couple might have felt like a protection against the catastrophic fears of falling that were prominent in Anthony's material.

On one occasion, however, when he must have felt more robust than usual, Anthony did allow me to catch his eye in the mirror. Smiling with pleasure, he spoke to the mirror rather than to me: "Hullo, mirror." He did not seem to be thinking of me as a human mirror, someone who could reflect him and reflect on him, but the ability to tolerate my face in the mirror appeared to liberate him for a moment from his imprisonment in sterile narcissism, and he found his voice to speak to the mirror as though it had human qualities. It felt as though the narcissistic couple that were mirror images of each other had become the kind of couple who could provide space for a child. In other words, when Anthony was briefly able to tolerate my reflection as a third element in his previously exclusive relationship to the mirror, it was as though the mirror had come to life as a benign presence.[5] Interestingly, it is within the framework of a triadic structure that many babies first learn to recognise their mirror reflection: while looking into a mirror in which they can see their own image next to the image of the person holding them in their arms. The baby who looks back and forth between the real adult's face and its mirror reflection seems to be learning the difference between real and virtual space.

The mother's internal family

Winnicott describes how the mother's preoccupations can interfere with her mirroring function so that they are what the baby sees in her face rather than himself. I have found it helpful to put together his conception of mirroring with Melanie Klein's idea (Klein, 1961, pp. 46–49) that young children experience the mother's qualities and behaviour as though they were the outward manifestation of a family that is imagined as living inside her. For example, in "Narrative of a child analysis", Klein's patient Richard wanted to turn off an electric heater, the glowing bar of which had previously been understood in terms of the oedipal father's presence inside the mother. Once he had turned off the fire, the mother-room seemed dead to him. Along these lines, the child might feel that the mother contains a benign internal family that willingly makes room for him and allows her to receive—and mirror—him with love, or he might misinterpret her preoccupation as being due to an internal family that physically occupies her completely and wipes out his presence, just as I was wiped out through Anthony's narcissistic relationship to the mirror. In this second scenario, the child might not experience eye contact as though the adult were paying attention to him, but as though it were evidence of a rival looking out at him through the windows of the adult's eyes (Meltzer, personal communication, 1972).

Such phantasies played a large part in the treatment of Lina, a girl with high-functioning autism who was nine at the time of the sessions I shall discuss. Lina seemed to have no doubt that significant people's facial expressions were determined by babies who she imagined lived inside them: for example, she brought along a plastic toy the expression of whose eyes could be changed from "happy" to "sad" to "angry" to "surprised" when she rotated its very pregnant-looking abdomen. She was also preoccupied with the difference between the reflective surface of the mirror and its opaque wooden back, which she compared to the wooden door of the therapy room. She had once collided painfully with this door when she tried to run through it in spite of its being shut. The shut door seemed like a concrete representation of not being able to get through, of literally banging her head against the wall, while the reflecting side of the mirror appeared to represent the converse situation of feeling that she could be seen and reflected upon.

Lina had begun intensive treatment in another country at the age of not quite four, when she spoke only a few words and appeared to be almost completely cut off from other people. This treatment had come to an end because of her therapist's fatal illness. I saw her twice weekly when she was between the ages of six and a half and thirteen, initially with the aim of helping her to come to terms with her first therapist's death. She had made gratifying progress when I began to see her and was speaking fluently and doing well academically, though her relationships were still very impoverished. Like her first therapist, I found working with her very rewarding: she had a gift for a poetic turn of phrase and could often make emotional contact at a profound level. However, she attempted to recapture important moments by reproducing the same material with the aim of getting me to repeat interpretations that had touched her, and this had a controlling and deadening quality.

Lina spent much time looking at the books and toys that she could see inside a tall, glass-fronted cupboard in my room. These belonged to a colleague and were, as she put it, "not playable". She was understandably very tantalised by being able to see things she could not use, and these toys soon took on the connotation of precious things inside me to which she had no access. This, rather than realistic deprivation, seemed to be the main reason for her fascination with them, as she had many of the same toys in her own box.

In the first session I wish to discuss, she held some water in her mouth without swallowing while she stood gazing into the cupboard. After swallowing the water, she cried out: "My sister Flo—I'm looking for my sister Flo", and rushed to the lavatory. She was still acutely distressed when she returned, and she went back to her position in front of the cupboard, repeating that she could not see her sister Flo. I said that perhaps, when she was cross about things in the cupboard or in me that got in her way, this made her worry that taking things in was something she did in order to empty me. That might make her feel guilty about keeping the water inside her, and instead she let everything "flo(w)" out of her into the lavatory. She calmed down, and checked her reflection in the mirror as though to make sure that she was still there. In the following session, she again swallowed a mouthful of water while standing in front of the cupboard. When I asked whether she was looking for her sister Flo, she answered confidently, "No, I'm looking for myself." It was as though taking up her hostility towards supposed rival siblings inside my cupboard (or me) allowed her to lay claim to her own reflection and identity without the danger of wiping them out. It also meant that she could retain the water she had swallowed instead of equating herself with me as someone that water "Flo'ed" out of.

A few weeks later, Lina took further the theme of her position relative to sibling figures inside the mother. This proved to be an important session from which I will quote in detail.

> Lina drew small circles in many different colours on the surface of the mirror. (In previous sessions, she had done this in the context of asking how babies were made, and she had said that the circles were produced by Mr Green, Sir Blue, and so on.) She commented, as though justifying herself, "I'm only trying to make stained glass." I said that perhaps she thought stained glass looked beautiful—all those colours with the light coming through—and that she would like to learn how to make it. That would be like feeling that it was she who was the cause of the expression—the colour—in my eyes when I looked at her, rather than a baby inside me like her sister Flo. Lina cleaned the colours off the mirror. She said, "It looks grey now", and moved her hand surreptitiously past her bottom as she threw away the tissue. The colours did, in fact, obscure her own reflection, but removing them seemed to make her feel that my mirror-gaze was grey—empty, messed up, depressed.
>
> Next she drew on the mirror a bull with angry-looking eyes, coloured in red as though it were bleeding. She then turned the mirror over, and seemed to be trying to see herself in its wooden backing, perhaps as though the bull were getting in the way of her reflection as the coloured circles had before. I said that one could not see oneself in that side; was she perhaps also wondering whether that was where the picture of the bull had come from? Holding up the mirror at an angle to the window, she said, "Now the light is shining through." This was not so, but I said she was trying to find a way for the light to shine through without being blocked by the picture, for there to be space for life to go on behind my eyes in a way that encompassed her, and did not get in the way of room for her feelings.
>
> Lina answered, "You can do something else, too." Taking the mirror to the sink, she carefully filled it up to the edge of the frame with water. The

picture of the bull was now beneath the surface. She bent over the mirror, as though again looking for her reflection. This time, she did not say that she was looking for herself: instead she said, "I can see myself." I agreed that the water was different from the mirror; that it had actual depth, and because of this the picture of the bull did not get in the way of her reflection in the water.

I would like to highlight the importance of two related conditions that were satisfied by Lina's mirror filled with water. First, she could coexist with my supposed internal occupant; and second, there was depth within the mother-mirror that this occupant did not fill. In such a situation, the child's way in is not blocked; space is available for emotional containment; the light "shining through" makes the child feel that he can elicit a response; and, at the same time, the presence of the internal object means that the child is not in danger of being engulfed or of feeling responsible for a depressed mother-figure who has been emptied of the child's double (Lina's sister Flo). In other words, mother and child are both complete and they can evolve reciprocal interactions. Lina's ninth birthday, soon after this session, encouraged her to feel that she was growing up and that one day she could have children of her own, as though she had identified with me as a woman whose internal husband and children left room enough for her own separate individuality to be reflected upon.

Discussion

Anthony's and Lina's material illustrates the way in which children with autism can use a physical mirror to convey the nature of the mirroring mother figure they relate to. Within the context of a session, and to varying degrees, the mirror can also serve as a bridge to more ordinary ways of relating to the therapist. Anthony, for example, usually resembled Britton's patient Ms A, who insisted that her analyst must purely reflect her words without adding anything of his own (Britton, 1989); even when my reflection in the mirror seemed to turn it into something with human qualities, it was still the inanimate mirror that he said "Hullo" to. Lina had less need than Anthony to be in absolute control, so that relating her play with the mirror to her feelings about me was not only tolerable, but led to developments in her material. In both children, a third element in their relationship to the mirror could be experienced as valuable, indeed essential, rather than being purely threatening. In Anthony's case, his fleeting ability to tolerate my reflection alongside his led to important developments, however temporary and limited. With Lina, the survival of her sister Flo was necessary to her own enduring identity, and the mother's mirroring gaze derived its colour and vitality from the coloured baby-circles deriving from Mr Green and Sir Blue. What seems to be at issue is a proto-oedipal constellation at the level of eye contact, on a very primitive level that concerns the child's experience of existing.

In order for the child to feel supported rather than intruded into, the parent's internal family must be felt to be located at the optimal "depth". Early in treatment, for example, Lina meticulously arranged two calves face to face, one on a plate, one outside it, in such a way that they were equidistant from the rim. Where the mother is preoccupied, so that, as Winnicott wrote, the child sees her preoccupations rather than himself, he might feel that his way in is blocked by an internal family that he (mis)interprets as lying too far forward. If the mother's preoccupation concerns transgenerational issues, as with Fraiberg and colleagues' (1975) ghosts in the nursery, the child might feel that his own "niche" is concretely filled by someone from the past.

Very schematically, one could speculate that, when the balance is right, the child can identify with the parental figure, as Lina did when she began to think of herself as containing unborn children like me. When the balance is not right, the child might identify instead with the parent's internal occupant, like Kate Barrows' adult patient (Barrows, 1999) who identified with her parents' dead or damaged siblings. For instance, the boy with Asperger's syndrome whom I previously mentioned and who appeared to have an experience of a "Lacanian" mirror image changed during treatment from being very withdrawn to being highly excitable, with much bizarre fantasy. In the first phase, the material suggested that he was identified with ghostly inhabitants of a parental figure, while in the second phase he seemed instead to be identified with a vengeful persecutory sibling figure who he thought was coming out of the television in order to attack him.[6] Such clinical experiences could have some bearing on the opposite interpretations of mirror reflections—sometimes dangerous, sometimes auspicious—reported by Rank and Roheim (Elkisch, 1957).

When maternal mirroring has been interfered with, as Winnicott wrote (1971, p. 113), "then a mirror is a thing to be looked at but not looked into". I have attempted to illustrate how exploring mirror reflections in the course of therapy can lead the child towards a fuller mirroring experience.

Notes

1. For a discussion of later work on the failures of mirroring, see Fonagy et al. (2003).
2. I have suggested elsewhere (Rhode, 2008) that Winnicott's approach to this primal sense of existing has much in common with Freud's (1923b) notion of primary identification and with the developmental researcher Trevarthen's (1979) concept of primary intersubjectivity.
3. See also Lemma (2009).
4. For some of "Daniel's" mirror material, see Rhode (1999).
5. Compare Lichtenstein (1964): "Someone who sees in the mirror nothing but himself has apparently a very special kind of looking that suppresses everything else except his own picture in the mirror" (p. 51).
6. It is essential to emphasise that I am in no way implying a causal link between mother–infant interactions and autistic spectrum disorder: there are far more depressed mothers or families with "ghosts in the nursery" than there are children with autism. What I suggest is that phantasies about the mother's internal occupants can get mapped on to the way the child experiences his life circumstances. These circumstances might sometimes include aspects of the parents' capacity to pay attention. They might also include experiences that are based in neurology: for example, the feeling of being invaded by loud noises is very common in children with autistic spectrum disorder, who can personify these noises as intrusive father or sibling figures (Rhode, 1997).

References

Athanassiou, C. (2006). *Représentation et Miroir.* Paris: Ed. Popesco.

Barrows, K. (1999). Ghosts in the swamp: some aspects of splitting and their relationship to parental losses. *International Journal of Psychoanalysis, 80*: 549–562.

Bion, W. R. (1962). *Learning from Experience.* London: Karnac.

Britton, R. S. (1989). The missing link: parental sexuality in the Oedipus complex. In: J. Steiner (Ed.), *The Oedipus Complex Today* (pp. 83–101). London: Karnac.

Britton, R. S. (2003). Narcissistic problems in sharing space. In: *Sex, Death and the Superego* (pp. 165–178). London: Karnac.

Elkisch, P. (1957). The psychological significance of the mirror. *Journal of the American Psychoanalytic Association, 5*: 235–244.

Fonagy, P., Target, M., Gergely, G., Allen, J. G., & Bateman, A. W. (2003). The developmental roots of borderline personality disorder in early attachment relationships: a theory and some evidence. *Psychoanalytic Inquiry, 23*: 412–459.

Fontaine, A.-M. (1992). *L'Enfant et son Image.* Paris: Nathan.

Fraiberg, S. H., Adelson, E., & Shapiro, V. (1975). Ghosts in the nursery: a psychoanalytic approach to the problems of impaired infant–mother relationships. *Journal of the American Academy of Child Psychology, 14*: 387–422.

Freud, S. (1920g). *Beyond the Pleasure Principle. S. E., 18*: 7–64. London: Hogarth.

Freud, S. (1923b). *The Ego and the Id. S. E., 19*: 3–66. London: Hogarth.

Haag, G., Tordjman, S., Duprat, A., Urwand, S., Jardin, F., Clément, M., Cukierman, A., Druon, C., Châtellier, A. M., Tricaud, J., & Dumont, A. (2005). Psychodynamic assessment of changes in children with autism under psychoanalytic treatment. *International Journal of Psychoanalysis, 86*: 335–352.

Klein, M. (1961). Narrative of a child analysis. In: *The Writings of Melanie Klein, Vol. 4*. London: Hogarth Press, 1975.

Lacan, J. (1977). The mirror stage as formative of the function of the I as revealed in psychoanalytic experience. *Écrits: a Selection* (pp. 1–7), A. Sheridan (Trans.). London: Tavistock.

Lemma, A. (2009). Being seen or being watched? A psychoanalytic perspective on body dysmorphia. *International Journal of Psychoanalysis, 90*: 753–771.

Lichtenstein, H. (1964). The role of narcissism in the emergence and maintenance of a primary identity. *International Journal of Psychoanalysis, 45*: 49–56.

Meltzer, D. (1987). On aesthetic reciprocity. *Journal of Child Psychotherapy, 13*: 3–14.

Meltzer, D. (1994). Adhesive identification. In: A. Hahn (Ed.), *Sincerity and Other Works: Collected Papers of Donald Meltzer* (pp. 335–350). London: Karnac.

Meltzer, D., & Harris Williams, M. (1988). *The Apprehension of Beauty.* Strathtay, Perthshire: Clunie Press.

Rank, O. (1989). *The Double: A Psychoanalytic Study.* London: Karnac.

Rhode, M. (1997). Going to pieces: autistic and schizoid solutions. In: M. Rustin, M. Rhode, A. Dubinsky, & H. Dubinsky (Eds.), *Psychotic States in Children* (pp. 231–244). London: Duckworth/Karnac.

Rhode, M. (1999). Echo or answer? The move towards ordinary speech in three children with autistic spectrum disorder. In: A. Alvarez & S. Reid (Eds.), *Autism and Personality* (pp. 79–92). London: Routledge.

Rhode, M. (2008). Joining the human family. In: K. Barrows (Ed.), *Autism in Children and Autistic States in Adults* (pp. 147–170). London: Karnac.

Rhode, M. (2010). The lost child: whose is the face in the mirror? In: E. McGinley & A. Varchevker (Eds.), *Enduring Loss: Mourning, Depression and Narcissism throughout the Life Cycle* (pp. 19–42). London: Karnac.

Roheim, G. (1919). *Spiegelzauber* [Mirror Magic]. Leipzig: Internationaler Psychoanalytischer.

Searles, H. F. (1984). The role of the analyst's facial expressions in psychoanalysis and psychoanalytic therapy. *International Journal of Psychoanalytic Psychotherapy, 10*: 47–73.

Segal, H. (1957). Notes on symbol formation, *International Journal of Psychoanalysis, 38*: 391–397.

Sinason, V. (1999). Psychoanalysis and mental handicap: experience from the Tavistock Clinic. In: J. DeGroef & E. Heinemann (Eds.), *Psychoanalysis and Mental Handicap* (pp. 197–198). London: Free Association Books.

Steiner, J. (2011). *Seeing and Being Seen: Emerging from a Psychic Retreat.* London: Routledge.

Trevarthen, C. (1979). Communication and co-operation in early infancy: a description of primary intersubjectivity. In: M. Bullowa (Ed.), *Before Speech: The Beginning of Interpersonal Communication* (pp. 321–348). Cambridge: Cambridge University Press.

Tustin, F. (1972). Psychotic depression. In: *Autism and Childhood Psychosis* (pp. 4–31). London: Hogarth [reprinted London: Karnac, 1995].

Tustin, F. (1981). *Autistic States in Children.* 2nd revised edn. London: Routledge, 1992.

Tustin, F. (1986). Spilling and dissolving. In: *Autistic Barriers in Neurotic Patients.* 2nd revised edn (pp. 197–214). London: Karnac.

Winnicott, D. W. (1971). The mirror role of mother and family in child development. In: *Playing and Reality* (pp. 111–118). London: Tavistock.

Zazzo, R. (1995). *Reflets de Miroir et Autres Doubles.* Paris: PUF.

CHAPTER THIRTEEN

Playing and Reality revisited: clinical practice with adolescents in the twenty-first century

Virginia Ungar

Revisiting Winnicott in *Playing and Reality* is a playful experience in itself. It is like going out to play a game that we have already played, but which, each time we do play it, it turns out differently. It is in this way that the spirit of Winnicott is renewed in us when he changed us forever by allowing us to live in and respect the intermediate space, the home of cultural experience.

Living in the times that we do, taking this perspective is unavoidable when tackling clinical work with adolescents. It is no longer possible to home in on this topic taking a solitary stance on the issue, whether it is from the internal world, environmental provision, or the historic–socio-political moment inside which the subject is experiencing his/her life crisis. Both the patient and the analyst are socialised beings who respond in one way or another to the cultural conditions of their times.

If we are to think of adolescence, it is then necessary to add to these dimensions another which is of the utmost importance: the presence of a body which gives rise to a crisis in the young person by imposing itself like an alien being which, in order to be integrated, will necessitate much psychic work. It is a sexualised body which houses the so-called secondary sex characteristics and which is, moreover, the centre of the impact drive, or *Trieb* (which is composed of, at one and the same time, re-edited elements and something of the new).

Adolescence, therefore, could be said to consist in a paradigm of the knotting together of all that is body, psyche, and social.

In the culture of the present day, this stage in life has been anointed as an ideal of yearning: the children of today dream of becoming adolescents as soon as possible, while older people would give anything to be teenagers once again. This phenomenon has been studied very closely indeed by experts in marketing who focus on adolescents as being their supreme target and tool.

This cultural landscape can be seen also to affect clinical work in testing our ability as psychoanalysts of patients of that age to maintain the analytical attitude. There is always the risk of being left transfixed when faced with young people who are so energetic, creative, vigorous, and ready to take on all comers. The almost inevitable corollary is that of entering into situations of seduction that unavoidably lead to an impasse.

At the other extreme, a possible attitude of condemnation (almost always unconscious) is present but latent when faced with the inescapable turbulence that analysis with an adolescent involves, turbulence that is much greater, we have to say, than that generated when treating patients of other ages, including children. Few situations affect the infantile structures of a psychoanalyst more than therapy with an adolescent.

The therapist's battle to maintain an equilibrium which allows him/her to remain flexible, tolerant, receptive, and at the same time firm in his/her position as analyst will run the whole length of the treatment with an adolescent.

We have "learnt from experience" that, even more at this stage of life than at any other, it is necessary that the setting is infused with a flexibility that allows us to receive the different modes of communication used by adolescents, among which the language of action prevails.

Indeed, in proposing to start analysis with an adolescent, we offer him/her a method that implies an emotional and intimate commitment with an adult at the very time when his/her relationship with the adult world is particularly conflictive. Moreover, it is a method which does not offer quick solutions in a period when the young person sees him/herself as being under pressure both to insert him/herself into the surrounding culture and to gain acceptance from the adolescent world, too.

We live in times where change happens faster and faster and this inevitably affects the practice of psychoanalysis and, especially, work with adolescents.

First of all, technology and the mass media have created new spaces and new modes of communication in which adolescents are at the forefront as users. Our times are characterised by direct access through the Internet to an immediate narrative which comes easily and is full of options. Today, the meeting place is predominantly virtual: texts, chat, social networking tools, such as Facebook, Twitter, blogs, Instagram, and Snapchat are just some of the possibilities. The Internet—the target of much criticism—offers a virtual option to connect to the world in general, to "get to know" people, to interact, have romances, and to play games online with others without even meeting them.

Chat, for example, is a virtual space which has an existence all of its own, like a city with neighbourhoods but without any specific location, populated by an imaginary community of transitory inhabitants of remote and diverse origins. This community has nothing to do with family, or with the neighbourhoods we all used to live in. Moreover, in cyberspace it is possible for the individual not to be defined by their self, or by any reference to their body; each and every one can have various gender, appearance, and age identities. On top of that, it is not necessary to meet personally; computers and mobile phones can be used, with their ever-increasing range of features.

If we look closer at this topic, two tendencies stand out: that of demonising the mass media, on the one hand, or entering into a type of idealisation and impassioned defence of them, on the other. We must think of those interchanges in each and every particular situation. It will always depend on what use is made of them: we cannot compare the young person who spends most of his/her day locked up in his/her room on the computer, watching television, and listening to music on headphones with that young person who, as well as chatting, gaming online, and watching television, goes out, plays sports, has a social life and contact with "real" people. It might sound a little daring, but I would suggest conceiving of the interchanges in virtual spaces as places of experimentation with links and, perhaps, as transitional spaces on the path leading out towards the adult world.

At any rate, the reality is that today young patients tell us that they will be late by text, and sometimes send us emails or YouTube videos, and we analysts, in spite of not working with the same codes, accept these and even learn how to handle these realities ourselves.

Secondly, the topic of the role of the mass media, with the unstoppable advance of technology, generates impassioned debate over questions such as the loss of privacy, the difficulty of conceiving the notion of intimacy, and stimulation tending towards omnipotence and omniscience.

Even if privacy is invaded by the mass media, there is a territory—that of intimacy—which can be looked after and preserved and which leaves the individual capable of making contact with the existence of a mental space in which emotional relations take place, relations that are the source of creativity in all its dimensions. One of these, that of generating dreams, is very highly valued by us psychoanalysts.

These days, for some people, the only private space that they have is that of the analytic session, and it is precisely there that the construction of the notion of intimacy may start.

These facts will undoubtedly produce changes in psychoanalytic theory, but this will not take place in the immediate future because, as historians say, you cannot write history while it is happening, and a certain distance is needed from which to observe changes, to describe them, and to think them through. That said, however, we can say that the mental mechanisms used by the children and adolescents of our times tend more towards those connected with splitting than repression. That is not to say that repression is not used, but, rather, that the type of interaction with the media whereby a young person can be watching television, chatting online, watching a YouTube clip, and sending a text message on a mobile phone appears to be closer to the splitting and dissociation of various levels of the self which allows the young person to, what would it be, "disperse" or "concentrate" attention on a number of elements at the one time.

Furthermore, technological advances have, in recent times, given to the prevalence of the image a special place in our society, and this has had a very direct impact on the young people of today. The image, in itself, is of fundamental importance to them as they try to process the anxiety that they feel about losing the representation of the self and the body of the infant in an accelerated change that the internal world struggles to keep up with. Along the path of the search for their identity, adolescents need to be looked at and reaffirmed by others, their peers, so that the latter, with their messages, return something to the former which, although it is almost always confusing and infantile, could bring a certain calm to the anxiety linked to the vacuum of existence.

Today, there has been an unanticipated and immeasurable spike in the number of postings on Facebook and other social networking sites. Young people upload their photos so that their friends post comments which are generally quite infantile and which contain very striking spelling "mistakes".

Another inescapable factor when we come to consider the youth of today is that of the changes in the configuration of the family.

Families that come to us are no longer traditional, monogamous and heterosexual, as was the norm in the times of the birth of psychoanalysis. When Winnicott started to work and write, some changes could be seen: for example, a rise in the number of divorces and a reduction in the rate of couples getting married. Adolescents who come to us today for consultation, on the other hand, often come from blended families or one-parent families, they can be the children of a teenage pregnancy or, in recent years, we have started to see those who are children or adolescents of gay couples by adoption or assisted reproductive technology. If we extend this thought, in this sense there is no longer a need that there be a mother, a father, and a sexual relationship between the two for a family to be formed. In a certain way, the egg and the spermatozoid are independent of the bodies of the mother and the father.

Patients force us to situate ourselves in a reality which obliges us to see that the family model that we have traditionally encountered has lost its validity; this is not what they now aspire towards.

In any case, the adolescent of today is faced with the task of undertaking the passage from the community world of family to the community of adulthood, while for a time residing in the world of their peers, as Meltzer (2011) explains. At some point in the evolutionary process, the adolescent will have to insert him/herself in the surrounding culture.

Culture has historically accompanied the moments of change in the life of human beings, such as birth, death, and marriage, providing rites of passage. The ritual ceremonies bear witness to, and validate, an event that has taken place. Many years ago—and, indeed, even today for some tribal societies—rites of passage still took place to mark the transition from childhood to adulthood and this has raised doubts for experts in the field as to the existence, or otherwise, of adolescence as a stage of life, in these cases at least.

If it is the culture that establishes rituals, it also provides the young people for the ceremonies that indicate that they are now adults. All they do is go through these practices.

In Western society in the past century, it was possible to identify mild equivalents of these rites in, for example, permission to wear long trousers for young men and high heels for young women, customs which have today either been replaced by others or, perhaps, been diluted.

If adolescence seems to have been an almost inexistent period in medieval times, today it is definitely much more extensive in time. The aforementioned fact that young people are the prime target for the marketing men of today gives some indication of the strong socio-economic pressure on them to prolong their adolescence. According to the statistics, the percentage of young people close to their thirties who still live with their parents is growing all the time, and with this comes the concomitant features of dressing in a way similar to teenagers, watching television programmes aimed at children (such as cartoons), playing video games, collecting superhero magazines, and even decorating their bedrooms with the dolls or action figures of whatever television series happens to be "in" at the moment.

What we are talking about here are adolescents from a chronological point of view, but they are straggling in their infancy in an emotional sense. They have remained stuck in the world of the child-in-the-family. They linger in a state of waiting, buoyed up by the belief that all they have to do is wait for their parents to introduce them to the adult world.

In this case, the period of dependency on their parents is prolonged by specific internal factors and because the world "out there" seems hostile to the possibility of some sort of personal project.

Coming back to the question of the rites of passage, contemporary society does not provide them for young people. In fact, young people are obliged to create or invent them for themselves in an effort to shake off the label of "the child in the family" and go on to form part of the adolescent community.

Rituals today, created by those same young people—and strikingly similar in different parts of the Western world—are reminiscent of the tests of courage which we often find in children's tales. They might consist in, for example, kissing someone that you have just met (and not necessarily of the opposite sex), drinking alcohol until you lose consciousness, or smoking marijuana. On one of these points, until not so many years ago, calling an adolescent homosexual was considered an insult; today, it is often the contrary, where telling others that you are bisexual can give you the status of being interesting, especially for young women.

We must recognise that young people today are more alone than they used to be and, undoubtedly, one of the major reasons for this is the accelerated pace of modern life and the pressure to succeed. Not only does it demand that adults dedicate much time in attempts to attain this success, but we must also take into account that there is a hijacking from the play space of both time and libido that could be shared with children. The latter also tend to have their agendas full, as, from a very early age, they are set on the road to promised excellence.

One factor which seems decisive in relation to the changes that have taken place in the organisation of the family is the decline or weakening of the paternal function, a subject which runs through the pages of psychoanalytic publications coming from many different referential perspectives.

The theme of the father has been linked to the Oedipus complex ever since this key suggestion, which runs through numerous texts of the creator of psychoanalysis, was made. We must add, however, that it was Lacan who developed the theme of the paternal function and the Name of the Father as a "joint" to the symbolic father.

Without questioning the fundaments of the Lacanian contribution, I have always queried the legitimacy of separating or isolating the three participants in the Oedipus complex (father–mother–son) who are inextricably linked in the focus of the complex in terms of the basic structure.

Moreover, clinical experience with patients of all ages has made me come to the conclusion that the paternal function does not just come about in a haphazard way; it is the product of a kind of daily and prolonged process of the weaving of the link with the child in which a man will become a father. It involves slow and silent construction and is reformulated at every step of a function that is tested at the same time as it is being constructed and applied.

In my opinion, the term parental is preferable, as this covers the area between two circles that intersect, producing a common space: the two circles are the fact of becoming a mother and the fact of becoming a father. To step outside the paternal function for a moment and approach the maternal vector paraphrasing, as I do, Winnicott, I allow myself an extension of the idea in asking: is it possible to ask of primary parental preoccupation also?

The changes in the parental function—in terms of the configuration of families that do not follow the traditional model of the family in modern times—are starting to be seen in our consulting rooms.

Since, up to now, the predominant model has been that of the classic organisation of the family, that is where I believe it is appropriate to talk about the weakening of the paternal function or, as the French authors say, the *défaillance*. The effect of this can be sensed in some of the presentations of current infant and adolescent pathologies that we encounter.

There is an idea that Winnicott brings up in the chapter on adolescence in *Playing and Reality* (Winnicott, 1971) that is striking because of its relevance today in relation to this topic. He speaks to us of "parental abdication", a situation where parents deliberately delegate responsibility to their children and leave them to sort out themselves all the hostility that the adolescent stage implies.

However, before going further into this topic, I shall now present a vignette from the treatment of an adolescent that might well give us some insight into what Winnicott has proposed.

This clinical story, which is increasing in frequency to an alarming extent, tells of young people, females in the main, who cut themselves. It is called self-cutting syndrome and consists of slitting, mostly the forearms, causing light superficial incisions close to the veins which are most visible. This behaviour carries with it the paradox that it is at the same time an act of extreme control in terms of the incision while also being one of an impulsive lack of control.

Last year, between consultations and supervisions in different contexts, I personally was able to follow the treatment of four adolescent females between the ages of fifteen and twenty whose cases have a certain similarity.

Let us have a look at one of the cases that I supervised, a girl whom I will call Emilia,[1] who was brought to her first consultation by her mother when she was on the verge of being expelled from her school for bad behaviour, in spite of having a good academic record. I asked her mother to leave the consulting room and, in a quite unenthusiastic way, having thrown herself into an armchair and ending up draped over it, she told me that she had felt alone for a long time, that she had no friends, and that her parents favoured her older sister. She added, "Since I was four or five I have thought of throwing myself out the window. When I was small, I decided I wasn't going to do it because we lived on one of the lower floors and if I threw myself out and didn't kill myself and ended up paralysed . . ."

Emilia told me that she had been seeing psychologists since she was a child because they had told her that she "was hyperactive, had ADD, whatever. . . . I felt fine, happy. . . . I was active and lively . . . my parents always thought that there was something bad in me." "When I got angry, I broke things, even ceramic things that I myself had made, or injured myself. . . . Anyway, nothing that I do is going to please my parents . . .."

At the end of that first interview, she said, "If they had brought me some months ago, I wouldn't have spoken. Women are unpleasant for me, but I could come again."

When she came for the second interview, she was covering up a tattoo that she had had done and that she did not want her parents to see. In this meeting, she told me that during the summer she had sniffed aerosols and cut her wrists. When her parents found out, they took her to a psychiatrist.

In the third interview, she said that the previous weekend she had drunk a lot of alcohol and blacked out in a very dangerous neighbourhood. Her friends had phoned her mother.

In the interview with her parents, her mother said, and I quote, "Emilia is going to kill me with her behaviour. I have a heart problem and I can't stand what she's up to, the problems that it all brings."

We have now heard from Emilia. We are neither her parents nor her tutors. We are thinking that we must try to stop her from killing her analyst as she did her former therapists. We also know that something of this, of the nature of death or murder, is implied in the adolescent process. I truly believe that nobody expressed it better than Winnicott in *Playing and Reality* when he puts forward his concept of adolescence as a period when the evidence of the success or failure of early care comes to the surface. He says that if parents help to promote the healthy growth of their children, it is then that they will see surprising results.

So, if the child meets him/herself, he/she will then want more, and that "more" includes aggressive and destructive elements as well those of love. At that point, a long struggle begins and what is required is that we simply survive this sequence.

The theoretical basis of this hypothesis is to be found in the concept that if, in the first growth there is death content, in adolescence the content is that of murder. The young person must take the place of the father and because of that the unconscious fantasy of growth is an aggressive act.

Winnicott left us with a phrase that communicates this very point in a quite vivid way: "You sowed a baby and you reaped a bomb" (Winnicott, 1971, p. 196). Furthermore, of great importance was when he stated that it is precisely when parents abdicate that the worst scenario appears. We must remember that the adolescent has yet to become capable of being responsible for his/her cruelty, hostility, and psychological pain.

The vignette that I have just presented sends us back to what Winnicott wrote in the chapter on adolescence in *Playing and Reality*. In the case of Emilia, death in the form of murder or the turning against herself in her thoughts of suicide is present from the very start of the encounter. We also come into contact with her helplessness in hearing her mother declaring that her daughter was going to kill her and that she could not put up with her any more. This configuration, compounded by a father who makes little or no appearance on the scene, leaves us with an impression of the abdication that Winnicott was referring to.

In a classical sense, the breakdown in the paternal function is seen as an absence of interdiction in the relationship between the child and the mother. Abdication, in this case, would be another form of failure in the paternal function and in this way violence, the homicidal impulse, is unleashed into the hands of a young person who brandishes some sort of knife because there is nobody around to take on the responsibility for the hostility and tolerate it, or stop it if necessary.

In the act of cutting, there seems to be a convergence of the mark or writing on the skin as a permanent feature and the experiencing of pain, something that often seems to be a dramatic attempt by the young person to truly feel alive.

Many different facets can be found to this problem and we may attempt explanations from perspectives such as sadism, masochism, narcissism, and an addictive streak, among others.

The skin is a surface and, at the same time, a limit between the psyche and the environment. The wound from which the blood flows and which is finely controlled so that it leaves its mark speaks to us of a mute ripping (made without the "Ow!" of pain) which is considered a symbolic deficit.

Freud told us of liberation from parents in "Family romances" (Freud, 1909c, p. 237), putting it thus:

> The liberation of an individual, as he grows up, from the authority of his parents is one of the most necessary though one of the most painful results brought about by the course of his development. It is quite essential that that liberation should occur and it may be presumed that it has been to some extent achieved by everyone who has reached a normal state. Indeed, the whole progress of society rests upon the opposition between successive generations.

The concept of liberation ushers into psychoanalytic theory the value of painful affection: not only do we have to go through this pain, but Freud goes so far as to say that it is a necessary precondition of progress (the ideal of modernity). In order to extricate oneself, to separate oneself, there must be a presence of somebody who testifies to the impossibility of actual murder.

As we have already seen, the skin is a limit and it may be turned into a scenario that indicates a breakdown in the question of limits. If there is abdication in the parental function, if generational differences are diluted, a vacuum is created which speaks of the untying of aggression and of a rapid movement to action and the turning against oneself.

The paternal function is, indeed, related to this limit. Winnicott, in the same article, tells us that "The term paternal must necessarily come a little later than maternal. Gradually the father as male becomes a significant factor" (Winnicott, 1971, p. 191). Even if, in Winnicott, this function relates more to the act of supporting the mother who, in turn, supports the child, in another article (1989, p. 237) Winnicott says,

> My patient is in this position that he always protects the mother because he must preserve her in order to be able to have any rest or relaxation at all. He therefore has no knowledge that his mother might survive his impulsive act. A strong father enables the child to take the risk because the father stands in the way or is there to mend matters or to prevent by his fierceness.

As we can see, he refers to the paternal function as the presence which permits the child to "run the risk" and dare to explore the world according to his/her impulses, given that the father "is present" to protect him/her from the dangers with which the world might injure him/her or he/she causes injury to him/herself.

This approach that Winnicott takes in terms of the function of the father relates to the act of imposing limits on aggression, modulating hostility—in the child as well as in the environment—as well as allowing, in that way, for the appearance of the creative gesture.

Taking this perspective, from the start the mother will provide the continuity of being—as long as she has the paternal function internalised—and she may yield her omnipotence somewhat in order to adapt to the necessities of her child. The father, in this case, could seem to be something of a late arrival on the scene but, if we look into it a little more, the paternal function is internalised in the mother so that she may then establish a relationship with a man, that is, the prospective father to her child. We could, in this way, say that the father, at the start of life, is channelled through the mother.

In order to make the space, as well as the transitional phenomena and the space for illusion, possible, what is required is not only mutual adaptation, but also a gradual disillusionment and this will be facilitated if, at some point, the mother looks away: "away" being nothing less than towards the father. It is at this moment, this mythical moment, that the third person appears and it could also be said that relationship then becomes three-dimensional.

This conquest of a three-dimensional mental state opens up a whole new world to the child, one with conflicts, undoubtedly, but also with all the possibilities of creativity and access to the symbolic world.

If we follow Winnicottian logic, the place of the father could be judged to be that of a buffer which attempts to limit the field of forces at those times when hostility predominates.

During the first growth period, he should support the mother so that she may then enter fully into the state of primary maternal preoccupation. It is precisely here that I dare to suggest the existence of the primary parental preoccupation based on the changes in models of upbringing and contemporary relationship set-ups.

Soon after, the presence of the father is crucial in the eyes, literally and figuratively, of the mother, and it is at this point that the third person comes into play. In adolescence, the role of the father will be decisive in setting limits to aggression so that the young person may "run the risk" and dare to explore the world. If the parents abdicate, as we have said, the young person will see their own aggression unleashed and this, depending on his/her emotional state, may be channelled outwards or come back against him/her, as in the practice of cutting.

Once more, Winnicott has helped us to consider situations in clinical practice in the present with concepts that, although now classics, as are those set out in *Playing and Reality,* still have the ability to be sources of creativity, just like the toys that our children continue playing with today.

Note

1. I would like to thank Nergis Guleç for her generosity in permitting me to use her material. I relate the material in the first person.

References

Freud, S. (1909c). Family romances, *S. E., 9*: 235–242. London: Hogarth.

Meltzer, D. (2011). Adolescent psychoanalytic theory. In: *Adolescence. Talks and Papers by Donald Meltzer and Martha Harris* (pp. 21–37). London: Karnac.

Winnicott, D. W. (1971). Contemporary concepts of adolescent development and their implication for higher education. In: *Playing and Reality* (pp. 186–204). London: Routledge [reprinted 2005].

Winnicott, D. W. (1989). Clinical illustration of "The Use of an Object". In: *Psycho-Analytic Explorations: D. W. Winnicott*, C. Winnicott, R. Shepherd, & M. Davis (Eds.). Cambridge, MA: Harvard University Press.

INDEX

For Product Safety Concerns and Information please contact our EU representative GPSR@taylorandfrancis.com
Taylor & Francis Verlag GmbH, Kaufingerstraße 24, 80331 München, Germany

www.ingramcontent.com/pod-product-compliance
Lightning Source LLC
LaVergne TN
LVHW021122300926
849160LV00010B/827
9781782200253